8/2016

Edie & Richard

To My Good ~

PRAISE FOR
WALK TO BEAUTIFUL

"Walk to Beautiful is a poignant, eloquently written book filled with vivid and memorable details that are so honest, moving, and intimate. It reminds me of the power of kindness, patience, understanding, acceptance, and endurance, but above all—love. And love should not be underestimated; it shapes, affirms, and blesses."

— Ms. Friday
Jimmy's sixth grade teacher (twice)

"Curveballs, sinkers, and changeups—life has thrown them all at Jimmy Wayne, and he has not only managed them; he has hit them out of the park! When Jimmy and I first met, we were two guys from Bessemer City High School who had big dreams and little more. Jimmy's incredible story in *Walk to Beautiful* is evidence that with faith and hard work, dreams still come true."

— Kevin Millwood
Major League Baseball player

"Incredibly engaging, emotionally charged—I rarely come across a book that turns my insides upside down. *Walk to Beautiful* did. From the beginning to the end, Jimmy's gutsy actions and survival instincts grab your attention. Having finished the book, I read it again, making sure I was not just imagining the story. God has a plan for Jimmy Wayne!"

— Sue Anne Wells, PhD
Chairman and founder,
Chattanooga Girls Leadership
Academy
Chairman and founder,
Mustang Leadership Partners

"Jimmy Wayne has written an extremely relevant book for our postmodern society and has done so with grace and love. Through his life's story he explains why we need to be aware of the crisis of kids without homes, without love, and therefore without hope. If I actually had another biological son I would want him to be Jimmy Wayne. I love what Jimmy has become in spite of adversity and a horrible, tumultuous childhood. His love for Bea—without whom he would not be the guy I came to love on our tour and still remain good friends with—warms my heart. I am honored to have played a very small part in Jimmy's life and stand in awe of his accomplishments and his courage in his fight for kids who need homes with love and stability. This is a great book. Sandy read it to me as we drove from Nashville to West Virginia. It made us cry, laugh, and feel pride in our 'son' Jimmy. Oh yes, I want to add . . . Jimmy, get a haircut, son. —'Papa P.'"

— Doug Paisley
Brad Paisley's dad

"Jimmy's story is our story. Struggle. Redemption. Hurt. Hope. It's all there. If your story could use a better chapter, take inspiration from Jimmy's."

— Max Lucado
New York Times best-selling
author

"We were blessed to hear Jimmy Wayne's stories as he shared them with our family at our home. *Walk to Beautiful* presents a challenge to all of us to live out the biblical charge to help children that are in need (Matthew 25:40). You can make a difference!"

— Bubba and Cindy Cathy
Chick-fil-A, Inc.

"*Walk to Beautiful* is Jimmy Wayne's unforgettably raw, honest, and yet tender story of how the power of one person changed the life of another. From despair to fame and on to self-actualization, Jimmy's life and this story of untold significance reveal the plight of foster children and the homeless. Inspirational, moving, and powerful, a page turner to the very end!"

— Anne Neilson
Fine art gallery owner, artist, and
author, *Angels in Our Midst*

"Jimmy Wayne's *Walk to Beautiful* weaves the complexities of life, love, faith, hope, and the eternal validity of the soul. This is a deep, down-in-the-gut story. A uniquely American tale of truth that exposes a shadow culture in our country in a way that cannot be rivaled by even the finest fiction. If a person is defined by his experience, then Jimmy Wayne and his story should be an example for all of us to believe that even the seemingly most insignificant actions can have a profound effect on the world and everyone around us."

— John Oates
Hall and Oates
Rock and Roll Hall of Fame
member

"This story peels back the stagnant skies and shows daily life at a street level—from the scattered trailer parks to the decaying mill villages. It challenges us all to take a close look at the faces we pass by each day, to listen to God's still small voice, and yes, to 'Bea' somebody!"

— Cindy Ballard
Jimmy's seventh grade guidance
counselor

"Jimmy Wayne's story is a powerful example of how foster parenting can change lives. I invited him to our church to share his music and testimony, and the story of Bea Costner, to challenge us to get serious about adoption and foster care. The results were overwhelming! His journey will deeply touch your heart and challenge you to get involved in the lives of foster kids and orphans."

— David Chadwick
Senior pastor, Forest Hill Church
Charlotte, North Carolina

"This book will break your heart and open your eyes. In sharing his tumultuous life story with such transparency, Jimmy Wayne illuminates the strength of the human spirit and the power of faith and love to change lives. His friend/mentor Bea Costner would be proud of the way he has carried on her legacy of compassion and kindness. From life as a homeless teen to country music stardom to working as a tireless advocate for foster children, Jimmy's story is inspiring. *Walk to Beautiful* is a journey worth taking."

— Deborah Evans Price
Music journalist and *Billboard*
correspondent

"*Walk to Beautiful* will open your eyes to the hurting people around you, but more importantly, to the opportunities to help others in large and small ways every day. This book will move you to action!"

— Frank Harrison
Chairman and CEO, Coca-Cola
Bottling Co. Consolidated
Chairman and cofounder,
With Open Eyes

"I was very touched by reading *Walk to Beautiful*. It is an incredible story, so well-written, and Jimmy Wayne is an inspiration. What a way God has of working things out. I guess if he can turn water into wine, he can certainly make lemonade out of lemons. It reads like a movie to me, and if so, I'll be the first one in a seat to see it."

— Dolly Parton

"For years, music fans from all over the world have enjoyed Jimmy Wayne's musical gifts. In *Walk To Beautiful*, he gives us an even greater gift by sharing his unbelievable life story to remind us all that even life's most extreme hardships can be turned to make the world a better place. Thank you, Jimmy."

— Pete Fisher
Vice president and general
manager, Grand Ole Opry

"Jimmy Wayne's story is as powerful as it is heartbreaking. *Walk to Beautiful* offers hope, inspiration, and incontrovertible proof that one person can make a difference."

— Cynthia Sanz
Editor, *People Country*

"Jimmy Wayne is the most remarkable and resilient man we know. He has achieved so much in his life in spite of adversity and has become an incredible man. We can all admire him for all he has accomplished. We are humbled to be called his friends."

— Tom and Gayle Benson
Owner, New Orleans Saints and
New Orleans Pelicans

"This is truly a remarkable and inspiring story of a young man's journey through rejection, abuse, and poverty to become a talented country music star. Everyone who reads this book or listens to his songs will feel his heartbreak and be encouraged by his overcoming spirit."

— Graeme M. Keith
Chairman, The Keith Corporation

"Beautifully written, honest, heartbreaking, and inspirational at the same time. Jimmy Wayne has a powerful life story and an amazing heart for God. He knows and acts on an everlasting truth: God does not make trash! His heart for our broken, scarred, and scared children in our foster 'care' system is inspiring, and we should all join him on this walk to help!"

— Mary Landrieu
United States senator

"As a morning radio host of over thirty years, I know Jimmy well, but didn't know half of the horrifying stories he tells. A radio station looking for local involvement could make a big difference by carrying the torch for *Walk to Beautiful*."

— Jim Mantel
Morning radio host
KNFM, KRYS, KKBQ, WGAR,
WRNS

"We never tire of hearing incredible testimonies. Jimmy Wayne's testimony is living proof that God is able to use the most painful experiences to affect people and change hearts and minds. Instead of allowing bitterness to take root in his heart, Jimmy has chosen to share his story and use the resources God has blessed him with to greatly impact the lives of others. We are proud to call Jimmy our friend, and we pray that this book will not only inspire people but will draw attention to children in foster care and promote positive changes that will give them a brighter future."

— Marcus and Cassi Smith
President and COO,
Speedway Motorsports, Inc.
Vice chairman,
Speedway Children's Charities

Walk to Beautiful is proof to the power of perseverance and the pure will that one human being can possess. After reading this book, there is no doubt in my mind that Jimmy Wayne's survival and success are destiny. His commitment to making a difference in the lives of homeless and foster care children is as inspiring as his story. God bless you, Jimmy!"

— Carole Christianson
Chief operating officer,
Western Association of Food
Chains

"I loved this book. Jimmy's story is moving and motivating. Read it and you'll be ready to join him in changing the world for our children."

— Michael S. Piraino
Chief executive officer,
The National CASA Association

"Words cannot adequately express how deeply impacted I was the first time I heard Jimmy Wayne tell his story. Because of the tragic and painful childhood that he experienced, and all that he has overcome, I knew his story would bring great hope to every resident in all of our Mercy homes. I am convinced that every person who reads the pages of this book will be both challenged and inspired to make a difference in the lives of others."

— Nancy Alcorn
Founder and president,
Mercy Ministries

"This is such a compelling read. Jimmy takes you though his ups and downs. He makes you laugh and makes you cry. What an incredible journey. You won't be able to put it down."

— Kerry Wolfe
Director of programming,
Clear Channel Media +
Entertainment

"A compulsive page-turner that tugs at the heartstrings while simultaneously demanding a call for action! Readers will be blessed by the inspiring story of Jimmy Wayne, who goes beyond overcoming adversity and leads by example."

— Lisa Rowland Brasher
Executive vice chairman,
Jelly Belly Candy Company
Executive board member,
Mission SOLANO Rescue Mission

"Ignored, abandoned, and disregarded by both family and society, Jimmy had one match left to keep warm . . . and find the way! *Walk to Beautiful* is a riveting, poignant look into the complex world of children in the foster care system as seen through Jimmy's eyes, words, and experiences. From unwitting victim to vocal advocate, his story underscores the flaws in the system, paints a face on these children, and becomes an effective plea for extending the dates where a child 'ages' out of the system from eighteen to twenty-one to give them a better chance. Finally, it shows that while love does not always conquer all, it does form the bridge to build the human soul."

— Paul Christianson
Executive vice president, sales,
Aqua-Zone Systems

WALK TO BEAUTIFUL

WALK TO
BEAUTIFUL

The Power of Love and a Homeless Kid
Who Found the Way

JIMMY WAYNE

with

Ken Abraham

W PUBLISHING GROUP

AN IMPRINT OF THOMAS NELSON

Published in Nashville, Tennessee, by W Publishing Group, an imprint of Thomas Nelson.

Published in association with Anvil II Management, 17721 Rogers Ranch Parkway, Suite 150, San Antonio, TX 78258.

Thomas Nelson titles may be purchased in bulk for educational, business, fund-raising, or sales promotional use. For information, e-mail SpecialMarkets@ThomasNelson.com.

Scripture quotations are taken from the Holy Bible, New International Version®, NIV®. © 1973, 1978, 1984, 2011 by Biblica, Inc.™ Used by permission of Zondervan. All rights reserved worldwide.

This is a work of nonfiction. The stories and anecdotes in this volume are true accounts drawn from the author's life experiences and have been reconstructed as the author has remembered them, to the best of his ability. In some cases, for the sake of the narrative flow, he has combined more than one conversation or adjusted chronology. Some names and details have been changed to protect identities.

ISBN 978-0-7180-3155-8 (IE)

Library of Congress Cataloging-in-Publication Data

Wayne, Jimmy, 1972- author.
  Walk to beautiful / Jimmy Wayne with Ken Abraham.
     pages cm
  ISBN 978-0-8499-2210-7 (hardcover)
  1. Wayne, Jimmy, 1972- 2. Country musicians—United States—Biography. I. Abraham, Ken, author. II. Title.
  ML420.W296A3 2014
  782.421642092—dc23
  [B]   2014012701

Printed in the United States of America

15 16 17 18 19 RRD 6 5

In memory of Bea Costner
In His early years, Jesus was a carpenter—and, to me,
it is no coincidence that Bea also worked with wood.
I love you, Bea!

CONTENTS

Prologue

FTW: TWENTY-SEVEN YEARS EARLIER

I SAT SULLEN AND SHIRTLESS TOWARD THE END OF THE day, alone in my room at the county home where Mama and her fourth or fifth husband had dumped me. My biological dad had left when I was a toddler, and Mama had already abandoned me several times as well. I'd lost count by now how many men she'd had in my fourteen years. A year earlier, Mama had married off my then-fourteen-year-old sister, Patricia, to an older, abusive man.

So I guess I shouldn't have been surprised when Mama ordered me out of the car at midnight in a bus station parking lot back then. I was barely thirteen years old; I stood there by myself, hundreds of miles from home, as I watched her pull away into the night with her lover. More recently, she and her husband had deceived a judge into designating me as a ward of the state. No doubt the judge thought the group home, known as Faith Farm, would be a safer, healthier environment for me than living in the chaos, drugs, alcohol, and other blatantly immoral behavior that constantly swirled around Mama's home.

He was wrong.

I hated my life. I hated living. I hated everything and everyone. I just wanted to die.

Faith Farm was an old frame house with creaky wooden stairs, so I turned off my heavy metal music so I could hear anyone coming up the staircase. I knew that if a staff member caught me doing what I was about to do, I could get into serious trouble. None of the other foster kids were around. It was just me, the evening sunlight, a small jar of black ink, and a sewing needle I'd found. I wrapped some thread around the tip of the needle so it could soak up some ink, like the wick on our old kerosene heater. I dipped the needle into the murky, dark liquid and watched it saturate the thread.

Carefully, I drew the needle out of the ink and then pushed the needle into my skin slightly above my left breast. *Ouch!* I screamed silently as the pain seared into my chest. It felt like a pinprick, but the burning sensation didn't disappear. Again and again I stuck the makeshift tattoo needle into my breast, the ink-soaked thread leaving an indelible mark as I pulled it through my skin.

Slowly, the letters began to take shape. First the *F.* Then *T.* Blood dripped down my chest, staining the top of my pants. With every prick of the needle, I was reminding myself of what I felt.

I knew what those letters meant. Most of the foster kids I'd met knew what the initials signified as well. Those who didn't would get it all too soon. *FTW.*

Again and again I stuck the needle into my breast, stabbing my skin repeatedly as I painstakingly drew, dot by excruciating dot, a cross and a battle-ax below the letters.

Blood now ran freely down my rib cage. Bitter memories of my childhood raced through my mind, and I became angrier yet somehow more numb as the pain of my childhood replaced the pain of the needle. I stabbed my skin faster and faster, until finally a mixture of blood and ink smeared my chest.

Only then did I stop. I sat there quietly with calligraphy ink covering my hands, my eyes searching all around the room. I didn't know what I was looking for; I was lost and alone.

After a few minutes I stood up, walked over to the mirror, and stared at the initials freshly tattooed into my swollen chest, the letters emblazoned in purple ink, the skin around each letter a sickly reddish-purple color. *FTW*—those initials expressed exactly what I felt inside. The cross and battle-ax below the initials represented my war with religion. *If God really loves me, as I've heard all my life, I wouldn't be in this situation right now.*

I stared into the mirror again, then lifted my eyes toward the ceiling. "Please, God; if you are really there, give me a reason to change the meaning of these letters."

It wasn't a prayer. It was a challenge.

Part One

A WAKE-UP CALL

One

BIG TIME!

I RAN TO THE EDGE OF THE STAGE AND SCANNED THE crowd of eighteen thousand screaming fans and flashing cameras. The pinpricks of light reminded me of the stars back in North Carolina. My childhood friend Rob Daniels and I had spent our breaks at the Osage textile mill, standing on the edge of the concrete loading dock, staring at the starlit sky. We were kids sharing our dreams about becoming famous musicians someday. I looked over at Rob and nodded at our images on the Jumbotron behind us. Rob grinned from ear to ear. We both knew what the other was thinking: *We did it, man!*

It was October 21, 2009, and we were playing Madison Square Garden along with Dierks Bentley as part of the closing leg of Brad Paisley's American Saturday Night Tour. Brad had already taken the tour to more than half a million people that year, but even he was excited to play "The Garden" for the first time.

"This place sure would hold a lot of hay," Brad had quipped as he gazed around the arena, as genuinely in awe as the rest of us.

Brad's crew had loaded into the arena, starting at eight in the morning for a seven thirty evening show, so the stage was already set when the artists and bands arrived midafternoon. After about a half-hour sound check for each artist, it was time for dinner. I went backstage to the dressing room area, where I could keep my voice warmed up in private. Shortly before seven thirty, my road manager knocked on the door. "Ten minutes, Jimmy," he called. I walked from the dressing rooms toward the main stage.

Even being backstage at Madison Square Garden was intimidating. Photos of entertainment legends Michael Jackson, Elvis Presley, U2, Paul McCartney, Billy Joel, Elton John—Elton played the Garden more than sixty times—the Rolling Stones, and more stars than I can name lined the hallway leading to the stage, a silent reminder of *you better be good*. They had all graced the stage on which I was about to perform for the first time.

My musicians—Radio Band, as I had named them—fidgeted anxiously. I adjusted my ear monitors and noticed I could hear the excited crowd through the ambient microphones located around the stage. The tour manager sent the band onstage to get set.

I'd been on tour with Brad since June—Brad had been out for twice as long—and I was still just as excited every night when the stage lights came up. But tonight was special. I was about to step out onto one of the world's most famous performance venues.

I waited offstage for my cue. The drummer hit the intro to our first song, one I had written called "Cowboys & Engines." Playing lead guitar, Rob struck a hot, quick riff and then the whole band joined him. The crowd was pumped and on their feet, instantly catching the rhythm.

It was *showtime*—my time!

My heart was pounding as I ran out on the stage, and the crowd greeted me with an enormous roar. Cameras flashed, lighting up the arena like a million fireworks.

Rob and I had dreamed about performing on this stage since our early days, when we'd played together in our first heavy metal band. Rob knew me as Jimmy Wayne Barber, long before the music world had ever heard of me and years before I dropped my last name. And now we were here, on the stage at Madison Square Garden. We had made it. This was not a dress rehearsal; this was the big time! The dreams of a couple country kids from North Carolina had come true.

I RAN TO THE RIGHT SIDE OF THE STAGE AND OUT ON THE ramp. The flock of fans on the right side of the arena screamed loudly. I bolted back across center stage and onto the left ramp. That side of the arena erupted in a huge roar. The crowd was going wild, and my adrenaline was pumping too. We rocked all the way to the end of the song, and when we hit the big ending, the response from the crowd was nearly deafening.

"Thank you!" I called out, knowing it was impossible for anyone to hear me. Without another word we lit into our second song. We performed "Stay Gone," my first big hit, then "Kerosene Kid," a song I wrote about a kid whose life was a lot like my childhood, living in a trailer park, going to school with the smell of kerosene all over my clothes, and being laughed at by the other students. The upbeat tempo of the song masked the message, but the crowd got it. Following "Kerosene Kid" came "Trespassin'," and then the band members cleared the stage, leaving only me as the lights went down.

All I could see were the runway lights, an exit sign on the far right corner, and the thousands of small camera lights. With my black Takamine guitar still in my hands, I walked out to the edge of the catwalk that extended into the audience and gazed into the crowd. It was a heady moment, to say the least.

A single spotlight came on, shining down from far up in the rafters, as brightly as a lighthouse beam. I blinked, allowing my eyes to adjust to the blinding light, and the pivotal events of my life flashed through my mind in a millisecond.

I thought of that day in the Gaston Mall, when I'd rummaged through a bargain box of old CDs and found a *Daryl Hall and John Oates Greatest Hits* album. I purchased it for one dollar, and when I listened to it, I was mesmerized. The song "Sara Smile," a megahit for Hall and Oates, caught my attention, and I fell in love. That's where this night all began for me.

I thought about Ellen Britton, the guitar teacher who taught me how to play the chords to "Sara Smile." My performance of the song got me my record deal. It opened every door for me, and in return I sang it nearly every time I opened a show or picked up a guitar and stepped onstage.

But for me, this moment wasn't simply about music. A movie was running in my mind. *This moment is for the hungry boy who asked the neighbor for food; the homeless teenager who carried around his belongings in a plastic trash bag; the young man who lost the greatest girlfriend because he chased his dream and prayed that God would bring her someone she deserved so she wouldn't have to wait on her dreams. This was for the man who believed in himself and wouldn't accept no for an answer.*

I performed "Sara Smile" acoustically, just my guitar and my voice. A few years earlier I couldn't even play guitar; now I was accompanying myself on a hit song in Madison Square Garden.

As soon as I struck the first few notes, the crowd recognized the Daryl Hall and John Oates hit and began singing along. More cameras flashed. I eased into the vocals and shivered when the crowd roared in approval.

The musicians were already back onstage when I finished the song to thunderous applause and cheers. The audience erupted again as Radio Band began playing "Do You Believe Me Now?" which had been number one on the charts for three straight weeks and had been instrumental in getting me on Brad's tour.

This was our last song of the evening, so I tried to soak up every sensation. I wanted these moments indelibly impressed in my memory. The crowd knew the lyrics and sang along as we finished our set. Young girls waved, looking up adoringly; others were still screaming on the front rows.

The band members looked at one another in ecstatic amazement. The crowd wanted more, and we wanted to give it to them, but we were out of time. I didn't want to leave the stage. I wanted to *live* in the light; I wanted to stay right there forever! I wanted to bask in the love that swelled up from the audience toward me; pseudo-love or not, I didn't care. It felt like love to me.

But the headliner, Brad Paisley, was backstage, gearing up, getting ready to come on and drive the crowd over the edge. My time in the spotlight was done.

I took one more bow and pointed to the screaming women in the front row, as well as the people in the balconies and side wings. I was living the dream—and it was real.

With a final wave, I exited the stage. The guys in the band were rowdy and slapping each other on the back, wiping sweat from their faces. I headed back down the long hallway toward the dressing room.

I had just played Madison Square Garden.

A SPECIAL BIRTHDAY CAKE, MADE FOR ME BY BUDDY Valastro, the "Cake Boss" on whom the TLC reality show was based, was sitting on a table as I arrived in my dressing room. *Who gets treated like this?* I thought when I saw the cake. I was a huge fan of *Cake Boss* and watched the show regularly while I was on the road. The room was already filled with people ready to celebrate my birthday a few days early.

This was totally different than my fifteenth birthday, when I had spent the night in a jail cell. Life sure had gotten better for me. I hardly remembered that boy who had been locked up in the detention center. That was all behind me now.

After the surprise birthday party, I freshened up and got ready to go back onstage. As we had done every night of the tour, Dierks and I joined Brad for his final, over-the-top number, "Alcohol."

The entire crowd was euphorically swaying with the music as Dierks and I burst out from backstage, entering the performance area through a door under the drum riser, which sat high above the stage. The scene was electrified with strobe lights as an enormous sign dropped down, flashing "Free Beer." The huge video screens were ablaze with images of brews from around the world, exploding like fireworks. Other images featured imaginary beers, such as "Bradweiser."

Dierks and I sang the chorus a couple of times with Brad, but more than anything we worked the crowd, the two of us striding back and forth from one end of the stage to the other while Brad continued to play and sing center stage behind his microphone stand. Near the end of the song, Brad launched into a phenomenal display of his guitar-playing ability, ripping a nearly two-minute-long guitar solo that whipped the crowd into even more of a frenzy. Meanwhile, Dierks and I continued to interact with members of the audience, racing now from side to side onstage, always careful to point the attention back to Brad but still having a blast improvising our own responses. We slapped hands with audience members and reached down and hugged women in the crowd; we even served as amateur photographers, accepting fans' cameras and taking quick pictures of Brad, still ripping on his guitar solo, then handing the cameras back to the ecstatic Paisley fans.

Two minutes on a live stage is a long time not to be singing, so as the standing crowd below the stage reached up toward me, I stretched out backward and fell into the waiting bed of fans. Dozens of hands held me high above the floor, moving my body along several feet away from the stage and then back again, catapulting me back onto the stage floor just in time to join Brad and Dierks for our final stage jump, the three of us huddling together in front of the drummer, then leaping into the air and landing simultaneously just as the band hit the ending note. To say the crowd went wild would be both redundant and an understatement. But they did.

Dierks and I quickly exited, heading backstage and allowing Brad to enjoy the adoration of his fans. Soaking wet from perspiration, I was glad when the stagehands handed us fresh towels as we made our way back to the dressing room area, the roar of the crowd still so loud it prevented any real conversation without yelling.

It was at least a half hour before my heart stopped pounding. Our road manager was pushing us to get out of the building, but my four band members and I stopped long enough at the exit door to pose for a photo in front of a Madison Square Garden sign. Then we rushed onto the tour bus waiting for us on a side street. Once aboard, I headed to the back lounge, slumped on the couch, and stared out the window.

Outside, I could see the busy, bustling New York City streets. The concert was over, so I could see the taxis and people flooding the streets, people streaming past each other, oblivious to everyone around them—including the homeless people, some of whom were lying in doorways on cardboard boxes to break the October chill of the cold cement below them.

Oh, yeah. The *homeless* people.

That used to be me, I thought.

Another thought flitted through my mind—this one of a beautiful, grandmotherly woman named Bea. I wished Bea could see me now.

I quickly closed the window blinds.

Two

BACK HOME

After being on tour since June, I finally got back to Nashville the first week in December 2009. I was so glad to be home. Sleeping in my own bed in my own comfortable Nashville townhome felt fantastic. Although I had traveled the country in a first-class, million-dollar tour bus, stayed in some fabulous hotels, eaten at fine restaurants, and enjoyed plenty of backstage food, there was no better feeling than to snuggle with my pillow and sleep in my own home.

Despite my road fatigue, I awakened early, as I usually do, the morning of December 3. Wearing only flannel pj's and a T-shirt, I rolled out of my toasty warm bed and instantly felt a chill in the air. It was unusually cold in Tennessee that year, so I reached for my Ugg slippers and threw on a heavy robe before ambling to the kitchen.

I yawned, stretched, and reached for the coffeepot. While on the road, traveling musicians learn to graciously accept almost anything that resembles coffee, but now that I was home, I brewed some of my favorite blend of GoodBean coffee that I had special-ordered from Jacksonville, Oregon. As the delicious brew slowly dripped into my coffeepot and the tantalizing aroma wafted through my townhome, I reached for one of the many specialty mugs I had collected. Today's choice was a large yellow cup with the words *Rise Up* imprinted on the side.

I'm trying; I'm trying to rise up, I thought, alternately gazing at the cup and the coffeepot, wishing I could hurry the brewing process. But good things take time.

When the coffee was finally ready, I filled my cup, careful to allow room for Coffee-Mate hazelnut-flavored gourmet creamer—another personal favorite. *Man, I have a great life!* I thought as I stirred the rich creamer into my GoodBean. *It doesn't get much better than this.* I took a sip of coffee and savored the taste while I reminisced about the sensational tour I had just completed, everything I had accomplished, and the many dreams that had come true for me in 2009, the memories of performing at Madison Square Garden still fresh in my mind. I moved about the kitchen then eased into the foyer to look out the front window, warming my hands with the coffee.

Brr, it looks cold outside, I thought. Despite the arctic blast that had gripped the southern part of the country, I saw people happily moving about the neighborhood. It was still relatively early in the Christmas season, but many Nashvillians had already decorated their homes; some had started holiday preparations more than a month ago. Others were out stringing Christmas lights in the frigid air. They appeared to be enjoying the cold weather. *Brr, not me.* A shiver shook through me as I looked at the frost-covered grass. Without even thinking about it, I reached over and pressed the button on the thermostat, nudging the temperature control higher by a few degrees. I raised the cup of hot coffee to my lips and allowed a sip of GoodBean to slip down my throat, warming me as it went, it seemed, all the way to my toes.

As I heard the furnace kick on, a sense of guilt suddenly overwhelmed me. I felt convicted by my oh-so-comfortable lifestyle. I wasn't rich, but I had some money in my bank account. I wasn't blowing money like a rock star, but I certainly wasn't hurting either. The amount mattered little. It wasn't that I had so much, but so many kids I had personally encountered had so little.

I recalled the faces of some foster kids I had met recently. Many of them were nearing eighteen years of age, the pivotal point when the system mandated that they would "age out"—in other words, the foster home system would turn them out of their care and back on the streets. Many of these kids had nowhere to go, no family members with whom they could live; some had few, if any, marketable skills with which they could find work; a large number of them were emotionally stunted and not yet mature enough to make it on their own in the world. They were the vulnerable ones, the ones predators lurking in the shadows salivated to see. For other, more street-smart foster kids aging out of the system, their past experiences nearly predetermined that, without help, they would return to lives of crime, drugs, alcohol, prostitution, and, inevitably, multiple prison sentences or an early death.

I knew that many foster kids aging out of the system would soon be homeless as I once had been; many of them would be condemned to sleeping on the ice-cold ground as I had done. Yet here I was, in my toasty slippers and robe in my comfortable home.

Another shiver rattled through me. I could feel the goose bumps popping up all over my skin, but this time it wasn't because I was cold. I had made some promises to those kids and to myself. Not to the kids individually, but the promises were real to me nonetheless. Years earlier I had vowed, "When I make it in the music business, I will not forget where I came from, and I will come back to help the kids in foster care."

But I hadn't done it.

When, Jimmy? When are you going to get involved? When are you going to do something? When will you do anything to help someone other than yourself?

I'd had hit songs on the radio and performed in some of the finest concert venues in America. I had been on tour with a country music superstar and had sung and recorded with rock stars. My name and music had topped the prestigious *Billboard* charts for three straight weeks at one point in my career. By every standard in the music business, I had made it.

Yet I hadn't kept my promise to those kids. I felt like a fraud.

My heart pounded; my mind raced. *You've forgotten; haven't you?*

Had I forgotten what it feels like to scavenge for food, shivering in the cold? How could I have forgotten that dreadful rejection and abandonment I felt when my mom drove off into the night, leaving me to fend for myself in a strange city, hundreds of miles from anything vaguely familiar to me? All those times in lonely, dark places, hands and bodies that weren't mine moving against me? My days spent wandering desolate roads, my nights spent crying tears that refused to form with my eyes wide open, my sleep-deprived body lying awake in fear?

Standing there in my warm house, staring at the frigid conditions outside, I felt the cold reality slap across my face. *I haven't kept my promise.*

Oh, sure, I'd performed a few concerts in foster homes; I'd done one not long ago for a small group of kids at HomeBase, a foster care facility in Phoenix. I was always willing and quick to say yes when people asked me to help raise money for foster care–related charities. But I wanted to do something more, something significant. I wanted to make a difference in the lives of kids who have been told over and over that they are nobodies, nothing more than trash, and that their lives are meaningless and don't count. I wanted to help kids who are lonely, hungry, and cold.

Lonely, hungry, cold. At Christmastime . . . or anytime.

Thoughts of Santa Claus cluttered my mind. But instead of Christmas cheer and gifts, the images reminded me that I was as much of a fake as Santa. Basking in the warmth of my home, with friends and fans galore, I had forgotten what it feels like to be lonely. With my belly full, and probably in need of losing a few pounds after poor eating habits on tour, I had forgotten that horrible ache in my stomach as it screamed for food. And as my hands wrapped around my warm coffee cup, I didn't even want to think about how it must have felt for those kids who slept outside in the cold last night.

Where'd you go, Jimmy Wayne Barber? What happened to you? Who are you anyhow, and why are you here?

I knew the numbers. Thirty thousand kids every year age out of the foster care system the moment they turn eighteen. Many of them will become homeless, addicted, or imprisoned. Some will never see their twenty-first birthday. I knew I wanted to help those kids the way somebody had helped me. But how? What could I do? It couldn't be simply another benefit concert. In Nashville we have benefit concerts out the wazoo. Every week a group of music artists is raising money for some worthy cause, and no doubt that is one of the reasons our music prospers. But I wanted to do something more than mere music. I wanted to do something bigger, something on a grander scale that would raise awareness about the plight of foster children who would soon be homeless with nowhere to go.

It has to be something big, something to catch people's attention.

In what seemed like a shot out of the blue, I suddenly had an idea. In a fraction of a second, I knew! It struck me that one of the foster care homes in which I had done volunteer work was Monroe Harding, located in the posh Nashville community of Green Hills. Another facility was HomeBase in Phoenix. To raise awareness for these foster kids I could walk from Monroe Harding to HomeBase. I realized that would be like walking halfway across America; I could simulate being homeless the entire way. The whole idea seemed to come together from out of nowhere as though all the myriad pieces were being drawn together by a powerful Master Planner.

Thinking of the homeless kid I used to be and the many kids I knew were still out there in the cold—physically, emotionally, and spiritually—I realized God had more for me to do than to hang around drinking expensive coffee. I needed to get back out on the road, this time not in a tour bus but on foot, sleeping wherever I stopped for the night, whether in the home of someone kind enough to invite me in or on the freezing ground. Just as I used to do, when I was homeless and on my own, away from foster care.

The at-risk kids who age out of the foster care system are not able to do it all by themselves; they need somebody to meet them halfway.

I walked back to the kitchen and placed my nearly full cup of coffee in the sink. I picked up the phone and called Jenny Bohler. A journalist who had cut her teeth in the Nashville music community as a writer and editor at *Cashbox* magazine, Jenny later served as Reba McEntire's publicist, then moved to MCA Nashville Records, where she continued to promote Reba along with other artists, such as Vince Gill, George Strait, and Trisha Yearwood. She eventually opened her own company and now, along with Mike Kraski, managed my career.

I could anticipate Jenny's response to what I was about to tell her, so I mentally prepared my case: I'm going to walk halfway across America to raise awareness about foster kids who age out of the system. It won't take long; I've looked at a map, and it doesn't look that far. I'm pretty sure I can make the walk in three or four months. No, I'm not going to walk halfway across Tennessee. I'm going to walk halfway across America and invite people to join me. I'm going to call the walk Meet Me Halfway.

I rehearsed my lines as Jenny's phone rang. As well as anyone in the business, Jenny Bohler knew that for me to take a quarter of the year to do a walk like this, I could well be walking away from a thriving career in the music business. Moreover, she had worked hard to help get me what millions of hopeful, struggling music artists would give nearly anything to have—a career making music.

But I knew I would spend most of the winter writing songs, gearing up to go back out on tour in late spring or early summer. *Now* was the best time.

I already could hear Jenny and other people telling me, "Jimmy, your star is on the rise. Why don't you wait until you are a superstar, and then do the walk? You can have an even greater influence." I appreciated their confidence in me, but I was also aware that the music business could be quite fickle. A rising star today can fizzle overnight and be snuffed out in the ashes tomorrow. I had a platform now. I might never be able to create greater visibility than I could right then.

Jenny answered her phone.

"Hey, Jenny; it's Jimmy."

"Hi, Jimmy."

"I've got this idea," I said, making sure I had Jenny's full attention. "I'm going to walk halfway across America."

There was a long pause before Jenny finally said, "What?"

ON NEW YEAR'S DAY 2010, WHILE MOST OF AMERICA WAS getting ready to enjoy a smorgasbord of football, food, and halftime shows, at 9:44 a.m. CST—I checked—I left my warm, comfortable townhouse and went across town to Monroe Harding foster care home where, after a brief talk to the kids, I began walking halfway across America.

Along the way I met some good people—some wonderful, fascinating, amazing people—and I had some incredible experiences, some fun times and some downright frightening ones. By the time I finished, I had walked seventeen hundred miles on foot, taking one excruciating step after another, facing everything from freezing temperatures in Tennessee to rattlesnakes on the road in Arizona. And in true dramatic fashion, I traversed the final fifty or sixty miles on a broken foot. It was the most incredible trip of my life.

But it wasn't the toughest journey I'd ever taken.

Part Two

THE CRAZY YEARS

Three

LIFE WITH CARROLL

MUSIC AND MAMA COMPOSE ONE OF MY FIRST VIVID MEMO-
ries of life in the Carolinas. Unfortunately, it isn't a good memory.

I was three years old and standing in the street, watching the taxi
roll away. My mom sat in the backseat of the cab, yelling at me through
the window to get back in the yard. I heard Glen Campbell singing
"Rhinestone Cowboy" on the taxi's dashboard radio as I stepped back
on the grass and the car pulled out of the trailer park where we lived. I
stood there alone, silently calling out for Mama to come back. It wasn't
the first time she had left, and it would not be the last time I would
experience a similar scenario during my early childhood. Indeed, it was
the type of good-bye that set the stage for the rest of my life.

Although I was born in Kings Mountain, North Carolina, a
little more than a year after my sister, Patricia, the three of us moved
to Johnsonville when Mama met a handsome, dark-haired, blue-eyed
gentleman named Carroll Collins. Patricia's and my real daddy had
abandoned us and was long gone before I could say my first word, but
Mama was never without a man for long. A petite, hazel-eyed beauty,
Mama was a bona fide man magnet. She and Carroll met and married the same year Elvis Presley died, and shortly after that, we moved
out to the country and settled in a small but picturesque two-bedroom,

white farmhouse nestled in the middle of a tall, green cornfield. At five years of age, I could not imagine what was in store for me beyond those straight lines of cornstalks or where the two-lane road in front of our house might lead. I just sensed that Mama and Patricia seemed happy, so I was too.

That's why I couldn't understand why Mama always wanted to leave. Anytime a man treated her well, she'd get antsy and feel suffocated. She'd bolt, sometimes with Patricia and me and at other times leaving us to fend for ourselves.

But Carroll was a good man—a salt-of-the-earth kind of guy—and he sincerely loved Mama, so he always took her back.

When Mama wasn't suffering from what later came to be called bipolar disorder—whatever that was—ours was an idyllic life, almost like a scene out of one of those black-and-white sitcom television shows. A chicken coop and tool shed stood behind the farmhouse in the backyard. One day I decided to crawl under the shed, where I found a batch of hen eggs along with an old, dirty army helmet. I filled the helmet with eggs then scooted back out to take them inside and give them to Mama. She was thrilled with my gift. "Oh, Jimmy, I love you," she said as she pushed me away.

Out in the country we made our own entertainment. For instance, Carroll stretched a clothesline across the backyard and clamped empty milk jugs to the line with wooden clothespins. He and Mama enjoyed target shooting at the milk jugs—and with a shotgun, Mama couldn't miss.

This was where I first caught lightning bugs in a jar and where the sound of the cicadas filled the air, creating their own music. It was where I caught and held a fish for the first time and where I picked a watermelon, along with peanuts and green beans, from the garden Mama tended. This was where my hands first shelled corn on an antique, cast-iron corn-sheller that sat in the corner of Carroll's welding shop.

This was the place where Carroll taught me to use a hammer and saw and later how to steer a go-cart and ride my bike without training wheels on our horseshoe-shaped sand driveway. This was also the place where I fell chin-first on a huge rock in the front yard while waiting for the bus to arrive and take me to the private Christian school that Carroll paid for Patricia and me to attend.

Oh, sure, there were those few weeks in the hospital inside an oxygen tent, recovering from pneumonia, and the time I had my tonsils removed. There was the time Mama accidentally closed the door on my left-hand ring finger—an important appendage for a future guitar player—and we had to race to the doctor so he could sew my fingertip back on. Some bad things happened during those years, but they never overshadowed the warmth of love that filled our farmhouse.

Always smiling, Carroll was a fantastic stepdad; he spent nearly every weekend with the family. He took us boating on Saturdays and to church every Sunday and every Wednesday night. Patricia and I participated in the church Christmas plays, and there were lots of gifts for all of us on Christmas morning.

This was life with Carroll, a safe, secure existence—a place where dreams could come true. Love and happiness flowed consistently, like a calm Carolina river. Even at five years old, I could tell the difference between the life we had left behind in Dixie Village Trailer Park and the new one we had in the middle of that cornfield in Johnsonville. To this day, I don't know why Mama never figured it out.

It was the calm before the storm.

PATRICIA STARTLED ME AWAKE IN THE MIDDLE OF THE night by shaking my arm. "Mama wants us in the car," she whispered.

"Wha . . ." I mumbled, rubbing my eyes and trying to blink the sleep out of them.

"Just hurry." Patricia repeated orders I recognized as coming directly from Mama.

In the darkness I crawled down from the top bunk bed and headed toward the front door. Even though I was barely awake, as I passed by Mama and Carroll's bedroom, I noticed that Carroll was still asleep in the bed. I crept silently past the doorway and outside to the car, where Patricia already had the door open for me.

For what felt like a long time, Patricia and I waited quietly in the car, wondering what happened, where we were going, why we were leaving, and why Carroll wasn't coming with us. Mama offered no answers. Instead she ran out of the house, carrying an armful of clothes. She threw them in the trunk and climbed behind the wheel.

Mama drove nonstop through the night, heading toward Crowders Mountain, North Carolina, to Grandpa's place. She wasn't in the mood for talking, and Patricia and I knew better than to ask questions. We simply shut our mouths and our eyes and tried to sleep. By midmorning we arrived at an old house sitting on a hill. When we walked in, it was impossible not to notice that the dark house reeked something awful—a combination of foul smells from pipe smoke, a waste chamber, and a musky basement.

I grappled with what was happening, unable to comprehend it, but it was obvious that this wasn't a pleasure trip to see Grandpa. I wanted to ask Mama, but she was acting strange. Her facial expressions were different; her demeanor was different. I couldn't figure out why. We stayed there for a week or two before Mama decided to go back home to the farmhouse and to Carroll.

After the seventh or eighth time this happened, Carroll stopped taking Mama and the rest of us back. He simply said, "I've had enough," and he banned us from ever returning to that farmhouse in the middle of the cornfield, the place where dreams lived and thrived.

I never understood why Mama left the wonderful man who treated her like a queen. But I slowly came to understand why he didn't take her back anymore.

Something wasn't right in Mama, and even a good man like Carroll could not cure her. Only God could do that—and back then He seemed a million miles away.

TODAY, A BLACK-AND-WHITE PHOTO OF MAMA SITS ON MY dresser. I keep it there because it explains a lot of things in her life and mine, and it helps me, all these years later, empathize with Mama and maybe understand some of the erratic things she did. She's approximately three years old in the tattered photo. Her eyes are sad, and she's frowning. Her hair looks as if the barber placed a bowl on her head and trimmed around it, leaving her sandy brown bangs a half-inch above her thin brows. She's wearing a floral print dress and holding a hard plastic baby doll by the leg. She's staring upward to the left of the camera lens, as though trying to please someone she must obey.

When I look at this photo, I see an innocent little girl who appears to be afraid of much more than a photographer. I would be an adult before I found out that during her childhood, Mama had been treated badly by a number of men. Maybe that's why she had such a love-hate relationship with so many men—including me.

Four

VANCE STREET VICE, MAYHEM, AND MURDER

MAMA AND CARROLL EVENTUALLY DIVORCED. I WAS SEVEN, and they had been married only a few years. Mama, Patricia, and I moved to Gastonia, North Carolina, a city of about seventy thousand people, located a few miles west of Charlotte. Gastonia has a long history in textile manufacturing and was home to the largest textile mill in the world, the Loray Mill. Author John A. Salmond exposed the horrible conditions of the industry in his book *Gastonia 1929.*

Similar to many inner-city areas surrounding factories in America, the local neighborhood went downhill as the manufacturing center took over. By the time we moved to Gastonia, the Loray Mill was an enormous five-story, red-brick structure with green windows, and the entire complex was surrounded by a high, rusty, chain-link fence. Inside the enclosed area the textile mill flourished; outside the fence the locality turned into nothing short of an American war zone. Mama found a place where we could live, an inexpensive, pale yellow house on Vance Street, in the industrial section of West Gastonia, right across the street from the mill. Mama thought she had scored a bargain; nobody told us it was the most dangerous section of town.

To say the least, Vance Street was not the best neighborhood in which to grow up. "Greasy Corner," as we called the intersection on the north corner of Vance Street and Franklin Boulevard, was the hot spot for the local prostitutes. I had no idea what the word *prostitute* even meant, but I was fascinated by the women who stood out on the corner at all hours of the day or night, dressed in tight pants and wearing lots of makeup while chain-smoking cigarettes. When Mama saw me staring at the women, she warned me, "Now, you stay away from those women. Do you hear me?"

I didn't understand why she'd say such a thing since the women seemed so friendly. After all, they waved at everyone who drove by.

Late one night a male friend of Mama's brought one of those women to our house and asked if they could stay the night. Mama made Patricia and me spread a quilt on the hardwood floor. That's where we spent the rest of the night, on the floor right beside our bed, while mom's friend and the *friendly* woman used our bed to have sex. When I woke up the following morning, they were still lying naked in our bed, on top of the twisted sheets and blanket. The woman's right leg draped over the man's left leg. She stirred, woke up, and caught me standing at the foot of the bed, staring at her. She smiled but made no attempt to cover herself.

That was the first time I had ever seen a naked woman in our home. It would not be the last.

MAMA HAD ONLY A FIFTH GRADE EDUCATION. SHE COULD read and write, as long as you didn't mind a lot of misspelled words. Although she made numerous foolish mistakes and unwise decisions, I always believed that Mama had a good heart and good intentions. In my naive seven-year-old mind, that explained why we always had such a strange assortment of people hanging around our house. Welcoming the freeloaders may have been a direct result of Mama's Baptist background.

A nearby Baptist church ran a bus route, picking up and transporting people who had no other means of getting to church. One wintry night Mama, Patricia, and I were the last passengers off the church bus. As always, the driver waited in front of our house as we walked to our front door.

It was late evening, and a light blanket of snow covered the ground. Mama fumbled with the keys, trying to unlock the front door, when she noticed two teenagers huddled close together behind a pine tree in our front yard. A streetlight shined down from behind them. Neither of them wore a coat, and they were both shivering so badly that their bodies were shaking. The boy held his hand against his mouth as if he were trying to keep warm by breathing on his hands.

Mama called out, "Who's there? Who are you?"

"Tate Coffee," the boy responded weakly, "and this is my sister, Barbara Jean."

Fresh from a rousing Sunday evening church service, there was no question in Mama's mind about her responsibilities. "Well, come in and get warm and get somethin' to eat," she said.

The church bus drove away as Tate and Barbara Jean followed us inside and waited in the living room while Mama built a fire in the fireplace. Tate continued holding his closed hand up to his lips, clutching a rag that looked like half of a sock and inhaling through his mouth. Every so often he would take a plastic bottle from his back pocket, remove the cap, hold the rag on top of the bottle, and then flip the bottle upside down, saturating the rag with paint thinner. He'd return the bottle to his back pocket and then hold his fist with the wet rag in it up to his mouth.

I noticed that his hand was raw and cracked. His eyes were red and glassy. Obviously, the paint thinner was making Tate look and feel the way he did. Barbara Jean never said a word the entire time they were there; she just sat quietly beside Tate. After Mama fixed something for Tate and Barbara Jean to eat, we all settled in for the night.

As kind and noble as Mama's gesture was, it set in motion a never-ending downward spiral. From then on Mama took in every Tom, Dick, or Sally who happened to come by the neighborhood and needed a place to crash. In the following months our house went from smelling like Pine-Sol—Mama's cleaning agent of choice—to beer and dirty clothes. It seemed every drug addict, sniffer, prostitute, and criminal who stepped foot on Vance Street found refuge at our house.

It got to the point where strangers wouldn't even knock before they would come in, raid the refrigerator, and find a spot on the floor to sleep for the night.

One of the addicts who'd been occupying our living room floor told Mama that a guy named Forrest Rose and his pregnant girlfriend, Dixie, were living in the woods near our house. Mama immediately headed out the back door and trudged into the woods until she found them, bundled up inside a cardboard box covered in plastic and snow. She begged them to come back to our house and stay until they could get on their feet. They came, but they never got on their feet. Quite the opposite. Once they moved in, Forrest invited all his lowlife friends to visit. Many of them became visitors who wouldn't leave. These druggies, alcoholics, and venereal-disease-ridden derelicts took over our home, adding to the lunacy of life on Vance Street.

We had people such as "Crazy Fletcher," who lived in one of the many mill houses—nearly identical small homes built by the textile companies and rented to their workers—near our house. One night Crazy Fletcher showed up at our house, carrying a record player along with an Ozzy Osbourne album, *Bark at the Moon*. Fletcher set up the stereo on the floor, cranked up the music, and then sat down in a chair beside it, staring at the odd menagerie of maniacs mingling in the living room.

After a few songs, Fletcher stood up abruptly and stormed out the back door. He returned a few minutes later, carrying an ax. Striding straight through the house, he reached the record player in the living room, raised the ax high in the air, and brought it down with all his might, crashing it right in the middle of the stereo and splitting the album and turntable in half. Everyone in the room scattered as Crazy Fletcher screamed while chopping his record player to smithereens.

A few of the remaining bystanders grabbed Fletcher and threw him out of the house. He never explained what set him off. Maybe he didn't know. Or maybe he *really* didn't like Ozzy Osbourne's music. Regardless, nobody thought much of Fletcher's escapade. It was just another day on Vance Street.

In addition to Crazy Fletcher, we had "Preacher Beaver," who lived in a mill house to the right of ours. I never heard him preach, but I often saw him sitting on his front porch swing with his Bible on his lap and some notebook paper beside him as he worked on the upcoming Sunday sermon, occasionally waving at those of us passing by. The only time I ever saw Preacher Beaver leave his porch was when I cut my foot in the neighbors' yard. Preacher Beaver saw me bleeding, ran and picked me up, and carried me home.

A meek, kind man, Preacher Beaver occasionally gave the kids in the neighborhood a quarter to buy an ice cream cone from the ice cream truck as it came up Vance Street. But one afternoon, with a bunch of slackers slouched on Mama's front porch, Preacher Beaver walked over to our house and yelled, "Who threw the beer can in my yard?"

The culprit could have been any number of drunks hanging around Mama's house, but everyone remained silent. We all noticed that Preacher Beaver brandished a pistol in his right hand.

"Well?" The preacher waved the pistol in the air.

No one said a word.

He then pointed the pistol in our direction, randomly aiming at each person sitting on our porch, as he asked again, "Who did it? Who threw the beer can in my yard?"

Preacher Beaver was clearly upset, but it was hard not to laugh because his hand was shaking so badly. He looked like Barney Fife, when Barney would get so nervous he could hardly hold on to the gun.

A couple of the preacher's relatives ran out of his house and up the sidewalk. They grabbed him and tried to calm him down. During all the commotion, one of the hippies sitting on our porch decided to stand up. I'm not sure if he was planning on confronting Preacher Beaver or if he was merely getting out of the line of fire. It didn't matter. One of the relatives stepped in front of Preacher Beaver and hit that hippie so hard in the jaw it knocked him off his feet and flat on his back. That was the loudest punch I had ever heard. No one on our front porch moved an inch. We all sat as quiet as convicts in a prison yard during count time.

The family finally managed to get Preacher Beaver under control and wrestled the gun out of his hand. They walked him safely back to his house. One of them carried the pistol as Preacher Beaver prayed loudly. I would have loved to have heard his sermon that Sunday. I didn't hold his outburst against him; I guessed that everyone has a breaking point— even Preacher Beaver.

With people such as Crazy Fletcher and Preacher Beaver living nearby, I wasn't surprised when I met another interesting character in our neighborhood. Carver, a freckled-faced, freckled-fisted, redheaded boy, would fight anybody. Carver was older and much bigger than I was, and he appeared to be cool, so I wanted to hang around with him.

The first time I met Carver, he growled, "Come with me." I didn't know where he wanted me to go or why, but I followed him obediently. We walked all the way through some woods that led to an open field. That's when he took a lighter out of his pocket and lit some of the dry weeds. Within seconds the small fire spread like a school of tadpoles in a pond, engulfing the dry field in enormous red flames.

I got scared and ran as fast as I could run back to the house, leaving Carver there at the edge of the burning field. Even from our yard I could still see the black smoke billowing over the tree line. I heard the fire truck sirens and their squawking CB radios through the trees. It took several hours for the firemen to extinguish the blaze, finishing the job before the flames fanned out to the wood-frame mill houses nearby.

I never squealed on Carver, but when Mama heard he was a trouble-maker and probably the one who had started the fire in the field, she told me to stay away from him. That was easier said than done. Telling

Carver I couldn't be his friend anymore made me just one more person in his life who rejected him. And Carver responded poorly to rejection.

One day Carver stopped me on the sidewalk and told me to get off my bicycle. I was scared and confused, but I said no. That was not the answer Carver wanted to hear. Sitting on my bicycle, I looked up to see Carver's face; instead, all I could see were his flaring nostrils. He looked like a giant compared to me. Carver reared back his cannonball-sized fist and belted me in the nose, knocking me clean off my bicycle. He then jumped on my bike and pedaled away. I never saw my Huffy bicycle again.

Carver stopped me another day, when my sister and I were walking home from Clay Street Elementary. This time I didn't have a bike he could steal from me, so I wasn't sure why he was picking a fight with me. He started thumping on my chest and, like most skinny, scared kids do, I looked down. That's when I saw the box cutter lying in the grass.

I quickly reached down, grabbed it, and slid it open, hoping that Carver hadn't seen or, if he had, that the blade might cause him to think twice before attacking me.

It didn't. Carver taunted me, "Come on, runt; cut me; come on, try it!"

I was more afraid now, thinking Carver was going to take the knife away from me and slice me to pieces with it. Instead of threatening him, I froze.

Just then a policeman pulled up in his patrol car. The officer yelled out the window and told my sister and me to get in the car and he would take us home. We immediately jumped in the car and closed the back door. As we rode away, Carver stood there snarling at me.

In a weird way I felt sorry for him. Carver was a broken, fatherless boy who took out his pain and anger on everyone else around him. I knew what it was like not to have a dad. I understood Carver all too well.

The police officer took Patricia and me to our house and let us out of the patrol car. But before I could get away, the officer said, "Son, I saw you pick up something back there. Can I have it?"

I lowered my head sheepishly and handed him the box cutter. He nodded and drove away.

SOMEBODY WAS ALWAYS FIGHTING ON VANCE STREET. WHEN the druggies and drunks weren't laid out in our yard, staring dumbfounded at the stars, they were slugging it out with leather belts wrapped around their hands, beating each other with their belt buckles. Violence was a normal, everyday occurrence on Vance Street, but one incident still gives me chills.

Leonard King was a kind, quiet guy who lived in our neighborhood, vying for Mama's attention. One night, in an effort to please Mama, Leonard agreed to give Cecil Cross a ride to his grandmother's house just off Airline Avenue. A fledgling artist, Cecil loaded his string art in the backseat of Leonard's car and got in the passenger's side backseat. I sat next to him, behind the driver's seat. Mama rode shotgun, and Patricia sat between Mama and Leonard in the front seat.

Along the way I peppered Cecil with questions about his string art. He patiently answered each query and explained how he drove nails in the board and ran yarn from one nail to the other, creating the artistic pattern. All the while, he continued giving Leonard instructions about how to get to his destination.

When we turned onto his grandmother's street, he said, "Just pull over there in front of that car," pointing at a car parked on the side of the road. Leonard complied and pulled the car over to the side of the dimly lit street. Cecil exited the car with his string art.

Almost immediately, a car rolled up behind us with its headlights off. The bright lights came on just as the car came to a stop, only inches away from our bumper. Instantly the headlights of the car parked in front of us came on as well. Both of the cars' headlights were on their brightest beams, illuminating the inside of Leonard's car. The four of us sat there like sitting ducks in a shooting gallery. Leonard mumbled something under his breath as he looked through his sideview and rearview mirrors.

I looked out the back windows but couldn't see anything due to the blinding headlights. I peered through the front windshield and saw nothing but blinding lights as well. Then suddenly a skinny man slid between Leonard's front bumper and the car parked in front of us, making his way around to the driver's side, where Leonard was sitting. The man shined a flashlight in Leonard's face then yelled back to someone standing by the trunk of the car parked in front of us. It sounded as if he said, "Yeah, that's him."

The skinny man turned back to Leonard and hit him in the face with the back of the flashlight. Leonard's head lurched toward Patricia.

The attacker then leaned inside the car and hit Leonard in the face and head several more times with the flashlight as he repeatedly yelled, "I told you, I'd get ya!"

Leonard tried to defend himself against the man's blows, but the attacker's leverage gave him an advantage over Leonard, who was stuck in the car's front seat. The skinny man slugged Leonard one last time then jogged away.

Leonard's face was bleeding. Mama wasn't saying a word, and Patricia was leaning into Mama's side, frantically holding on to her. We sat there stunned and scared. Then the man's silhouette came sliding between the bumpers again; this time he carried a hatchet. He quickly maneuvered his legs between the two cars' bumpers and ran around to the driver's side, where Leonard was still sitting, dazed and only semiconscious.

I looked up from the backseat through the driver's side window into the attacker's angry eyes as he jerked open the front car door. Leonard tried to pull the door closed, but he was too weak, and the skinny man had already stepped between Leonard and the door.

The man then raised the hatchet back as far as he could reach and swung it downward, burying the blade into Leonard's body with a horrifying thud. Leonard let out a bloodcurdling scream that sounded like three lions roaring at once. Mama and Patricia screamed and bolted out the passenger's side door.

But the attacker wasn't done. The next chop split Leonard's leg open.

There was a third, fourth, and fifth chop to Leonard's torso and arms. I sat paralyzed by fear, wanting to flee but too afraid to move. At one point I saw what looked like a sickening cord of blood stretching three feet in the air, like crimson chewing gum, from Leonard's body to the blade of that hatchet.

Now in a full rage the maniac began swinging the hatchet wildly, at times hitting the top of the car as he brought the hatchet down again and again. Each time the blade sank deep into Leonard's body, it sounded like a belt popping, followed by another of Leonard's hysterical screams.

Somehow Leonard mustered enough strength to turn over on his stomach and crawl out the passenger side, slithering onto the asphalt, and then he staggered to his feet. Blood saturated his clothes and dripped on the road.

The attacker saw Leonard standing and quickly ran around to the front of the car, attempting to catch Leonard before he got away. Leonard seemed to realize that the skinny man was not going to stop until he was dead, so with what must have been a burst of last-ditch-survival adrenaline, Leonard staggered off toward Airline Avenue.

The attacker was right on his heels and swung the hatchet one last time, hitting Leonard in the back of his head, close to his neck. He stumbled forward and disappeared around the corner.

By then I had gotten out of the car and was standing in someone's yard. I looked around for Mama, but she and Patricia had already fled the scene.

I glanced backward and saw the skinny man along with several other men knocking all the windows out of Leonard's car. I didn't know what to do other than run in the same direction Leonard had gone, so I ran down Airline Avenue. Not far away I saw lights and an open bay garage door at a warehouse. As I got closer, I could see people standing around Leonard as he lay on the floor in a puddle of blood. I ran up and told the people there what had just happened.

The paramedics arrived shortly afterward and loaded Leonard's unconscious, barely breathing body into the back of the ambulance. I crawled inside, as well, and sat down beside the paramedics. They worked on Leonard the entire time as we raced to Gaston Memorial Hospital. When we arrived, I got out and stood at the back doors of the ambulance and watched the paramedics pull Leonard's bloody body from the ambulance and rush him through the emergency entrance. I didn't know where else to go, so I followed them.

The hospital staff stopped me and then led me to a separate room, where they asked lots of questions. I did my best to tell them who I was and what I saw, but I'm sure I must have sounded like a traumatized kid who had just seen a nightmare—because I had, and the scene was burned forever in my mind.

After a while a few of Leonard's family members arrived; then Mama showed up. She had left Patricia at a friend's house.

Leonard's family grieved over why this had happened to Leonard and who might be to blame. While Leonard's family was consumed by grief, Mama quickly grabbed my hand and stormed out of the hospital. We ran across the hospital parking lot and onto the dark highway. Mama held out her thumb as cars approached.

Finally a stranger in a black hot rod with loud mufflers pulled over and offered us a ride. I crawled in the backseat, and Mama sat in the front. The windows were down, and the cool night air was blowing in on my face as we drove off into the night with another strange man.

I never found out for sure what happened to Leonard. Some say he died from complications stemming from the attack, and the crime remains unsolved to this day. Others say he is still alive, living under a different name. But I can't help thinking that someone in Mama's circle of friends knows the truth.

THE CHURCH BUS CAME RIGHT ON TIME AND SAT IN FRONT of our house the following Sunday morning. The driver blew the horn as he always did.

Mama staggered to the front door and yelled out, "We ain't going this morning!"

I heard the church vehicle drive away, and I cursed the day we'd ever moved to Vance Street.

Five

MATINEE MADNESS

I TEND TO BLOCK OUT MANY OF MY MEMORIES OF VANCE Street because most of my early years spent there were filled with visions of violence. But I did have one happy experience while living there. When I was about seven years old, Mama wanted to get away from the negative environment for a few days, so we went to visit our grandmother's sister, Patricia's and my great-aunt Wilma, who lived on Hill Street, on the west side of the Loray Mill. Hill Street was just a few blocks away from Vance Street, but it was an entirely different world.

Aunt Wilma was a pleasant and kind woman who always had a homemade cake sitting on the table. Her home smelled like someplace people actually wanted to visit.

One day while visiting Aunt Wilma, a bunch of kids were playing outside, so Patricia and I joined them. A lady in the neighborhood gathered some of us kids together and said, "I'm taking my daughter to a movie, and you can come along. But first, you must ask your parents if it is okay for you to go to the movie with us." Kids scurried in every direction, begging their parents for permission to go to the theater.

Patricia and I didn't budge. We knew Mama didn't have the money for a movie ticket. Nevertheless, I wanted to go, so I told the lady that Mama wouldn't mind if my sister and I went to the movie. We joined the other kids and followed the woman closely. Together we all crossed the busy street and headed up the sidewalk to the theater's ticket window with our movie money in hand—well, at least the other kids had their money in hand. Patricia and I didn't have a dime.

The other kids excitedly handed the woman their money, and she purchased their tickets. When she realized Patricia and I had no money, she was a bit irritated. This obviously put her in a jam; she could either buy tickets for Patricia and me or we'd all have to walk back home together without seeing the movie. She had enough wisdom to know that she didn't dare leave my sister and me outside while she and the other kids went inside to watch the movie.

She eyed us suspiciously as she slowly reached into her pocket and pulled out some money. She handed the money through the small opening at the bottom of the ticket window, and the person inside handed her two tickets, one for me and one for my sister.

We all went inside and sat down in chairs that were like those in our school auditorium, but it was a dimly lit room. Some people were already inside, sitting and eating popcorn and drinking colas while waiting for the show to begin. A beam of light came on from behind us and shined on the white floor-to-ceiling screen hanging in front of us. I couldn't believe it. *This is the biggest television I've ever seen*, I thought.

I sat there mesmerized, on the edge of my seat the entire show, with my eyes glued to the screen. The man on the screen ran down the streets of Philadelphia and up to the top of some steps, where he began shadow-boxing. Children followed him just as we had followed the lady to the theater. The boxer held his fists high above him as if he had already won the fight. Children surrounded him, and the sound of French horns made me believe I could be him.

It was the first time I'd ever been inside a theater to watch a movie and the first time I saw *Rocky*.

Mama enjoyed movies, too, I discovered, but her movies weren't as inspiring.

Mama had a friend with whom she liked to watch movies. He was a balding old man, twice her age, who looked as though he could be her father, and Mama always acted like a silly little girl every time he was around. In the middle of the day, Mama took us to her friend's house to visit. Some other men and women were already there. "Sit here on the couch, and do not get up," Mama instructed. "You better not move," she warned us. Then Mama and the old man and the others went into a back bedroom.

Patricia and I sat there and looked at each other. We had no food or water and nothing to do. We sat . . . and sat . . . for as long as we could. Like most seven-year-olds, I had an extremely limited ability to sit still. I could hear a staccato sound, almost like a rattlesnake, or a ticking like that of a machine gun firing nonstop in the distance, and I was curious. I wondered what could be making that noise. The sound was coming from the bedroom, where Mama and the others had gone.

Still, Patricia and I waited. After what seemed like hours, I couldn't sit any longer. I stood up, quietly walked to the front door, and slowly opened it, careful not to make any noise. Although Patricia was only a year older than me, she often played the role of caretaker. "Don't go outside," she said fearfully, "or you'll get in trouble."

I ignored my sister's warning and went outside anyway. Once I stepped off the porch, I heard music coming from a few houses down and across the street. I'd never heard this style of music before, but it sounded good. I walked down the street to that house and stood in the road, staring at the people who were dancing on the porch and in the dirt of their front yard. A number of the dancers wore polyester pants and colorful silky shirts, and many of them had a lot of hair on their heads. This was my first experience with black music.

Their bodies were moving in perfect rhythm with the sound belting out of the tall cabinet speakers in the yard. At one point a man leaned forward so low that his Afro haircut nearly touched the ground as he danced. Never before had I seen anyone move like that.

They were dancing to the music of a new group that I later learned was known as The Gap Band. The dancers were having so much fun; I could feel the energy coming from them, and I wanted to be a part of it.

The song finished, and everyone in the yard applauded, laughing out loud, hugging, slapping each other on the back, and wiping sweat from their faces. One of the dancers noticed me staring at them, and for some reason, I got scared.

I thought, *Oh, no; Mama's probably looking for me.* I ran back to the old man's house and up the steps, quietly opening the front door. I walked inside and saw that Patricia was still sitting on the couch right where I'd left her. I noticed immediately that she'd been crying. "You weren't supposed to leave," she whispered hoarsely. I could tell she was scared and had been worried about me. She knew better than to cross Mama. "Mama's going to get you."

I stood there in the living room for a second, and then, despite Mama's firm instructions, I walked over to the bedroom door and turned the doorknob. When the door opened, the sunlight illuminated the room, and I saw two reels turning on a film projector that was casting a beam of light onto a sheet hanging on the wall at the foot of the bed. The sheet was a makeshift movie screen, and on it were naked people. There were also naked people in the bed, and one of them was Mama.

"Get out of here!" Mama yelled loudly when she saw me. I quickly backed out of the doorway, toward the couch where Patricia was still sitting. A few minutes later Mama came out half-dressed, clutching some of her clothes to her chest. She was not happy.

"Come on, let's go!" She nodded toward the door.

Matinee madness was over; it was time to go back to Vance Street.

Six

HANGOVER STREET

WE MOVED A LOT WHEN I WAS A LITTLE BOY, MOSTLY within a twenty-mile radius and usually every time Mama ran out of rent money. Although we were flat broke, Mama always worked out some way to satisfy the landlord, even if it didn't last for long.

Not surprisingly, when our landlord evicted us from our house on Vance Street in the middle of the winter, we didn't move far—just a short distance away to Hanover Street, which wasn't exactly a step up. Mama negotiated with a landlord who allowed us to live in an empty mill house, but we couldn't afford to pay the gas bill, so there was no heat. A wood-frame mill house without heat in the winter affects the body much like rigor mortis does after a person has been dead three hours, only quicker. The cold seeps through the floors, walls, and windows into your skin, chilling to the core of every bone in your already cold body.

Pipes burst under the house and kitchen sink. Doorknobs felt ice-cold, almost sticking to my hand when I tried to turn them. Even the water in the toilet bowl froze like a mini ice skating rink.

Mama persuaded some of her Vance Street cohorts to haul our few possessions and what little furniture we owned to Hanover Street. That was the good news. We now at least had blankets and a bed. The

43

bad news? Mama's shady friends now knew where to find her, and they did. Often.

Eventually Mama scrounged up enough money to get the gas turned on, and almost immediately our house became the favorite party spot, especially on weekends. Mama's friends brought booze and drugs, and they began piling in every Friday before dusk. They partied late into the night, winding down early Saturday morning, and then starting up again Saturday afternoon. Mama soon began referring to Hanover Street as *Hangover* Street.

Sloan was a newbie who came around on Fridays, always with a pocketful of cash and some alcoholic beverages to drink. Straight, relatively conservative, and clean-cut, Sloan's short haircut made him an obvious target for the roughhousing hippies. After they'd all been drinking heavily and smoking pot for a few hours, a few wild and crazy hippies grabbed Sloan and held his arms and legs while another drunk or druggie peeled off Sloan's clothes. Sloan put up good fight, kicking and screaming, but he was no match for the thugs.

Laughing uproariously and yelling the entire time, between gulps of beer or whiskey, the bullies stripped Sloan naked and then bound his hands and ankles with duct tape. One of them continued taping Sloan's legs together as the others helped hold his body. Together, they circled that roll of duct tape around and around his entire body from his feet up to his neck, wrapping him like a mummy.

Sloan begged Mama to make them stop, but she thought it was funny. The hippies continued torturing Sloan by tickling him and doing obscene acts to his body parts. Finally, before things turned more violent, Mama yelled, "Okay, that's enough! Leave him alone." The drunks and druggies laughed and rolled Sloan onto the floor, where they left him, "accidentally" tripping over him each time they caroused through the room.

At some point one of the dopers had mercy on Sloan—well, a warped sort of mercy, anyhow—ripping the duct tape off his hairy body. Ironically, Sloan came back for more abuse every weekend. I guess he figured a painful acceptance was better than none at all.

ONCE MAMA'S FRIENDS ARRIVED ON FRIDAY, ANY FOOD WE might have had in the cupboards or in the refrigerator disappeared. The freeloaders scarfed up every morsel, regardless of how hungry Patricia or I might be. By Saturday they had eaten everything in sight, but since they were so high, nobody seemed concerned about going out for food. And nobody noticed that Patricia and I hadn't eaten since our last meal at the school cafeteria through the free lunch program.

With my stomach growling, I came up with an idea of how to get food for my sister and me. I watched Sloan and the others drink until they passed out. When I was certain they were blitzed, I slid my hand down into their pants pockets and removed all their beer money. Saturday morning, while they remained hung over, I walked down the street to a small mom-and-pop convenience store, where I bought hot dogs and drinks.

Even at seven and eight years old, I knew that if I didn't do something, Patricia and I would not eat until we went back to school on Monday. So as I grew more street-smart, I also became more skilled at relieving the drunks and druggies of their excess cash. Sometimes, I intentionally bumped into one of the inebriated bums while he was still awake. He'd think it was an accident and throw his hands in the air. I'd run around him a few times, and before he realized what was happening, my hand was in and out of his pocket.

Duct-taped Sloan was an easy mark. He foolishly carried an entire week's worth of pay in his pants pockets. Usually by about three in the morning, whatever money he hadn't spent on alcohol was mine. I'm not proud of stealing, but it was a means of survival.

Getting robbed and duct taped didn't deter Sloan from coming back to Hanover Street. But one night after the dopers taped Sloan, one of them punched and kicked him as he lay on the floor. Another jumped on him and did worse. Sloan squalled from the floor, begging Mama to stop the abuse, but Mama couldn't help him. Another druggie placed a piece of duct tape over Sloan's mouth, and the bullies continued beating him. When they had satisfied their bloodlust, they left Sloan lying on the floor, still taped, tears streaming down his face. It was sick.

I felt sorry for Sloan and guilty that I had taken his money, but it was too late, and there was nothing I could do. I had spent his beer money on food. I thought about trying to pay him back, but after that humiliating beating, Sloan never returned to our house again.

PATRICIA AND I ATTENDED WOODHILL ELEMENTARY. I WAS a slow student, not because I wasn't bright but because I had too many other things on my mind besides learning about Dick and Jane. To me, school was just another place to eat a free lunch and play dodgeball.

One day my second grade teacher made me stay after school but wouldn't explain why. When she finished her duties, she told me to get in her car; she wanted to drive me home. On the way to my house, she lit a cigarette and took a few draws.

I spoke up and reminded her of what she'd said earlier that day: smoking is harmful to your health.

She looked over at me and rolled her eyes. "You're right," she said. But she continued smoking.

When she pulled in our driveway, she snuffed out her cigarette, got out of the car, and walked to the front door with me. She asked if she could speak to my mom. I opened the front door, invited the teacher inside, and yelled for Mama.

The moment Mama saw the teacher, she assumed I had done something wrong. "Whatcha done now?" she yelled at me, her eyes flashing, right in front of my teacher.

The teacher intervened. "Jimmy hasn't done anything wrong, ma'am," she said flatly. "Look at his shoes."

The three of us simultaneously looked down at my feet. The entire front of my shoe was torn open, and my dirty sock was exposed. I had been wearing those shoes for several months, and the kids in class had been making fun of me. I had become oblivious to their comments, but the teacher had not.

She glared at Mama and said, "Go buy your kid a pair of shoes." The teacher turned on her heels and walked out of the house. I didn't realize the significance of the teacher's words, but Mama recognized that the teacher was not making a suggestion; she was issuing a warning.

I'm not sure where Mama got the money, but a few days later I got a new pair of white tennis shoes with black stripes on the side. I thought surely those shoes would make the kids stop picking on me. When I showed up at school, wearing my new shoes, one of the kids pointed at them and started laughing. "Those aren't real," he told everyone in the class. I didn't understand what he was talking about; the shoes felt real to me.

But apparently my new shoes were Adidas knockoffs. Some of the kids who were sitting near me got up out of their desks and ran to the other side of the room, as if my new, cheap shoes had cooties. Ironically, most of the kids in my class were poor, so why they would make fun of my shoes never made sense to me.

But those knockoff Adidases did one thing for me that none of my detractors could deny. Perhaps to help ease my pain at being teased by our peers, Anne, a fellow second-grader who lived next door and was the love of my young life, laid a big kiss on me.

She and I were playing inside a cardboard box I'd found behind a factory near her house and dragged into her front yard. We had gotten inside the box and were just sitting quietly, staring at the walls. Anne leaned over and put her lips on mine. When she finished kissing me, we sat there again, awkwardly looking away from each other. I couldn't believe what had just happened, but I knew I wanted to do it again!

Seven

GHOST TALES

Poverty is a relative thing. When we moved from Hanover Street to Pine Manor Apartments in Kings Mountain, North Carolina, it was the first time I had ever lived in an apartment. I couldn't believe the luxury! We had heat and air conditioning, running water, and electricity, and the apartment complex had its own Laundromat that also served as the school bus stop during the winter.

I was afraid to go inside the Laundromat, and I didn't most of the time unless it was freezing cold outside. Then I would go inside and stand in a corner, where I could remain inconspicuous, staring through the window toward our apartment door, down the hill.

One morning a few of the bigger kids wrestled a smaller boy into one of the dryers and held the door closed while one of the bullies put a quarter in the slot and turned the machine on. Everyone laughed as the boy rotated around inside that hot tumbler as he tried hard to brace himself with his feet and hands. But the dryer eventually turned hot, and he lost his grip, bouncing around like a Ping-Pong ball, the dryer fins beating up the kid something awful with every rotation. When the bullies finally pulled him out, the young boy was burned and bruised. Being of small stature myself, I decided to wait for the school bus outside in the cold from then on.

In warmer weather one apartment became a canteen store, where the kids could buy ice cream and other snacks. The African-American woman who lived there would answer the door and invite us in, then lead us to the kitchen, where she had an assortment of snacks for sale. The price for each item was more expensive than what the local convenience store charged, but that's how the old lady made a profit. I didn't have much spare change to spend, but when I did, I liked helping the canteen woman.

We also had an openly gay guy who lived at Pine Manor. He, too, was African-American and had long, painted red fingernails. He never spoke; he just danced like a robot, and all the kids in the apartment complex loved to watch him.

Despite growing up in a racially charged section of the Carolinas, I never thought twice about someone's skin color, but that didn't mean it wasn't an issue. The "N" word was a common term among both blacks and whites, and although our schools had been integrated since the mid-1960s, there was a lot of leftover racial animosity. My best friend George was an African-American kid, much bigger and taller than me. When George's parents realized that we had become buddies, they told him he couldn't hang around with me anymore. I thought it was because I had begged George to ask his parents if I could have a piece of his birthday cake. "No, Jimmy," he told me sadly. "It's because you are white." I tried making new friends in the complex, but none of the new kids were as cool as George.

One day a group of kids and I were walking through the pine trees, getting ready to cross over a barbed wire fence, when I heard sirens. I turned and saw a fire truck stopping in front of our apartment.

I ran as fast as I could, past the firemen who were just arriving, and into our apartment, where I saw Mama sitting on the couch crying. Both her arms were severely burned. A young black man had pulled both empty vegetable drawers out from the bottom of the refrigerator and ran to the neighbor's to fill the drawers with ice. He quickly brought them back and then filled the remaining space in the drawers with water. He carried each drawer over to the couch and placed a drawer on both sides of Mama. By then the fire company's paramedic was in the house, and he told Mama to place her forearms inside the drawers. Mama sat there crying as the paramedics prepared to take her to the hospital.

When she calmed down enough, Mama explained what had happened. The grease had caught fire on the oven range when she was frying potatoes for Patricia. She tried putting the fire out with a towel but to no avail, so she grabbed the handle on the pan and rushed to the back door, holding the pan of burning grease. When she opened the back door and attempted to toss the grease out and away from her, the grease apparently flew upward and came back down on her arms.

About that time the young black man, who was in the neighbor's yard, looked up, saw what was happening, and came running to her rescue. I didn't know him, but it was another reminder that when someone is in trouble and needs help, skin color or other external circumstances are irrelevant.

MAYBE THE FIRE WAS A WAKE-UP CALL. MAMA TRIED HARD to get her life on the right track after that. She even got a job, working the third shift at the Mauney Hosiery Mill, a textile mill that produced stockings. She began dating Joel, a security guard who monitored the mill, but that relationship ended as soon as Mack, a former lover of Mama's, came back into the picture.

I'd heard that Mack waited on Joel to get off work one morning and attacked him as he walked across the parking lot. The last time I saw Joel, he had a broken arm and was wearing a sling.

Mack didn't hang around too long this time—probably because he didn't want to frequent our apartment complex. A large number of African-Americans lived in the Pine Manor Apartments, and Mack was extremely racist.

SINCE MAMA WAS WORKING NOW, THAT RAISED THE ISSUE of childcare at night. Patricia and I were too young to be left alone, so

Mama asked the Chesters, a family who lived in a house near Kings Mountain battleground, to babysit my sister and me while she worked.

Mr. Chester was a quiet man who worked outside in his yard a lot. Mrs. Chester was an old-fashioned Baptist woman who always wore a dress and kept her hair up in a bun. She cooked over a woodstove in the kitchen, and her chicken and dumplings were some of the best I had ever eaten. I was always glad when Mama dropped Patricia and me off at the Chesters' home before their dinnertime. No matter how much or how little food they had, Mrs. Chester made it stretch to fill two more mouths.

The Chesters had an adult son, Karl, living at home. Mama said Karl was a bit slow, and that's why he still lived there. But Karl had a lot of people fooled; he was smarter than most people realized.

He and his mother shared an unusual ghost story. I didn't know all the details, but the gist of the story was this: if three lightning bugs get inside the house, it means you'll see a ghost that night. Most likely this story was part of Mrs. Chester's strategy to make us do our best to keep the front screen door closed. Nevertheless, I was always thinking about ghosts whenever Patricia and I stayed with them overnight, which we did often when Mama worked the third shift.

One night I was lying in Karl's bed. It smelled of firewood and dirty socks. The quilts were old and heavy, and the sheets were stained with perspiration. I was nearly asleep when I heard a creaking sound and saw the wooden bedroom door slowly open. The moonlight was shining through the windows, creating strange shadows on the bare walls and antique furniture.

I was thinking about the ghost tale when I saw a silhouette of a large person standing in the doorway. The figure crept toward the bed, and when it passed the window, I could clearly make out that it was Karl.

I was scared and wanted to say something, but I didn't; instead, I pretended I was asleep. Peeking out from under the covers, I saw Karl stand beside the bed and take off his pants, carefully making sure they didn't hit the floor with a thud that might awaken me. It wasn't all that unusual that Karl would get undressed; it was, after all, his bedroom in which I was sleeping. But then he braced himself with both hands on the bed and sat down. He lifted his legs and eased back onto the bed, apparently trying not to wake me. He lay there for what seemed like forever and didn't move. Nor did I. In fact, I barely allowed myself to breathe.

After a while Karl repositioned himself as if he was trying to get comfortable. He remained in that position a little longer, then rolled over on his left side, facing me. He was so close I could smell his breath and his dirty body. I tried hard to pretend I was asleep.

Karl reached over with his right hand and took my right hand, then slowly pulled it back toward him, placing my hand on his privates.

I flinched in horror, but I was so afraid, I dared not move. Instead, I continued to pretend I was asleep. Karl tried to manipulate my hand, so I jerked it away and rolled over to my left side, up against the wall, tucking both of my hands under my body. I laid awake like that the rest of the night, doing my best to give no indication that I was aware of what had just happened.

Karl finally sat up in bed, then stood, grabbed his pants, and walked out of the room. The following morning I was terribly sleepy from being awake all night, but I had to get up and go to school.

Mama met Patricia and me at our apartment when the school bus let us off later that afternoon. As soon as I saw Mama, I told her what Karl had done and urged her to confront him or at least tell Mrs. Chester. I just knew Mama was going to believe me and take us to another baby-sitter from then on—but she didn't.

When Mama told Mrs. Chester about my accusations, Mrs. Chester simply smiled and said, "I think Jimmy's imagining things. He must have dreamed he saw a ghost in the bedroom." She looked at Mama, waiting for her to agree.

Mama nodded, and that was that.

I begged Mama not to take us back to the Chesters' house, but she did anyway. "Jimmy Wayne Barber, you shut your mouth and stop lying about Karl."

"I'm not lying, Mama," I said through my tears. "I'm not."

"Well, we need the Chesters to babysit, so just shut up your mouth."

My sister and I went back to the Chesters' house that evening. When we walked in the kitchen, Mrs. Chester was cooking, as always, and Mama immediately started bragging on what a great cook she was. It was as though nothing had ever happened.

Karl was in the living room watching *The Incredible Hulk*. He had taken off his shirt and was growling and flexing his muscles in front of the television, along with the Hulk. I sat down in a wooden chair at the kitchen table and glared at him. I couldn't believe what this pervert had done to me. I looked at Mrs. Chester and then at Mama as she was going out the door, leaving for work.

As she did every day, Mama said, "Jimmy, you behave."

Me behave? What about this guy? I wanted to say. Of course, I didn't. I merely smiled a fake smile and waved good-bye.

That night I lay there in Karl's bed, staring up at the ceiling. Every so often I saw the flickering of a lightning bug in the corner of the room. I counted, "One . . . two." I lay there and waited until my eyes refused to remain open any longer, and I eventually fell asleep.

Mama never said whether she believed me or not, but I was thankful when she found another sitter in the neighborhood who volunteered to watch Patricia and me; we never had to go back to the Chesters' house again. I missed the dumplings, but not the ghost tale.

Eight

I THINK I KNOW
HOW JESUS FELT

PATRICIA WAS NINE, AND I WAS EIGHT WHEN MAMA informed us that we were moving out of Pine Manor and into a small, yellow house on Second Street in Kings Mountain. Although at the time I could not have imagined myself ever meeting her, much less singing with her on an album, country music legend Patty Loveless once lived in the brown trailer on the opposite end of Second Street. Patty had been singing with the Wilburn Brothers when she married the group's drummer, Terry Lovelace; but to avoid confusion with porn star Linda Lovelace, Patty had changed the spelling of her last name. When she and Terry divorced, she kept her stage name.

The Second Street neighborhood was filled with kids, and there was always something exciting going on—a baseball game, hide-and-seek, skateboarding, or building clubhouses from cardboard boxes or scrap lumber we scavenged from discarded factory pallets.

I experienced a number of firsts on Second Street. It was where I first heard a curse word on public television and where I first tried Beech-Nut chewing tobacco. I nearly gagged on the stuff, so I glued the pack closed and returned it to the store.

Most significantly, it was while living on Second Street that I first met my biological father. I had seen him before, but I was too young to understand who the stranger was and why he was reading a book to me. But I guess at nine years old, Mama considered me "of age."

She was driving down Second Street one day when she pointed at a man sitting on a porch swing. "Jimmy," she said matter-of-factly, "that's your daddy."

What? My daddy? Really?

I scooted up to the edge of the backseat and looked out the window to see the man Mama was talking about. He was wearing a white T-shirt and faded blue jeans. His hair was combed back neatly, like James Dean's. His arms were spread out resting on the back of the porch swing, and he looked as though he was relaxing without a care in the world.

Mama continued on to our home, only a few blocks away. The moment she pulled into our driveway and parked the car, I jumped out and ran as fast as I could back down Second Street. I found the house with the man on the front porch, raced across his yard, and bounded up the steps onto the porch. Apparently surprised at the intrusion, he stopped swinging and simply stared at me.

I was out of breath, but I was so excited to let him know who I was. I could hardly contain myself as the words tumbled out of my mouth: "Mama said you're my daddy!"

He peered at me intently, then smiled and said, "Well, how ya doing there, buddy? It's nice meeting ya." He leaned over and patted my head with his right hand. Then before I had a chance to say another word, he stood up, pulled at the waist of his jeans, and said, "Well, you take care of ya self, all right?" He walked inside the house and closed the door behind him.

No! Wait! I screamed silently. *Don't go. Please don't go; don't leave me again!*

But he was gone. I stood on the porch, peering through the windows on the door, waiting . . . waiting . . . and waiting for him to come back out. But he never did.

After a while I turned around and dragged myself back down the steps, then down Second Street to the small, yellow house, only three blocks away.

There's an old saying: "You don't miss something you've never had."

That's just not true.

My dad's mother, Mary Jane Stewart, had despised Mama even before I was born. Maybe she knew Mama's reputation because when Mama became pregnant with me, Mary Jane refused to believe I was her grandson. "My son will not be responsible for another man's baby," she declared.

I can remember seeing my paternal grandmother only once in my entire life. It was Halloween, and Mama dressed Patricia and me to go trick-or-treating. She must have been thinking about how my dad treated me that day on the front porch because our first stop was at Mary Jane's house.

With no hint of a warning, Mama pulled her car in front of my grandmother's house and said, "Go to the front door."

Patricia and I excitedly headed to the house, carrying our empty trick-or-treat bags. Just as we got to the front porch, Mary Jane flung open the door and called out whimsically, "Trick or treat?"

But as soon as she said it, she looked over our heads and saw Mama sitting in the car. Patricia and I stood there with our trick-or-treat bags open, looking up expectantly at Mary Jane. But Mary Jane didn't budge, and she offered us no candy. Instead, she stood there in the doorway, holding a handful of candy, looking back and forth, first at us, then at Mama, then back at us. When she realized Patricia's and my identity, she yelled a few mean words to Mama. Not to be outdone, Mama returned fire and sent a blistering litany of expletives and other nasty words right back at Mary Jane.

My grandmother quickly stepped back inside her house, slammed the front door, and turned off the front porch light. She never gave us the candy. Patricia and I stood there at the bottom of Mary Jane's steps in the dark until Mama yelled, "Come on, git in the car."

For us, trick-or-treating was over.

MAMA WAS A STRANGE MIXTURE OF THE HOLY AND THE profane. If Mama and Canadian Mist were a mixed drink, it would be called *Intemperance*. Mama drank too much, got drunk, and did stupid things, like driving her green Ford LTD around and around the yellow house at a very high speed.

She'd crank up her music to blaring levels as she listened to "Night Moves" in the comfort of her home. There was nothing unusual about that, but then she'd raise all the windows in the house, open the front and back doors, and turn "Hollywood Nights" up as loud as that stereo would go, so the whole neighborhood could hear it. Like a vinyl Bob Seger record, Mama had an A side and a B side. The only consistency in her life was her inconsistency.

She could be sitting Indian-style on the living room floor singing "Highway to Hell" on Saturday night, then come Sunday morning, she'd be at the Baptist church, front and center, singing "I'll Fly Away."

In a similar manner, after several months of late-night partying and early morning toilet-hugging, Mama would eventually crawl her way through the beer cans and liquor bottles strewn across our floor, back into the loving, forgiving arms of Jesus.

Mama got saved just about every other month, or whenever the rent money ran short. Patricia and I always knew when Mama had invited Jesus back in the house by the overwhelming smell of Pine-Sol. When Mama was off the bottle, she was in the Bible; and when she was in the Bible, she made Patricia and me clean the house all day long and read Scripture to her before bedtime. Mispronouncing a biblical term was our worst fear, but words such as *propitiation* or names like Melchizedek and Nebuchadnezzar were simply not in my nine-year-old vocabulary. When we couldn't pronounce the words, Mama would yell at us, and then she'd whip us—sometimes severely.

Although Mama didn't know how to pronounce all the words in the Bible either, to her, anyone who couldn't read the Bible was either purposely insulting God or was demon possessed, and she was not about to allow her kids to be either.

I almost hated to hear Mama say, "Jimmy, read to me," as she handed me the Bible. Mama made me afraid of Christians, Jesus, and Pine-Sol.

THAT SUMMER A GROUP FROM A CHURCH UP THE STREET came knocking on doors in our neighborhood, informing parents about their upcoming Vacation Bible School. It was a good deal for parents in our neighborhood—several hours of free babysitting, some snacks, and even some cute crafts, combined with some good moral teaching—what lazy parent wouldn't want their kid to go to Vacation Bible School? Mama sure did.

I didn't want to hang out with people like Mama, who hit kids when they mispronounced Scripture, but Mama made me go anyway. I arrived on Monday morning at the big, brick Baptist church, carrying with me a big, bad attitude. I knew I couldn't buck Mama's decision that I go, so my best alternative, I figured, was to misbehave and get kicked out as soon as possible.

I walked into the classroom, where all the other kids were already seated. The teacher was handing out beads and wire to be used in making a craft. "Hello!" she said, sounding genuinely happy to see me. "Just have a seat over there." She pointed at an empty chair in the back left corner of the small room. I took my seat as the teacher walked around the room, handing out supplies.

Intent on getting kicked out, I made a few funny noises, trying to interrupt the class as she talked, but she pretended she didn't hear me. She then walked back to the front of the class and told everyone to take the wire and begin threading it through one of the beads. As we followed her instructions, she began telling the story about Jesus and why He died on the cross. I made a few more noises but soon realized she wasn't going to allow me to disrupt her or to control the class. After a while I gave up and listened to the story. As much as I didn't want to admit it, I was intrigued.

The class continued threading beads and twisting wire while the teacher explained how the nails were driven into the hands of Jesus and how a crown of thorns was cruelly forced onto His head. She emphasized that, by giving His life for us, Jesus paid the penalty for all the bad things we had done, and He did that because He loved us.

Mama had taken Patricia and me to church periodically throughout our lives, but I'd never heard the story told that way. Mama tended to emphasize the fear of God rather than the love of God. She knew she deserved to go to hell, and she was determined to keep us on the straight and narrow path by scaring the hell out of us. But as I listened to the teacher in Vacation Bible School, I was inspired to learn that Someone actually loved me, that Jesus loved Mama and my sister and me so much that He would die on a cross for us.

By the end of the teacher's story, we all had made crosses out of the beads and wire, and the craft was ours to take home with us that day. But I couldn't have cared less about the handmade cross we had just made. I wanted to learn more about Jesus—the One who didn't smell like Pine-Sol.

WHEN I GOT HOME, I GATHERED A FEW PIECES OF SCRAP wood left over from the tree house I had built several months earlier. I positioned the wood into crossbars and nailed them together. I dropped the bottom of the cross into a shallow hole in the backyard and tied a piece of rope to each end of the cross, forming a loop where I guessed that the nails would have been driven.

I backed up against the cross and slipped my hand through the rope on the right side of the cross and then my left hand through the other loop. I stood there, roped to the cross, thinking about what the teacher had said earlier. I had always thought that Jesus must have been angry at those who had hurt Him so severely, that He surely must have been bitter toward even the people for whom He was dying. After all, it was their sins that drove Him to that cross. But the way the teacher had told the story, it seemed to me that as Jesus was dying to make a way for us to go to heaven, He didn't feel like hating anyone; He felt like forgiving everyone.

I stood against the cross for quite a while, thinking about what Jesus felt. After a while I tried pulling my hands out of the ropes, but my hands were stuck, the ropes like handcuffs around my wrists. I raised myself up on my tiptoes and lifted the bottom of the cross out of the hole and began dragging it to the front yard, calling for Mama to come outside and help me get my hands out of the ropes.

Mama had been standing in the kitchen, watching me through the window above the sink the entire time, and to my surprise she was already on her way out—but not to rescue me. Oh, no! In her hand she wielded a large leather belt.

The moment I saw the strap, I knew exactly what she was thinking. She thought I was mocking Jesus. But before I could explain why I was on the cross, Mama began hitting me with the belt. All I heard between every powerful swat was, "Don't . . . you . . . ever . . . make . . . fun . . . of . . . Jesus . . . again!"

"I wasn't making fun of Jesus, Mama!"

I tried to run from her with the cross on my back, but it was awkward moving, and I couldn't get away. My feet must have gotten tangled up with the bottom of the cross because, suddenly, both the cross and my body tumbled backward toward the porch, landing hard against the steps.

Mama continued beating me with the belt, swinging it as though she were some kind of modern-day Roman soldier. She finally stopped, mumbled a few words I couldn't understand, and then marched back inside the house, leaving me still attached to the cross. I was stuck, with my legs side-saddling the cross and my hands still trapped in the ropes. I squirmed every way possible but could not free myself from the cross. Then after a few more minutes, I looked up and saw that a car had stopped in front of our house. *Thank God!*

An elderly woman stared at me from inside the vehicle. She was crying, but she made no attempt to help me. Whether Mama saw the woman or not, I may never know, but for some reason, Mama came back outside and pulled my hands out of the ropes. I slumped down on the porch, glad to be free of the cross.

It wasn't long before Mama stepped off her Jesus soapbox and down to eye level with the devil. Soon the usual assortment of unusual men appeared back in our lives, followed by the debauched partying and violence.

Not surprisingly, Mama's food stamps disappeared, along with the electricity. Mama was too broke to buy kerosene and too hungover to build a fire in the wood heater.

The bitter cold North Carolina mornings made getting ready for school without heat an enormous challenge. In an attempt to warm my school clothes for the morning, I placed them in the bed with me every night. Trying to stay warm as long as possible, I dressed under the covers in the morning.

I'd lie there until I heard the bus coming up the road, then I'd jump out of bed really fast and run out the front door down to the bus stop.

I was so happy to see the spring buds appearing on the trees. Warmth would soon return to our home. But, unfortunately, with the coming of springtime Mama's already erratic behavior grew worse. One spring afternoon I walked into the bathroom, where Mama was standing in front of the sink, washing her hands.

She looked back over her right shoulder and screamed at me, "Git outta here!"

I obediently started to turn and run away, but when I heard Mama crying, I turned back around and quietly eased up behind her. That's when I saw Mama wasn't washing her hands. She was drowning our newborn puppy in the bathroom sink.

"No, Mama! No!" I screamed and cried for her to stop, but she continued holding the pup under the water, yelling all the while, "He's sick, Jimmy. He's sick!"

I was old enough now to know that it wasn't the puppy who was sick. It was Mama.

Nine

FOSTER KID

DURING THE FIRST NINE YEARS OF MY LIFE, MAMA BOUNCED in and out of jail on numerous occasions for varying lengths of time, most often incarcerated for shoplifting or other misdemeanors. While Mama served her time in jail, Patricia and I lived with Grandpa or friends or relatives until she returned. Increasingly, her bipolar personality produced more erratic behavior, sometimes even violent. When I was still nine years old, Mama was committed to Broughton Hospital, a state-operated psychiatric facility. Since the doctors expected her to be there for quite a while, Patricia and I were sent to a foster care receiving home in Dallas, North Carolina, which at the time felt like the loneliest place on earth.

In the foster care system, a receiving home is a house set up to accommodate the daily living needs of any number of children, depending on the size of the facility and the number of staff members. In most receiving homes, kids are housed two to a room and eat their meals together in a family-style dining room. The kids go to a public school and take part in activities meant to simulate an ordinary family. An abandoned child or a child whose parents have been killed, incarcerated, or otherwise indisposed is placed in a receiving home while he or she is waiting for an available foster parent or family willing to provide a more permanent home. The receiving home is meant to be a temporary situation, but sometimes, if foster parents aren't readily available, the time can be extended.

The receiving home in Dallas actually comprised two houses facing each other, one home for the boys and another for the girls. Myrtle and Clyde Edgewood were the house parents, and when we first checked in, Patricia and I were the only two kids there. Since we were siblings, we were allowed to stay in one house together.

Myrtle and Clyde often invited their friends over for dinner. I hated these dinners because, for some reason, Clyde felt compelled to demonstrate in front of his friends what a great disciplinarian he was and how much authority he had over me.

One evening we were sitting at the table with guests, and Clyde ordered me to "Eat that," referring to some food on my plate. I had eaten most of my meal, but I didn't care for whatever it was that Clyde wanted me to eat, so I said, "I don't want it."

Clyde interpreted my refusal to eat as rebellion, and he was having none of that—especially in front of the guests to whom he wanted to show off. He yelled loudly from across the table, "You'll eat it, or I'll knock your teeth out!"

I was quickly learning that there are good, kindhearted foster parents and staff members working within the system—and then there are others.

PATRICIA AND I SPENT MUCH OF OUR TIME OUTSIDE DURING our stint at the Dallas receiving home. Sometimes Patricia simply sat on the swing, neither talking nor swinging. She would stare at the ground and rake her foot across the sand. I could tell she was sad and depressed, and I was concerned for her, but I didn't know how to help.

It was thirty days before Patricia and I were finally sent to a foster home. I know now that thirty days is not an exorbitant amount of time for the system to find appropriate, approved foster parents, especially for two siblings. But at the time, a month with Clyde constantly on my back seemed like forever.

Pat and Don Miller, our first official foster parents, were just the opposite of Clyde and Myrtle. They were wonderful! Don was a tough US Navy veteran, and Pat was a schoolteacher of British descent. She spoke with a strong British accent. They met in England while Don was in the military. Prior to Patricia and me, they had taken in at least six other foster kids over the years.

Pat and Don Miller also had a daughter of their own, Tina, who was about the same age as Patricia. The three of us became inseparable, and the Millers treated us as their own kids; they did so many kind things for Patricia and me.

Don took the entire family to Sims Ball Park to watch baseball games. We ate hot dogs and drank Coca-Cola. He taught me how to target-shoot with a BB gun. Pat made hand-sewn dresses for Tina and Patricia to wear to a special event; she joked that she was going to make me a matching shirt, but she didn't. She gave us cookies and milk every night before bed. We attended church together every Sunday, and Tina invited us to the horse stables every time she went. It was an ideal foster home experience.

Nevertheless, despite the Millers' unconditional love and kindness, I was still an angry nine-year-old boy inside. I was in the yard one day when I caught a frog. I put that frog inside a can and began kicking the can around the yard. When I finally opened the can, the frog was dead.

A profound sense of sadness overwhelmed me. I knew I shouldn't have treated that poor frog like that. The frog was just trying desperately to survive; he did not deserve to die. Worse than that, I realized I had killed that frog for probably the same reason Mama had drowned our puppy—it was all about exerting power and control over something. I felt awful.

The memory of killing that frog has haunted me to this very day. Even now, I have a brass frog that sits on my windowsill in memory of that innocent frog. I see it every morning, and it is a reminder not to take out my problems on others.

Years later a woman working with foster children in Wyoming told me that she collected trinkets of frogs and gave them to kids. "Why?" I asked.

"Because FROG means to Fully Rely On God," she explained. I liked that and vowed never to take my anger out on someone or something else; instead, I choose to fully rely on God.

PATRICIA AND I LIVED WITH THE MILLERS FOR NEARLY SIX months. Although I missed Mama, when Pat and Don told us our mom was out of the hospital and wanted us back, it was a terribly sad day. We had no choice in the matter; we were going back home.

As I was packing my clothes, I spied the Bible that had been sitting on my dresser. I hadn't read much of it, but I placed it in my bag. I knew it was stealing, but I didn't think Don and Pat would mind.

A female social worker soon arrived, and after patiently waiting as we exchanged tearful good-byes with the Millers, she took Patricia and me to reunite with Mama. The social worker didn't stay long when dropping us off; she made sure Mama was home and asked her to sign a few papers.

Mama's faded yellow house on Second Street looked dingy and dreary with beer bottles and other garbage strewn everywhere, as though a disaster had struck. It smelled damp and musty and reeked of kerosene, exactly as it had before Patricia and I were taken away by the state and placed in foster care. Old blankets were nailed to the woodwork and draped over each bedroom doorway where strong wooden doors once hung. Where the doors had gone, we had no idea, and Mama wouldn't say. After living in clean, comfortable conditions with the Miller family, coming back to Mama's dump was depressing. It was like stepping back in time. It all looked the same, just as filthy as the day we left it.

The only thing different was the new man in Mama's life.

MAYBE IT WAS HER WAY OF SEEKING SECURITY, OR PERHAPS it made sense to her that she must first arrange some means of feeding Patricia and me, but retrieving her children was not Mama's top priority when she was released from the psychiatric hospital. She had to find a man.

And she did. While we were living in foster care, Mama met and married Robert Davis. Patricia and I disliked Robert from the moment we met him because we felt he monopolized Mama's time. No doubt we were right, but I'm not sure it would have mattered.

Soon after we were reunited, Mama and Robert decided we were moving a short distance away to Stanley, North Carolina, a town of about thirty-five hundred people in Gaston County, in the southwestern part of the state. The per capita income of the town was around $17,000, and more than 10 percent of the population lived below the US established poverty line.

During the 1700s, a prospector named Stanley came to the area, panning for gold. The creek and town were named after him, but ironically, he didn't stay in the area. During the Civil War, the town's railroad depot, Brevard Station, was a major departure point for soldiers leaving for the war and for sending supplies to soldiers in the field. People were leaving Stanley from the beginning—and for me, leaving Stanley could not come soon enough.

But living there was cheap, so it appealed to Mama and Robert, neither of whom had a job or wanted one. We moved into a small, two-bedroom duplex, with thin interior walls between us and our neighbors and a wood heater in the living room.

It was a low-income community much like Vance Street and the other rundown neighborhoods where we had lived, and similar to them, this part of Stanley had its own identity. The railroad tracks ran east to west through the center of town, and being a young boy living south of the tracks had big disadvantages.

Once you get picked on and don't stand up for yourself, you are more than likely going to become the neighborhood punching bag. I learned that the hard way.

It seemed like every kid in that neighborhood, including one of the boys' oldest sisters, wanted to take a swing at me. One day a kid called out my name, and when I turned around, he punched me in my nose so hard it made my eyes water. Blood poured from my nose onto my shirt.

Mama saw the kid hit me, and she came running out the front door of our apartment. Instead of taking up for me, she started yelling at me, "Hit him back!"

I looked at her, somewhat dazed.

"I said to hit him back," she hollered again.

I didn't really want to punch the kid, but Mama kept yelling and repeating her command over and over. She was probably right; she understood the survival-of-the-fittest mentality much better than I did. Unlike most parents who want their children to avoid fighting, my mom actually became angry at me because I *wouldn't* hit the boy.

Now I was more afraid of Mama than I was the kid who had decked me. I thought for sure that Mama was going to whip me if I didn't punch the kid, so I finally hauled off and smacked him in the jaw as hard as I could with my fist. The look on his face reminded me of how I had felt when he'd hit me. I just stood there and stared at the boy, feeling sorry for him. He didn't swing back, so I turned around and walked home. At least there would be one less bully to bother me after that.

Seth and Brice were the only two good kids I found who lived near the apartment complex in which we lived. Seth's dad was the associate pastor at the church where Mama took my sister and me. When I met him at church, Seth and I instantly became friends; he later introduced me to his friend Brice. The three of us spent most of the summer goofing off at the water treatment plant, walking along the edge of the reservoir walls, throwing debris into the dirty water below that had been stagnant since the plant closed many years earlier. We played war in the fields near the apartments and had sleepovers in Seth's living room, where we would stay up late at night, watching television and talking loudly.

Unfortunately I had to walk through my dangerous neighborhood to get to theirs, which meant a bully challenged me nearly every day along the way. To avoid conflict and the likely possibility of being beat up by the bullies, I ran to my friends' apartment complex and back. I became a fast runner, too, but not nearly as fast as Brice.

Unlike Seth or me, Brice was a quiet kid, very humble. I once asked Brice, "How are you able to run so fast?"

"My mother is in a wheelchair," he replied, "and when she calls for me, I need to run to her quickly. So I've developed some speed."

Brice's unselfish example really touched my heart.

VIOLENT INCIDENTS HAPPENED SO FREQUENTLY IN OUR neighborhood, few people bothered to call the police. Conditions continued to deteriorate around our apartment complex. And though I could live with the external corruption, what affected me most was internal hypocrisy and conflict.

For instance, when I was at Seth's one evening, I overheard his dad tell his sister to take off her roller skates while indoors. Seth's sister was slow to obey.

A few seconds later Seth's dad yelled, "I said take those [curse word] skates off!"

Hearing Seth's dad curse shocked me. I had grown up with profanity; I'd heard profanity in our home, in my school, and on the streets. But I couldn't believe the associate pastor had just taken the Lord's name in vain. It was terribly disillusioning. I ran outside and never went back to Seth's apartment.

Not long after that Seth and his family stopped attending the church within walking distance from our apartment, but I continued going to services nearly every Sunday and Wednesday. Church was the only place where I felt safe.

After each sermon the pastor encouraged the congregation, "If you want to give your life to God, come down to the altar area at the front of the church." As the preacher implored, a woman softly played the piano, enhancing the mood.

I stepped out of the pew, walked down the aisle, got on my knees, and bowed my head almost every time the preacher extended an invitation. Sometimes I'd be the only person kneeling at the altar, but I didn't care. I felt a strong connection with God, despite my disillusionment with people who claimed to know Him, and going down to the altar and praying was my way of staying connected.

NEITHER ROBERT NOR MAMA HELD A JOB THE ENTIRE TIME they were married to each other. They depended on the government to provide food for the family and pay all the bills. At the beginning of each month, Mama received a welfare check along with food stamps, so the whole family walked to the grocery store in downtown Stanley to stock up on a month's supply of groceries.

There we were: an able-bodied family of four, slowly following a shopping cart up and down each crowded aisle, staring at the name-brand foods but having to choose the generic brands because they were cheaper. Finally Mama eased the cart up to the checkout lane and unloaded the mountain of free groceries onto the conveyer belt. The cashier scanned each item, and the bag boy placed our groceries in brown paper bags. I watched intently, carefully checking that the cereal got into the bag, knowing that for Patricia and me, the two large boxes of cornflakes and powdered milk would be the staples of our meals for the next month.

Sometimes I finished my box of cereal before the month was over and another stash of food stamps arrived. When I did, Patricia shared the remainder of her cereal with me.

The cashier rang up the total, and Mama counted out the food stamps while Robert, Patricia, and I grabbed the bags of groceries and prepared for the long walk home. Rainy days and winter evenings were the worst times to go grocery shopping, but the wet, brown paper grocery bags were the least of my worries. My biggest concern was how fast we could get out of town before another bully from Kiser Elementary, where I attended, saw me carrying groceries down the sidewalk.

Grocery shopping was the hardest work Mama and Robert did the entire month. Occasionally Robert chopped a load of firewood, but once he learned I could chop wood, he laid down the ax.

When a new load of firewood arrived in the backyard—apparently, someone from the church had donated the wood along with more groceries—Mama yelled to me, "Get out there and chop some wood."

I lifted the heavy ax in the air and brought it down hard, driving that blade through the heart, splitting a block of wood in half. I then split the halves the same way. Once the block of wood was cut into quarters, I loaded Patricia's arms with each piece of fresh pine, and she carried the wood inside the apartment, where she let the wood roll off her arms onto the floor beside the wood heater, and returned for another load of kindling that I had chopped. Meanwhile, Robert and Mama remained in bed.

I LOOKED FORWARD TO GOING TO KISER ELEMENTARY EACH morning for two main reasons: free lunch and Nicole Lindsay, the prettiest girl in the world. Nicole had big blue eyes and long black hair, just like Wonder Woman. From the very moment I saw Nicole, I couldn't keep my eyes off her. I was too bashful to express my feelings for her, but wherever Nicole went, I went, too, following her around like a puppy follows its owner. Surprisingly, Nicole never said a negative or rude word to me. She didn't encourage my affections, but she tolerated me. She just pretended I wasn't there, in a nice way.

Shadowing Nicole as closely as I did, I naturally heard her conversations with her friends, many of which centered on a new Steven Spielberg movie about an extraterrestrial. It would be many years later before I finally saw *E.T.* and understood why Nicole and her friends were so enamored by the movie; by then it had already become a classic.

Extra money for movies was not available in our household. I did, however, earn two dollars once by doing an odd job while we were living in Stanley. Instead of spending the two dollars on a movie, I decided to give it to the church. To spread out my joy of giving, I traded the two dollar bills for eight quarters. My plan was to take one quarter to church each week for eight weeks and drop the twenty-five cents in the offering plate.

The first week, I took one quarter to church, but I foolishly left the other seven quarters in a Band-Aid can sitting on the stereo in the living room. When I returned from church, the can was gone, along with my seven quarters.

Robert didn't go to church that morning, but he swore he didn't take the quarters. I looked all over the house, but I never found the quarters or the can.

I was devastated. I felt as though I had let God down. I cried for several days.

Mama had borrowed a small black-and-white television from the preacher so Patricia and I could watch *The Wizard of Oz*. She promised to return the television right after the movie aired, but she didn't. About a month later the preacher came to our apartment in search of his television. Mama answered the door, but before he got a sentence out of his mouth, Mama cussed him out and threatened to fight him in the front yard.

The kindhearted preacher was stunned. So was I, along with being embarrassed. The preacher didn't get his television, and Mama never took us back to his church. Instead, Mama tried to remain "in the Word" by watching Jimmy Swaggart, an evangelist she had discovered while watching that little black-and-white television. She made Patricia and me watch Jimmy, too, every time he was on. The fellow playing the white grand piano seemed like a rascal to me, but I enjoyed his music, and Jimmy could sure preach up a storm.

Mama still demanded that my sister and I read Scripture to her at night by her bedside, as she'd pray and cry and then pray again. These prayers went on for what seemed like a half an hour, as did the beatings when we mispronounced words.

I believed in God, and I had embraced the message of Jesus, but as I encountered the cussing preacher, the soon-to-be public scandals surrounding televangelists, and Mama's confusing combination of faith and foolishness, I was becoming increasingly disillusioned with religion. *If God really loves me*, I thought, *He sure has some strange ways of showing it.* Unfortunately, staying away from church was not the answer and resulted only in a total spiritual decline for my entire family.

We stayed only a short time in Stanley; then we moved a few miles away, back to Dallas, North Carolina, where Mama found us a house with no electricity. We lived there for two weeks before moving back to Gastonia. Again. I was thankful that Mama didn't try to take us back to Vance Street; instead, she found some people vacating a house on Walnut Avenue, right behind R.O.'s Bar-B-Que restaurant.

I should have known we were in trouble when I noticed the cockroaches carrying out the furniture!

Ten

HUNGRY

HUNGER WAS THE WORST PAIN I EVER ENDURED AS A CHILD. Mama's beatings were abusive, and I took some shots from the bullies I met along the way, but no physical pain I encountered affected me quite so deeply as our lack of food and the perpetual gnawing I felt in my stomach. I grew accustomed to the abuse and the bullies, but I never got used to being hungry. Nor could I understand why there were so many cockroaches in our house, when there was hardly ever any food for them to eat.

Of course we had food for the first week of each month, when the food stamps arrived in the mail. But after that there'd be no food for the next three weeks because there'd be no food stamps left.

Going to bed hungry became a familiar way of life. Sometimes I tried to stay in bed as long as possible in the morning so I wouldn't feel the emptiness in my stomach quite as severely.

But one Sunday morning I noticed something different. The night before, Mama had dragged a mattress out in the yard; because the roaches were so bad, we couldn't sleep in the house, so Patricia, Mama, and I had slept outside. Her husband was passed out in some sort of stupor and probably didn't even notice the roaches crawling over his face.

As usual, when I woke up, my stomach was aching from not having eaten since school on Friday, when Patricia and I last received a free lunch. I sat up on the mattress and sniffed the morning air. A distinct aroma of bacon wafted through the air. And it sure smelled good! *Bacon? Surely not. Mama's not making bacon for us, is she?* I sniffed the air again. It was bacon, all right, but it wasn't coming from our kitchen. It seemed to be drifting in my direction from the neighbors' house next door—the same neighbors who didn't like us much. Those neighbors rarely spoke to my family, and they never opened their back door, the one that faced our house.

But today the back door was open, except for a screen door, through which the tantalizing scents were flowing. I sat there for a few moments, breathing deeply and looking longingly at the neighbors' door, and then, like a zombie drawn to the cemetery, I stood up and slowly walked toward their back door.

I stopped short of their steps, dawdling as though I were looking for something but, every so often, peeking toward their screen door. No one was in the kitchen or sitting at the table, so I gingerly walked up the steps, put my face against their screen and got a closer look. With my nose pressed against the black screen, I could see the food they had left on their table, and the smell of bacon was even stronger now.

I slowly pulled open the screen door, making sure the spring didn't squeak. It didn't, so I slipped carefully into the neighbors' kitchen. I could hear voices in the next room; it sounded as if the family was getting ready to go to church.

I tiptoed over to where it appeared they had just finished eating breakfast but hadn't yet cleared the table. For a moment, I stood still, listening intently to make certain no one was coming. I sure didn't want the neighbors to catch me inside their house. But then I saw it. Just an arm's length away from me was a plate with some scraps of bacon. A short distance away was another plate with more breakfast scraps; a little farther away was yet another plate half-filled with leftovers. I smacked my lips, and I could feel my mouth salivating. I reached over with my right hand and grabbed the bacon someone had left on the plate. At the same time I used my left hand to hold up the bottom of my shirt, forming a pocket where I could stash the leftovers and partly eaten food. I quickly began filling up the front of my shirt with the table scraps I retrieved off the food-smeared plates. I was so excited! My eyes were as big as silver dollars; I couldn't wait to dig in to this feast.

That's when I heard a man's voice, yelling, "Hey!"

I didn't take time to look or to figure out who was yelling at me.

"Hey, who are you? What are you doing here? Why you . . . get out of here!"

I didn't answer; I turned and ran through the kitchen and out their back screen door, clutching the front of my shirt to my chest, trying desperately not to jostle too much and lose my stolen scraps. The screen door smacked the doorframe loudly behind me as I leaped off the porch, raced across the yard, and hid behind our house.

When I was certain that I had not been followed, I sat down on some wooden steps and ate every piece of scrap stuck to my shirt, leaving behind nothing but a big greasy circle. I hate to admit it, but I didn't even share the table scraps with Patricia; I ate every morsel myself.

BEING HUNGRY SOMETIMES EMBOLDENED ME TO DO THINGS I wouldn't ordinarily do. On one occasion, I walked across Walnut Avenue to where an elderly lady was standing in her yard. "Excuse me, ma'am," I said, trying to be polite. "Do you have any bread I could eat?"

The elderly woman looked at me pathetically and said, "Stay here. I'll be right back."

I waited at the bottom of her steps. She returned with a half loaf of bread and a pack of ham.

"Oh, thank you, ma'am," I said. "Thank you!" I ran up the steps and took the bread out of her hand and then raced back toward my house.

The woman called out, "But I brought you some ham too . . ."

I stopped in the middle of the street, turned around, and said, "That's okay. I have mustard."

Say what? *Mustard?*

The dear woman watched me as I ran all the way home. I charged into the house, carrying the bread like a football and immediately began making mustard sandwiches for Patricia and me. I was so hungry that it never occurred to me that the bread and mustard might have tasted better with a bit of ham. But I didn't mind; after all, I was grateful the woman gave me what I had asked for—some bread.

MAMA KNEW WE WERE HUNGRY MOST OF THE TIME, AND every so often she would take some special steps to help. No, she didn't get a job. Instead, one night Mama woke Patricia and me around one o'clock in the morning. She had gone down the hill, sneaked into the preacher's garden, and stolen a few ears of corn. No doubt the preacher would have given Mama the corn had she asked nicely for it. But begging wasn't in Mama's nature. Stealing? That was okay. Using men to get what she wanted? Oh, yes, that was acceptable too. In fact, almost any means of obtaining what she wanted was legitimate to her—anything but hard work and common decency.

But I didn't think about scolding Mama for stealing. Patricia and I hadn't eaten all weekend, and we wouldn't eat again till we got back to school on Monday, so when Mama boiled us some corn on the cob in the middle of the night, I certainly wasn't going to complain.

FOR ALL HER VACILLATING VALUES, MAMA STILL TRIED TO instill within Patricia and me a sense of personal pride. Before we went out to wait for the bus one morning, Mama said, "Make sure your hair is combed; it's picture day at school."

Picture day! That was always exciting. We bought few of our school pictures, but it was fun to have our picture taken and look at the proofs. Sometimes the photographer even sent them home, though that was rare since we weren't the only family with a less-than-100-percent return record. When the school sent home the thumbnail-sized proof stapled to the sales pitch, Mama peeled off the proof. That was our school picture for that year until it faded away.

I stood on the side of the auditorium stage that morning, along with my classmates, and waited for the teacher to call my name. Since my last name was Barber, I was one of the first to be called. I walked onto the stage and sat down in a wooden school desk the photographer was using as a prop. Right before he took my picture, I yelled out, "Wait a minute! Mama said I had to comb my hair."

"Okay, fine, kid," the exasperated photographer said. "Comb your hair. But hurry up. I have a lot of pictures to take today."

I reached in my back pocket and pulled out a small black comb, the kind you could stick a piece of white paper in and form a makeshift harmonica by blowing on it.

But the white flecks on my comb were not from paper. And my teacher noticed. As I ran the comb through my hair, the teacher walked over to me and looked more closely. "What kind of comb is that?" she asked suspiciously.

"It's the comb my mom gave to me," I told the teacher. "It's a lice comb we had to use a few days ago."

The teacher said, "Go to the principal's office."

"But my picture . . ."

"Go! Now! And take that comb with you."

All my classmates stared at me, some making hideous faces as I left the auditorium.

I didn't get my picture taken that year.

Eleven

BAPTIZED

It's a wonder that today I don't have a warped concept of God because so many of my early experiences with church
folks—and more specifically with people who claimed to know God—
were definitely out of the ordinary. Despite my disillusionment with
religion, from the time I put my trust in Jesus at Vacation Bible School,
I have maintained a simple, childlike faith. Despite all the craziness that
was around me, I continued to believe even though I haven't always lived
the way the Bible teaches.

So when Mama and Preacher Davis said that I should be baptized
if I really believed in Jesus, I said, "Absolutely. I want to be baptized."

I'm not sure that at age ten I understood what baptism was all about,
and nobody bothered to explain to me that it is supposed to be a significant statement that *my* way of life has come to an end, and a new life has
begun. Preacher Davis simply said, "Boy, ya need to be baptized," so that
settled it in Mama's mind.

Preacher Harry Davis was the pastor at Mountain
View Agape Church, located right across the road from the front door of
our trailer. The small, white brick building boasted ten blood-red steps

leading up to the front entrance, with a cross hanging above the double doors and yet another cross on the steeple above. Three additional large white crosses lined the front yard to the left of the steps. Nobody doubted that Agape Church was all about the cross and the blood.

When Preacher Davis delivered the Word, his very demeanor evoked images of blood. His normally round, freckled white face grew increasingly tomato-red as he preached, screaming fire-and-brimstone messages at the top of his lungs, pacing up and down the aisles of the church, shaking, gesturing, and beating his Bible with his open hand as though he were trying to slam the Word into the minds of the small but enthusiastic group of devout listeners. With every "Amen!" "Hallelujah!" or "Glory!" shouted out by members of the congregation, Preacher Davis screamed louder, laboring on, his red face dripping with perspiration, his eyes flashing, his red hair disheveled as he preached us all right into hell. He looked like a heart attack waiting to happen. Preacher Davis didn't present short sermons, but fortunately for us, he lost his voice during every message. That usually calmed him down for a while.

Rather than baptizing converts in the church, Preacher Davis encouraged a public commitment of getting baptized in a cold, muddy river nearby the church. The day I joined the congregation to be baptized could have been a scene right out of the movie *O Brother, Where Art Thou?*

The women of the church gathered in "holy" garb, apparently having worked hard to avoid looking even somewhat attractive. With long hair and no makeup, wearing long, bland dresses, the women stood on the riverbank along with the short-haired men, most of whom wore polyester pants, suspenders, and white button-up shirts with the sleeves rolled up. Some of the men and women were singing; some had their arms raised above their heads, their eyes closed and lips quivering, mumbling, "Jesus, Jesus, Jesus." Others were speaking in tongues. The uninitiated looked on in wide-eyed wonder.

My eyes remained open the entire time, looking at Preacher Davis, his red face appearing even brighter against the background of the blue sky and the white clouds above him, as he dunked one person after another beneath the brown water, retrieving each person after a few seconds or whenever he felt sure the convert was ready to shout "Hallelujah!" or "Praise the Lord!" which each person did upon being pulled up out of the water. When my turn came, I slowly stepped into the cold, dark water, glancing over toward the bank every few seconds to see if Mama was watching me. She was, as she sang and swayed. I finally reached the reverend and presented myself for baptism.

"Have you been born again, son?" he asked loudly enough for all the folks on the riverbank to hear.

"Yes, sir," I answered hoarsely, getting more nervous by the second. I didn't know what being born again meant, but fortunately I came up with the right answer.

Preacher Davis covered my nose and mouth with his left hand, cradled the back of my head with his right hand, and began to pray.

A million thoughts raced through my mind as the preacher prayed. *I hope he doesn't drown me*, I fretted. *He sure looks different without his church suit on. I don't like his hand on my mouth. Why is his face so red?* Trying not to worry, I imagined, *Maybe his face is sunburned from all the fire and brimstone he preaches about.*

Preacher Davis finished praying, loudly shouted, "Amen!" then pinched my nose, and slung me backward, lowering me down into the muddy river. As soon as the cold walls of water caved in on me, I panicked and fought loose from his grasp.

I sprang up out of that river, coughing, sputtering, and hacking, with my arms flapping and flailing around in every direction. I wiped my eyes and searched for the trail that led up to the top of the bank where I'd last seen Mama. I staggered out of the river like a drunk boy, thinking that possibly Mama might come running to my rescue. But when my eyes cleared, I saw the look on Mama's face.

Oh no! I knew that disappointed demeanor all too well, and I could guess what she was thinking. It was my fault the baptism "went to hell," and I was going to pay dearly for that when we got home. I had embarrassed her in front of the church folk, so I knew I was in trouble.

But at least I had been partially baptized. For my Methodist, Anglican, Catholic, and other more liturgical groups, I was definitely "sprinkled." And for my Baptist, Church of Christ, and Pentecostal brethren, I was at least partially immersed for a fraction of a second. Despite the amount of water, I've heard that God looks on the intent of the heart. And even in that muddy river, my intentions were pure.

But I knew I was going to have a hard time convincing Mama of that. When she was off the booze, Mama was the epitome of the uneducated Bible-thumper. Every current event was a sign of the times, and we were all going to burn in the lake of fire. She loved the church and believed anything the preacher said. I'm certain she would have grabbed the tail of a copperhead if the preacher had told her to do so. The only thing Mama wouldn't do for the church was permanently change.

Twelve

GRANDPA'S PLACE

PATRICIA AND I CAME HOME FROM SCHOOL ONE DAY AND, to our shock, found our trailer wrapped in police tape. We weren't allowed to go inside.

Mama had stabbed Ronnie Brown in the chest and was in jail. Mama had met Ronnie in Reed's Trailer Park, where we were now living. Ronnie was a good man and a nice man—maybe too nice for Mama's crowd. When another tough guy showed up and started coming around our house, Mama soon grew sweet on him. Her new flame started picking on Ronnie. A fight ensued, and somehow in the middle of it, Mama stabbed Ronnie, apparently trying to kill him with a large steak fork. Somebody called the police, and the authorities hauled Mama off to jail again. Although Ronnie lived, Mama's arrest was a violation of her probation. Eventually she was convicted and sent to a state prison in Raleigh, North Carolina.

The Department of Social Services (DSS) didn't take us back to the county-run receiving home. Instead, they escorted Patricia and me to the far end of the trailer park to trailer number 34—Grandpa's place. Grandpa had moved to Reed's Trailer Park, so the DSS asked Grandpa if we could stay with him for a while.

Most kids have fond memories of spending time with their grand-parents. I don't. When I recall visits to Grandpa's place, it makes me retch. Grandpa was a mean, grouchy, nasty man, so we rarely stayed with him for long. But this time we were moving in.

MOVING IN WITH GRANDPA WAS MUCH WORSE THAN LIV-ing in any foster home. Grandpa constantly reminded Patricia and me that he didn't ask the DSS to bring us there. He wanted us there about as much as he had wanted a litter of kittens he had put inside a potato sack along with a brick. Then he tossed the sack into a deep creek.

Truth is, Grandpa didn't care about much of anything except smok-ing hand-rolled cigarettes and watching *Rawhide* on his small television. He especially couldn't have cared less when Mama had someone dump Patricia and me at his place from time to time, whenever she had to go back to the mental hospital or when the law came and took her off to jail. Sometimes Mama simply took us to Grandpa's and told us to get out of the car before she romped away on another escapade. But this time was different. We had no idea when Mama might return. Attempted murder was a serious charge.

Grandpa got up every morning before the sun rose. Weekends were no exception. Grandpa always said you could get more accomplished before the sun came up than any good-for-nothing-late-riser could accomplish all day. Of course, Grandpa hadn't really tested that theory; Grandpa never had a job or a hobby.

Grandpa didn't teach me how to fish. We never worked on a bike together or talked about school or anything else that grandfathers and grandsons ordinarily do. The only time he voluntarily spoke to me was to yell something like, "Ya darn punk, go outside!" or "Git outta the way, boy!"

We had one real conversation in my entire life. I asked Grandpa about the scars on his neck and how they got there.

He replied, "I was sitting in my car at a drive-in theater. Someone walked up beside the car, reached in through the window, and cut me with a knife." That was it. The entire explanation.

I didn't believe him, but then again, Grandpa was an old-school entrepreneur from the mountains of North Carolina, where they hauled the sunshine in and the moonshine out. He sold moonshine and carried a gun in his right front pants pocket. There was no telling how those scars got there. A part of me wished it had been Grandma who had put them there.

My mom said Grandpa treated Grandma really badly. I never met her, but I heard my grandmother was "a good, God-fearing lady," as some might put it. Grandma passed away when Mama was seventeen years old, before I was born. People who knew her back then said that Mama was never quite the same after her mom died.

I DO CREDIT GRANDPA FOR ONE THING—HE TAUGHT ME how to earn money at a young age. His teaching method was simple. When he lived near the golf course, he'd say, "I'm not givin' ya nothin'. Git yourself out there on the golf course and hunt golf balls outta the weeds and bushes and sell 'em to the golfers."

I spent every summer day searching for golf balls in the creeks and brush that surrounded the golf course. The bushes scratched my arms and legs, and there was always the danger of deadly copperhead snakes, but I plunged right into the weeds and ponds, searching for those balls. One by one, as I found them, I'd wipe them off and toss them into a tube sock. I filled an entire tube sock with golf balls and tied the sock to my belt loop. Then I'd do the same with another sock. I'd wait quietly at the greens with tube socks filled with golf balls attached to both sides of my shorts. I must have been a funny sight, but I didn't care. I was in business.

Once the last golfer putted, I yelled, "Wanna buy some golf balls? Quarter apiece!"

Almost always, the golfers replied, "Let's see what you have."

I untied the socks and shook all the golf balls out on the ground alongside the green. The golfers searched through them, picking out a few they liked.

Sometimes a golfer might ask, "Will you take one dollar for five balls?"

"Sure thing, mister."

On a good day, a golfer might make a special offer. "I'll give you ten dollars for all the golf balls you have there."

Sold.

Sure, he was ripping me off, but ten dollars was a lot of money to a nine-year-old boy.

MANY TIMES MAMA SIMPLY LEFT PATRICIA AND ME ALONE with Grandpa for several days or weeks at a time. She gave us no warning or advance instructions. If she wasn't in the mental hospital or jail, we had no idea where she was, and sometimes it could be quite frightening.

For instance, I woke up on my tenth birthday, and Mama was gone. I wasn't sure where Grandpa was either, and that concerned me because from the back of the trailer, I smelled smoke. By now I had lived around trailer parks enough to know that most of the mobile homes were tinderboxes, tragedies waiting to happen. If the trailer was on fire, I didn't have much time to get Patricia and me out of there.

I slid the bedroom door open, ran through Grandpa's bedroom area, and slid the door open between his bedroom and the kitchen, looking for Patricia. Then I saw her; she was standing in the kitchen, bawling.

She had gotten up early and had tried to bake a birthday cake for me, but she had burned it, smoking up the whole trailer. I felt so sorry for her that I told her I liked burned cake.

"No, you don't!" she said, tears streaming down her face.

"Sure I do. Watch, Patricia," I said. "Look; it's good. I'll eat it." I laid some canned pineapple slices on top of the charcoaled cake and cut a piece.

"See, I love burned cake," I told her, as I stuffed the piece of blackened cake into my mouth. It nearly gagged me, but I ate the whole thing. And Patricia stopped crying.

It really is the thought that counts.

AFTER MAMA WENT TO PRISON FOR STABBING RONNIE, Patricia and I stayed with Grandpa for a few months before we moved in with Sarah Moses, a childhood friend of Mama's. Growing up, Mama and Sarah often got together and baked homemade biscuits, fried fatback, and fried chicken, along with all sorts of other soul foods. Sarah's old house always smelled like cooked grease, but it was better than Grandpa's. Plus, we were accustomed to staying at Sarah's.

Even when Mama wasn't in jail, she sometimes left us at Sarah's for a few days, weeks, or even months at a time. Truth is, we spent much of our childhood at Sarah's. Her house was a second home to us, and during my preteen years, Sarah was as real a mom to us as Mama—often, more so. Sarah was good to us, especially considering that she had three children of her own: Lawrence, the youngest; little Sara, who was disabled; and John Wayne, who was meaner than the devil himself. Making matters worse, Sarah's husband, Bill, was an alcoholic and unwilling to work.

When we realized that Mama wouldn't be coming home anytime soon, I stayed at Sarah's a few months before Sarah and Grandpa made me move back to Grandpa's. Patricia remained at Sarah and Bill's. Sarah needed Patricia's help around the house since Sarah had to go to work to support the family. Patricia washed all the clothes, cut the grass, and cleaned the kitchen while Sarah walked to and from work in the textile mill. Meanwhile, most days, Bill laid passed out drunk on the bed.

I worried a lot about Patricia that summer.

Thirteen

A LIGHT IN THE DARKNESS

Surprise, surprise! Patricia and I had another brother and sister, Charlie and Rhonda. They were five and six years older than me, born to Mama by a different biological father than ours. We didn't know Charlie or Rhonda until one day they showed up at the trailer park and Charlie said, "Your mama is our mama too."

That kind of news will rock your world.

Mama confirmed the truth of Charlie's statement, that we had older siblings even though they didn't live with us. Charlie showed up again when I was around eleven. Mama told him that he couldn't stay with us unless he provided some food. Charlie left in a huff but returned a few hours later, carrying several bags of groceries he had stolen. Mama let him in, and he stashed the stolen food in our refrigerator. Just as Charlie finished unloading the food, Mama screamed at him, "Get out of here. Leave now, or I'm callin' the cops!"

Charlie bolted out the front door, but I could still hear him yelling back at Mama. "You tricked me!" he railed at her as he fled.

Mama didn't answer. She simply slammed the door.

I didn't see Charlie again until Mama went to jail for stabbing Ronnie Brown. Charlie showed up at the trailer park with a gorgeous new girlfriend on his arm and a gun in his hand as he strutted around the trailer park with his chest bowed out like a rooster. For some reason, I was impressed by him. I guess because he stood up for himself.

By then his arms and neck were covered in tattoos. He had everything from a swastika to the words *White Power!* inked onto his skin.

To say that Charlie was a racist would be a gross understatement. One day Charlie handed me two business cards soliciting new members for the Ku Klux Klan. The information on the cards included a sketch of a hooded KKK member and the message, "Join the KKK and fight for race and nation." An address and a phone number to call for free information about joining were boldly printed on the cards.

I didn't know much about the Ku Klux Klan or its activities, but Charlie told me Klan members did not like black people. I thought that was cool, especially since my sixth grade teacher at school, Ms. Friday, was an African-American.

"I'm going to take these cards to school," I told Charlie, "and flash them to let Ms. Friday know she better not mess with me again."

Charlie nodded approvingly, and I could tell he thought I had a great future as a racist.

CRYSTAL FRIDAY WAS ONE OF NINE CHILDREN IN A CHRISTIAN family with traditional values and a strong work ethic. She had been teaching professionally for about six years when I showed up in her sixth grade class at Bessemer City Central Elementary School. A rotund woman with a vibrant personality, she was one of very few black teachers in a predominantly white school system in North Carolina, but she kept a firm grip on the class. She strengthened that grip with the help of a leather strap she used for corporal punishment when anyone in our class stepped out of line—which I did often.

I acted out horribly, doing everything I could to make Ms. Friday mad. At one point I received more than sixty citations denoting poor behavior.

Although she was a strict disciplinarian and didn't take any guff from anyone, Ms. Friday was an angel. She loved her students and called us her "kids." She often made Rice Krispies treats and brought them to school for us.

Despite Ms. Friday's kindness, I was determined to make her miserable. I gave her dirty looks and made nasty comments about her in class. Since Mama was in prison and I was living at either Grandpa's or Sarah's, I often showed up late for school, conveniently just before lunch. I did everything Ms. Friday told us not to do. If I knew something might get on her nerves, I did it intentionally.

Ms. Friday kept the leather barber strap in her desk—the sort of strap barbers used to sharpen their razors. She whipped me with that strap at least once a week. I never sensed that she took any joy from disciplining me; in fact, I knew she was trying to help me, and she disliked paddling me almost as much as I disliked her doing it. Ms. Friday didn't know Mama was in prison; she had never met anyone else in my family, but she recognized that I had no discipline at home. As she liberally applied the leather strap to my behind, she said, "You're not getting this at home, so you're gonna get it here."

It made no sense that I should constantly attempt to irritate Ms. Friday. But I did. Sometimes I'd sneak up to the front of the classroom when she wasn't looking and erase something she had written on the chalkboard.

Whenever she caught me being mischievous or disobedient, Ms. Friday sent me out to the hallway to wait for her. She corralled another teacher as a witness before Ms. Friday reminded me of what I had done wrong. "Okay, bend over and touch your toes."

Ms. Friday grabbed my belt loop, pulled it up, and then reared back and hit me three times with that leather strap. She hit so hard the force made my face hurt!

When I returned to the classroom, I wore an expression on my face daring any kid in that room to think it was funny that I had just been whipped. None of my classmates even looked at me after a whipping.

I tried everything to make Ms. Friday mad, and that included flashing the Ku Klux Klan business cards that Charlie had given me and writing derogatory comments, such as "Save the land, join the Klan," on the back of my T-shirts with magic markers.

"Jimmy, why is that on your shirt?" Ms. Friday asked me.

"It's a new club I've joined."

"Do you know what that means or what the Klan does?"

"We just get together to talk."

"Well, Jimmy, whether you realize it or not, that is offensive to me and to many other people."

As much as I tried to agitate Ms. Friday, deep down I really loved her, and it hurt my heart to think that I had insulted her. She noticed my pained expression and said, "I want you to go to the restroom and turn your shirt inside out. You can wear it like that the remainder of the school day."

"Yes, Ms. Friday," I said obediently. I went to the restroom and turned my shirt inside out, cursing Charlie the whole time.

One day Ms. Friday kept me after school because of my behavior. I don't recall what I did wrong, but I remember Ms. Friday making me write over and over on a piece of paper, "I will not do this again. I will not do this again. I will not do this again."

As soon as Ms. Friday said I could leave, I went outside and lowered the flag on the flagpole that stood near her classroom window. I hooked my book bag on the latches that held the flag, hoisted the bag up to the top of the flagpole, and left it dangling outside her window next to the desk where she was sitting. She took one look and knew that it was my blue book bag.

Seconds later Ms. Friday came to the open window and placed both of her hands on the windowsill. She leaned out the third-floor window and yelled at me, "Take that book bag down!"

I cursed her from the road and told her, "I don't have to, and you can't make me. School's out." I eventually took the bag down and walked home to Reed's Trailer Park, approximately five miles away.

The following morning every kid in the school heard Ms. Friday whipping me once again with that leather strap.

I failed nearly every subject in sixth grade. I think I even failed lunch. Although it would have been much easier for Ms. Friday to pass me on to the seventh grade simply to get rid of me, she didn't. She held me back in sixth grade, so I had to repeat it. And when I repeated, she again was my teacher.

Nowadays I like to tell people that Ms. Friday was my sixth grade teacher—twice. The second year, Ms. Friday pulled my desk up to the front of the class. This was not an honor. She put my desk right next to hers so she could keep an eye on me. She motivated me by giving me simple chores to do: washing the chalkboard or sweeping the floor or being the leader of the line were big deals. Slowly but surely I responded to her love and discipline.

Ms. Friday instilled in her students the concept that nobody was any better or worse than anyone else, regardless of color or social status. I didn't mind playing with any of my classmates, but one student with whom I had a good friendship was African-American, Nigel Smith. We both enjoyed music and dancing, but I never volunteered to sing.

At the end of each school year, we had a talent show, and students had to earn the opportunity to perform. I earned my shot by making a beard out of brown construction paper and a guitar from cardboard. I lip-synched to ZZ Top's "Sharp Dressed Man." There were no cash prizes, but that talent show was my first public performance. Nigel did a rap song and was the best performer in our class by far. For years after that I tried to write some poems I could turn into rap songs, but I never could get the groove like Nigel. It probably wouldn't have worked—a white kid from North Carolina with KKK on his shirt—no wonder my rap songs were horrible!

Anger was a big part of my life during that time, and it had little to do with school. The first year, I refused to cooperate with Ms. Friday. I wasn't belligerent, but I definitely displayed passive-aggressive characteristics. During my second stint in sixth grade, I was much more cooperative. I knew Ms. Friday might hold me back for a third year.

Ms. Friday was a Christian, but out of respect for school policy, she didn't discuss her faith with her students. She simply lived out Christian values every day in front of us. She filled a desperate need in my life for order and also for a role model, someone who exemplified moral character.

She emphasized the importance of education. "You need an education, and you need a job. It's not going to be fun all the time," she said, "but if you don't get a good education, there are two places waiting for you—either the prison or the cemetery."

Ms. Friday was also big on taking personal responsibility. She tolerated no excuses for laziness. Although it wasn't unusual for kids in our class to wear the same clothes over and over, she expected the clothes to be clean. "You're in the sixth grade," she said. "Don't tell me you can't wear clean clothes. You can wash them yourself with hand soap in the sink. You may not have much, but you can be clean."

In addition to encouraging self-control, one of the greatest gifts Ms. Friday gave me was a desire to write. Ms. Friday taught me to keep a journal and write out my experiences. At the time, I called the practice of writing down my experiences "stupid journaling," but Ms. Friday would not accept any excuses. She didn't necessarily read our journals—we could write anything we wanted, including deeply personal thoughts—but she did check every day to make sure that we had written *something*. It is a practice that I've continued to this day.

MS. FRIDAY WAS A LIGHT IN THE DARKNESS OF MY LIFE; SHE remains one of the most positive influences I've ever known, and I will be eternally grateful to her. More than anything, Ms. Friday taught me that your circumstances do not define you. If you really want to do something, if you make up your mind and put forth the effort, you can do it.

Ms. Friday is not merely a teacher; she is an educator, and educators hope that their students will eventually catch on. Although I gave her a difficult time during my two years in the sixth grade, I did indeed catch on. Gracious woman that she is, Ms. Friday still sends me birthday and Christmas cards every year, and we have remained good friends.

Fourteen

MONEY FOR MAMA

Mama tried her best to stay in touch with Patricia
and me while she was in prison. It was always exciting when she called to
talk to one or both of us. Since Grandpa didn't have a phone and Sarah
was working during call time, Mama called Mr. Reed, the owner of the
trailer park. Mr. Reed searched for me all over the trailer park until he
found me and told me that Mama was on the phone.

"Hurry," he said. "She's calling collect." Out of the kindness of his
heart, Mr. Reed had agreed to pay for Mama's long-distance call from
prison. Mr. Reed was more than our landlord; he was a very good man
indeed.

I ran barefoot all the way across that trailer park and into Mr. Reed's
house, where, huffing and puffing, nearly out of breath, I picked up the
phone and yelled, "Mama!" Despite her erratic behavior, she was still my
mom, and I was always glad to hear her voice.

There's a certain tone mothers have when they speak to their babies,
and that's how Mama spoke to me even though I was now twelve and
would soon be a teenager. She'd tell me how much she missed and loved
me and asked if I was behaving.

"Yes, Mama," I replied dutifully. "But when are you coming home?"

"How's Grandpa doing?"

"He's fine, Mama, but when are you coming home?"

Occasionally I heard other inmates in the background telling Mama to hurry up or demanding that Mama get off the phone.

"I'm talkin' to my young'un!" Mama retorted brashly, but I detected an uncharacteristic fear in her voice. I could tell that she was afraid of those women in prison.

"Well, honey, I gotta get off here; these women want to use the phone."

"I love you, Mama," I cried into the phone, hoping she could continue talking for a few more minutes. She rarely did.

"I love you, too, Jimmy," she replied. "Now, you better listen to your grandpa."

"Oh, I will, Mama, I will," thinking of the filthy geezer with whom I was living. Mama and I said our hasty "I love yous" one more time, and then she said good-bye. I hated hanging up that phone more than anything in the world.

It might be another month or so before I would talk to Mama again, but meanwhile, we'd communicate through letters. I would get so excited when I received a letter postmarked from Bragg Street, Raleigh, North Carolina. It didn't have the prison name on the envelope, but I knew it was from Mama.

I read every letter she ever sent at least twice. Funny thing is, Mama's letters always reminded me of a church service. They'd start off by saying how much she loved me—and end by asking for money.

IN A WEIRD SORT OF WAY, MAMA'S LETTERS INSPIRED ME TO work harder. Not necessarily for myself, though. I felt compelled to earn some money that I could send to Mama in prison. She needed cash to be able to buy food and cigarettes from the commissary and to purchase anything beyond the basic prison fare. She didn't always tell me why she needed money, but she rarely wrote without mentioning it. So rather than the parent taking care of the child, we experienced a role reversal in which I was providing for my parent, even though I was only twelve years old.

Grandpa had moved out of the old trailer near the golf course, so retrieving lost golf balls and selling them was no longer an option. I knew I had to figure out how to earn some money, and I had to figure it out fast. After all, Mama needed me.

One day an elderly woman in the neighborhood asked me if I'd walk to Ingles grocery store to get her some washing powders (laundry detergent).

I gladly obliged. She gave me some money, and I made the trip to the grocery store. When I returned with her soap, I handed her the change, but she waved her hand. "No, Jimmy, you keep it," she said. "Thank you for helping me."

I thanked the woman. I was indeed grateful, not simply for the money but for the idea she had sparked in my mind. If this woman needed help with her grocery shopping, maybe there were others in the trailer park who needed help too. There were a number of older people living there. I canvassed the trailer park, asking if anyone needed a young man to go to the store. I took grocery orders from a large number of the elderly folks living nearby.

I wrote their orders on a piece of paper, accepted their money, then walked to Ingles and bought their groceries. Approximately twenty cents was left over from each order, and in almost every case, the elderly folks allowed me to keep it. That was great, but a few dollars a month wasn't enough; I needed to earn more.

Unfortunately that job ended shortly after it began when one of my customers sent me to Hardee's to buy some French fries. Those fries smelled so delicious, I couldn't resist. I ate half of them on the way back to the trailer park. My customer was furious and made it a point to tell everyone he encountered what I had done.

They all fired me. I was right back where I'd started, but I had learned a valuable lesson: integrity matters. Whether running grocery orders or guarding a jewelry store, a person is only as good as his or her word.

Once trust is broken, it is difficult and sometimes impossible to rebuild. Running grocery orders is like any other business; customers talk to one another about your service, so you better not eat one of their fries.

Nevertheless, when one door closes, another one opens—except in prison. The thought of Mama behind bars and needing money for cigarettes and shampoo was more than I could stand. I decided that I had to earn some money before the week's end.

A few days later, while playing cards with some of the old men from the trailer park, a guy named Rick said he needed some blackberries to make some homemade wine.

I perked right up as I envisioned opportunity knocking. I immediately said, "I'll pick 'em."

Rick agreed to pay me two dollars for every gallon of blackberries I picked. *Two dollars! Just for picking berries?* I was going to be rich!

I got up early the following morning and trudged down the hill behind trailer number 34, where I knew there were some dense blackberry patches. I knelt down and began picking. And picking. I picked blackberries until my fingertips turned a bluish-black. It took me an entire day to fill a single gallon jug.

By evening I had welts and scratches from my neck down to my ankles from reaching around blackberry thorns. It was still hot outside, so when my perspiration trickled into those red thorn cuts, it burned like fire. It was as though those thorns were trying to tell me, "Son, there's got to be an easier way to make a few dollars."

True to his word, Rick paid me two dollars for my day's work, the one gallon jug full of blackberries. When I got home that night, I was finally frustrated enough to ask Grandpa if he'd just send Mama some money.

I should have known better.

Grandpa was rolling a cigarette and never even looked up. "I didn't put your mammy in there," he drawled, "so I'm not supporting her."

Thanks loads, Grandpa.

Feeling defeated, I sat in the hot living room and watched him.

Grandpa's fingers twisted the rolling paper around that Half and Half smoking tobacco, packing it into a tight cigarette. He licked the edge of the paper, making sure it all held together. *That's it!* I thought, as Grandpa's cigarettes gave me another idea how to earn some money.

His homemade cigarettes reminded me of marijuana joints, growing ever more popular among the poor, working-class people in the Carolina textile mills. Workers paid good money for the buzz that soothed their minds but didn't cripple their ability to function, as too much alcohol might.

I didn't know much about weed, but I'd heard that a marijuana leaf and a tomato leaf looked similar. I ran out the door and down to the trailer rented by our neighbor, Drew. I pounded on the door until Drew answered. When he did, I begged him for some pot seeds. I knew Drew would have some seeds because he was the neighborhood drug dealer.

Drew handed me a pill bottle half full of marijuana seeds and said, "Now get outta here, boy."

I hid the seeds in the tree house I had built near our trailer. Late that night I pulled up some of Grandpa's tomato plants and hung them inside the tree house to dry. Two days later the tomato plant leaves were shriveled up and completely dried.

I removed some rolling paper from Grandpa's supply and laid a tomato leaf inside the paper, just as I had seen Grandpa insert his Half and Half. I sprinkled a few marijuana seeds on top of the tomato leaves so when it was smoked, the seeds would pop just as they do in a real joint.

One by one I rolled "marijuana" cigarettes in my tree house. When I had approximately fifteen cigarettes, I climbed down and ventured out into the trailer park, selling each fake joint to the local potheads for one dollar each.

My first customer was Drew, the drug dealer. He didn't say anything as he smoked the fake joint. He just smiled at me with a sick sort of approval. Only one skeptical guy balked at giving me a dollar before he had tried the smoke. He made me stand in front of him as he smoked the joint. But once he heard the seeds popping, he gave me a dollar.

No one ever asked me where I got the joints, not even Drew. I guess they thought I was running marijuana for someone in the trailer park, and they weren't about to start butting into someone else's business.

I sold most of the joints and had enough money to purchase a money order and send Mama at least nine dollars by the end of that week. I did something similar every week until Mama was released from prison, doing whatever it took to earn some money that I could send to her.

The day Mama got out, she came straight to Grandpa's. I was so happy to see her, but she didn't stay. Instead, she left to go celebrate with some of her old friends. She was gone most of that week, making up for lost time, filling her life with fresh men and old liquor. She eventually showed up with some guy who owned a restaurant, but then she left again.

For the first month following her release, it was as though Mama was still in prison; she was gone all the time. She'd surface for a day or two but then disappear again for days at a time.

I often wondered if she appreciated my working so hard to send her money while she was in jail. If she did, she never mentioned it. She never even said thanks.

Fifteen

SPARKLES

Throughout the spring and summer of 1985, I stayed with Grandpa in Reed's Trailer Park, and Patricia stayed with Sarah Moses. Grandpa didn't care what I did, so I basically ran wild all hours of the day or night, going to school if I wanted and staying home and roaming the neighborhood if I didn't. That had been a running theme of Mama's letters while in prison: "I heard that you weren't going to school." She wasn't really worried about me so much, but for some reason, Mama thought it made her look bad in prison if I didn't attend school. So while Mama was in prison, I received numerous requests from teachers and guidance counselors for a family meeting. I'd have Sarah Moses sign the requests, or I'd sign them myself and return them, declining the meeting request.

One woman, Debbie Dillinger, who lived just beyond Reed's Trailer Park, noticed that I was a lost soul and made a special effort to keep me from self-destructing. Debbie and her husband, Terry, were both especially nice to me, watching out for me. They had a daughter named Dana and a son with a disability, Dusty, who wore metal braces on his legs, impeding his ability to run or to even walk well. Other kids ignored Dusty or didn't want to play with him because of his disability, but I knew what it felt like to be ostracized; so not surprisingly, Dusty and I became best friends. We played together in his yard almost every day. Debbie fed me as though I were one of her own kids. She often allowed me to take a bath or a shower in her house. Maybe it was in self-defense on the Dillingers' part, trying to fend off my body odors, but the bath sure felt refreshing to me, especially since I was living in Grandpa's pigsty. On many occasions the Dillingers permitted me to stay overnight with their family in their simple but clean home.

ONCE MAMA WAS FINISHED RUNNING AROUND ALL OVER town, she finally came home and blazed a trail from one side of Reed's Trailer Park to the other. She even called Debbie Dillinger out in the yard and threatened her for no reason at all. She wanted to beat her up. "Do you think you're the mother of my kid?" Mama shrieked at Debbie, shaking her fist in Debbie's face.

Terry heard the commotion outside and came out of the house. Quickly sizing up the situation, he stepped between Mama and Debbie and said, "You're not going to hit my wife. Go on; get out of here."

Mama slunk away. "Come on, Jimmy. Get on home." Mama was acting nothing like the scared woman on the other end of the telephone line when those other prisoners were demanding her to get off the phone. Now she wanted to show how tough she was. I've since learned that showing off is a common trait of many ex-convicts after they have been released from prison. They want to let everyone know, "I just got out of prison." It's a type of intimidation game.

"I'm sorry, Dusty," I called back to my friend, as Mama steered me away from the Dillingers' yard. "Sorry, Mrs. Dillinger," I said softly so Mama wouldn't hear me.

"I'll see you tomorrow," I waved at Dusty.

IT WAS ABOUT THIS TIME THAT I MET MY FIRST TRUE LOVE. Her name was Sparkles, and she was my absolute best friend in the world. With her sparkling brown eyes and her short legs and her tongue constantly hanging out, she was quite a sight. Her white curls were matted and looked like a saddle. Her fur was full of fleas, but I didn't care. I loved my dog, Sparkles, more than anything in the world.

Sparkles slept under Grandpa's trailer. When I went outside, she quickly surfaced and greeted me with her tail wagging. Sparkles and I went everywhere together—to the swimming hole, to Dusty's house, to Ingles grocery store. Sparkles and I were inseparable.

Sparkles had pups while Mama was in prison, so I had to work extra hard to earn enough money to support Mama's habits and still have enough money to feed Sparkles and her pups. Only two of the pups survived, but Sparkles was a great mother to them.

Like me, Sparkles had the run of the neighborhood, so it wasn't unusual for her to wander off for a few hours at a time. One morning I saw Sparkles walking away from the trailer, and she looked worn out, her body tired, her head hanging down. I didn't think much of it at the time and felt sure Sparkles would return soon to feed her pups.

But by midday there was no sign of Sparkles, and the pups were crying, obviously hungry. I tried to feed them some canned dog food, but they wouldn't eat it. They wanted their mother. I could relate to that.

Later that afternoon a friend of mine, Randy Miller, walked down to Grandpa's trailer. Most people avoided Grandpa's trailer, so immediately my sensors were up.

"I saw Sparkles lying by the road," Randy told me, "and she wasn't moving."

"What? No!" I ran all the way up the long dirt road to the main highway, and there I saw her. Just as Randy had said, Sparkles was lying on the side of the road—and she wasn't moving.

I ran to her as fast as I could and knelt down beside her, holding her in my arms. Her curly fur was bloody, and she wasn't breathing. The love of my life was dead.

I tenderly picked up Sparkles and carried her in my arms, back down that long dirt road, crying all the way to Grandpa's trailer. With tears streaming down my face, I buried her in the front yard. My heart broke in a million pieces that day. I missed Sparkles terribly, but at least we still had two of her pups.

A short time later Mama returned and decided that we were moving to a new location, Sante Trailer Park. A family friend, JR Wilson, had an old red pickup truck and was helping us move. As I prepared to load Sparkles's pups onto the truck, Mama stopped me.

"They don't allow animals there," she said. "We'll have to take the pups to the pound." That news broke the remaining pieces of my heart. JR took the pups to the Matthews Animal Shelter near Gastonia, and a few days later he brought me a clipping he had cut out of the *Gastonia Gazette*.

It was a black-and-white photo of Sparkles's pups! They each wore a collar with a numbered tag. Below their photo was information in case someone wanted to adopt them.

I guess I should have been happy that the pups were going to get new homes. But I wasn't. Staring at that photo and knowing that Sparkles was dead and her pups were up for adoption devastated me, crushing a part of me that's never healed. I know it sounds exaggerated, but that was the worst heartbreak I had known up to that point in my first twelve years of life. A piece of me died.

Today weeds have overgrown the area where twenty-five or more trailers once stood in Reed's Trailer Park. But you can still find a few bent rusty nails in the side of a tree, where the two-by-four ladder led to my tree house. More importantly to me, that tree marks the spot where Sparkles is buried and where I wrote my first poem—a poem about a mother and her child being separated.

Of course my writing as a twelve-year-old was elementary by today's standards, but to me, writing the poem expressed my innermost thoughts. Part of the poem reads:

> I wish I was like a flower,
> Who was loved by a bee.
> I wish I had a family

That really cares for me.
I wish I was like a whole
And wish I was like a well.
I feel like in this place
That I'm locked up in a jail.
I have feelings like everyone else does
I was loved at one time
I know I really was.
I love someone
And they love me true
And if you love me,
I will love you too.

Sixteen

THE NIGHTMARE BEGINS

SANTE TRAILER PARK IS A SMALL TRACT OF LAND TUCKED back in the trees off Highway 74, near Gastonia. Unlike Reed's Trailer Park, tall pine trees stood in statuesque pride throughout Sante Park, providing plenty of shade in the summertime and protection from the elements in the winter.

I was sad to leave Reed's, but I was pretty good at making new friends. One of the first kids I met in Sante Trailer Park was Mike McBride. Mike was a few years older than me and had a little brother, Stevie, as well as an older sister, Theresa, who had a son named Chris. All four of them lived together with their mother, Bernell, in a small one-axle camper parked between two trailers. The camper was so tiny that I wondered how they could all fit inside to sleep. A neighbor allowed the McBrides to run a drop cord from their trailer to the camper so Mike's family could have electricity. Mrs. McBride served the family a lot of macaroni since that was an inexpensive meal. I never met Mike's dad.

Despite their poverty, the McBrides were some of the richest people I had ever met. They may not have had much money, but they were rich in love. The family members loved each other and worked together. Mrs. McBride was devoutly religious and wouldn't tolerate any cursing in her presence. Although she was very poor, her kind and loving demeanor was a picture of dignity. She modeled a truth to her family—and to me—that it is not what you have materially that matters but who you are as a person.

Mike, Stevie, and I loved to go camping—which was ironic, considering that they lived in such a tiny camper—along with two other brothers who lived on the hill behind the trailer park. We thought the brothers were rich because they had an inground swimming pool.

Sometimes Mike and I played football behind the nearby convenience store or rode bikes to the Diane 29 drive-in theater to watch a movie. We crawled under the white wooden fence and found a spot where no cars were parked. We took a speaker off the pole and placed it on the ground beside us so we could hear the movie. We watched movies like *Return of the Living Dead* and *Back to the Future*, along with plenty of B movies. We were just boys, living every second of life the best way we knew how. Thanks to Mike and his family, I was beginning to think that Sante Trailer Park might turn out to be a good place to live after all.

My sister, Patricia, had already moved out and was living back in Reed's Trailer Park with Steven Burgess, a twenty-five-year-old man who had courted Patricia with cheap gifts and empty promises. Mama saw an opportunity to get rid of Patricia, so she signed marital rights documents granting permission for Steven to marry Patricia, even though she was only fourteen years old. I didn't know Steven, but I noticed that Patricia was crying when he escorted her out of the courthouse where they were married. The tears streaming down her face did not appear to be tears of joy.

ONE SUNDAY MORNING MAMA DIDN'T WANT TO GO TO CHURCH, so I went outside to play. Later that morning, on a whim, I walked over to a vacant trailer and opened the back door. I peeked inside and discovered Mama lying on a dirty mattress with Tim Allen, a man she'd recently met in the trailer park.

A clean-cut, slender man in his midthirties, Tim lived in the trailer park with his dad, Charles. Tim had diabetes and depended on insulin, but he was a strong, hard worker nonetheless. It didn't take Mama long to get Tim's attention. They quickly became a serious couple, and since Mama and her previous husband were divorced when she went to prison, Mama and Tim soon got married. The three of us moved into a trailer together.

Despite our awkward first encounter, Tim seemed to be a pretty good guy. In the early months of our relationship, he actually reminded me of Carroll, the best of Mama's previous husbands. Tim was good to Mama, and he tried to be a great stepdad, treating me as his own son. I enjoyed doing things with him; we laughed together and had lots of fun. Tim discovered that I enjoyed building clubhouses in the woods, so he often brought home boards and large pieces of cardboard that I could use in my clubhouse. As far as I was concerned, Tim was awesome. I even thought we might be a real family—whatever that was.

One of the things I most admired about Tim was that he and his dad, Charles Allen, were so close. Having lived my entire life with an absentee father, I had never before seen the sort of strong father-and-son relationship shared by Tim and Charles.

Both Tim and his dad had drinking problems, but when Tim and Mama married, Tim used the occasion to challenge Charles to give up the booze. They agreed to stop drinking alcohol completely. Tim held up his end of the deal, but Charles struggled to stay away from alcohol. Whenever he could, he slipped away from the trailer park and found a drink.

One summer day, about six months after Tim and Mama got married, the three of us were driving up Highway 74, toward the Dixie Village Shopping Center, when Tim spotted Charles sitting at a picnic table on the other side of the busy highway. "Look at that!" Tim said with obvious disappointment in his voice. "There's my dad, and he's drunk."

Mama and I looked across the road and saw Charles staggering around the table. Tim reduced the car's speed as though he was going to stop, but then decided against it. "I'll come back and pick him up after I take you two home," Tim said. He drove past Charles in the direction of Dixie Village.

I could see Charles looking toward us and waving as we drove away. His eyes were glassy. He may have been drunk, but he recognized us, and by the look on his face, he must have realized that Tim was sorely disappointed in him.

Tim drove on to the store, where we purchased the items Mama wanted, and then we headed back toward Sante Trailer Park. As we passed the spot where we'd seen Tim's dad, Tim peered across the highway, searching for Charles around the picnic tables. But Charles was nowhere in sight.

Tim was disgusted. "He's probably passed out on the ground beside the picnic table," he said. We continued on home, and Tim dropped us off at the trailer. Then he hurried back up the highway to get Charles.

But it was too late. By the time Tim arrived at the picnic area, Charles had already stumbled out onto the highway, apparently staggering back toward Sante Trailer Park. He was struck by a car and was killed instantly.

It was a few hours before Tim returned home, sharing this horrific news with Mama and me. He was devastated and beside himself with grief mixed with regret. "I could have helped him," Tim cried over and over again. "I could have rescued him. I could have saved him! But I didn't."

Tim loved his dad more than I could even understand. The decision to pass by his dad was one that Tim would regret for the rest of his life.

Tim had a teenage son, Charles, named after his grandpa. Charles Jr. lived in Bessemer City, North Carolina, with his mother, Kathy, Tim's former wife. Charles and I were both thirteen, and we became instant friends. I spent most of my time hanging out with him the summer that his grandpa died. We did all sorts of things together—camping, hiking, boxing, and most of all, chasing girls, though we weren't quite sure what we'd do if one of the young ladies returned our interest. Still, we had fun.

As the Fourth of July 1986 drew near, Tim was still grieving the loss of his father, so Mama allowed me to spend the weekend with Charles at Kathy's apartment in Bessemer City. Meanwhile, my oldest brother, Charlie Barber, whom I barely knew, visited Mama and Tim.

While Charlie Barber was with Mama and Tim, he and Tim got into a fight. The two of them exchanged strong words and threats, getting into a raging argument that spilled all over the house. Charlie Barber decided to leave, but on the way out of the yard, he picked up a brick and slammed it against the top corner of the windshield of an Oldsmobile Delta 88 that he had seen Tim driving. The windshield shattered where the brick had hit, but it held together due to the safety glass. Charlie Barber hustled into his car and roared away.

But what Charlie Barber didn't know was the Olds Delta 88 was not Tim's car; it belonged to Tim's recently deceased father, Charles Allen. When Tim saw what Charlie Barber had done to the windshield of his father's car, he was furious and vowed to get even.

I came home from Bessemer City that evening, and when I saw the broken windshield, I ran inside the trailer. "Mama, what happened?"

"Charlie came over, and he and Tim got in an argument," she said.

"Why?" I asked.

Mama gave me a brief synopsis, but it was obvious she was in no mood to talk about it. Apparently, she and Tim had gotten into an argument, too, with Mama sticking up for her flesh and blood. She didn't say much; she simply left the trailer without telling us where she was going. We later learned that she went across the trailer park to Grandpa's trailer. Grandpa had recently moved to Sante to stay close to Mama.

About that time, I heard Tim thrashing around in the back bedroom. He stormed out to the living room, and when he saw me, he said, "Come with me; let's go for a ride."

I could tell that Tim was upset, but I didn't have any concerns. We all lived with anger in the trailer park. That was nothing new.

Tim and I went outside, and I pulled open the big, heavy passenger door on the Olds Delta 88 and got in. I closed the door and sat there wondering where we were going.

Tim got in the driver's seat and placed a fifth of vodka on the seat between us. He cranked the Oldsmobile's motor and drove out of Sante Trailer Park. "Let's stop by the store and get a Mountain Dew," Tim said in his usual friendly voice.

A Mountain Dew? Gee, thanks, Tim! I was excited because that was my favorite soda, and it was rare when I got one.

Tim pulled into the parking lot of a convenience store and parked in front of the entrance, leaving the engine running. I waited in the car while he went inside and bought two twelve-ounce bottles of Mountain Dew, one for him and one for me. He hopped back in the car and handed me the Mountain Dews.

We headed west on Highway 74, passing by Sante Trailer Park, traveling instead toward Crowders Mountain. Wherever we were going, we weren't going home.

Tim was driving fast, and I was a little nervous, but the Carolinas are NASCAR country, so driving fast was the norm. I wasn't *too* worried.

Then Tim said, "Pour me some liquor in that cup," as he pointed to a cup on the floor.

I opened the bottle and carefully poured the vodka into the cup, filling it halfway.

Tim nodded in the dark. "Now pour a little Mountain Dew in there," he ordered.

I quickly obeyed and handed the mixed drink to Tim. He guzzled the drink in one swig. He extended the cup in my direction. "Again," he said.

Like a passenger-seat bartender, I repeated this process several times before we reached Crowders Mountain. By then Tim had downed four full cups of the vodka and soda in rapid succession.

We took a left turn off Highway 74, in front of the property where Grandpa formerly lived. We passed Mountain View Agape Fellowship, the little white church on the hill, and zoomed past the old bus stop where I had stood and waited so often for the school bus. As we topped the next hill, Tim lifted his foot off the gas pedal, slowing the vehicle. He then turned the car into someone's driveway and stopped.

We sat there in the dark for a few minutes, not saying a word, with the engine still running. Tim peered into the darkness in the direction of a lone trailer. His eyes remained fixed on the rectangular shape in the darkness. Finally, he whispered, "Load this gun." He handed me his .22 caliber, nine-shot revolver.

Without hesitating, I loaded the gun and handed it back to Tim. I had no clue what he had in mind to do, but I wasn't about to disobey his orders.

We sat quietly for a few more minutes, with Tim idly caressing the gun. After a while the front door on the trailer opened, and we could see someone standing in the shadows of the doorway. But all the lights were off in the trailer, which made it difficult to identify the person.

Tim hissed to me, "Ask him if he's Charlie."

What? He wanted me to ask the figure in the dark for his name? I shrugged, and obeyed. I yelled out the passenger window, "Hey! Are you Charlie?"

The man grunted and said, "Yeah, who wants to know?" He sounded a lot like my older brother, Charlie Barber.

That's all Tim needed to hear. He backed the car out of the driveway and into the road, and then pointed the gun out the driver's side window at Charlie. Before I realized what was happening, Tim fired off six shots. Whether he was too drunk to aim straight or just trying to scare Charlie, I'll never know; but all six bullets tore through the aluminum exterior of my older brother's trailer and miraculously missed Charlie.

Tim stomped on the throttle, and while peeling out with the tires spinning, he fired three more shots into the trailer. He looked like an outlaw, riding the back of a horse through a town and shooting up the saloon.

The big Olds roared off, and Tim slapped the gun down on the front seat as we headed back toward Highway 74. Just before we reached the main road, he steered the car off onto a side road, where we parked and watched through splintered trees as the police raced by in the direction of Charlie Barber's trailer.

We sat there for a few moments in the dark before Tim pushed the gun toward me and said, "Load it again."

Why, Tim? What are we doing out here? I thought but didn't dare say aloud. This was the first time I had ever questioned Tim. He had always been such a good guy. But that night, at that moment, he wasn't the stepdad I'd quickly grown to like and trust.

A voice whispered in my ear, *You're in danger. Get out of the car.*

It was a familiar voice, one that I had heard on Vance Street in times of trouble and another time at a campground when I was ten. Whether it was intuition, the voice of an angel, or the Spirit of God, I don't know.

I emptied the gun's cylinder, then reached down and picked up some used shells off the floorboard. I loaded the spent shells in the cylinder, hoping that Tim was too drunk to notice. I snapped the cylinder shut and handed the gun back to Tim.

He shoved the gun back at me and yelled at the top of his lungs, "I saw what you did. Put some bullets in the gun!"

My hands were shaking, and I was getting more scared by the minute. I nervously emptied the used shells out of the cylinder and reloaded the gun with live ammunition from a small cardboard box Tim had on the seat. I handed the gun to Tim and sat motionless in the front seat while Tim finished off the vodka.

Tim lowered the cup from his lips and threw it on the floor. "Do you know how fast I am?" Tim asked, without turning toward me.

Before I could even respond, his right arm flashed in the darkness, smashing me in the face with the knuckle side of his closed fist. My head snapped sideways as I felt warm blood squirt from my nose, running down my neck onto my favorite shirt.

I wanted to scream, cry, or yell out, *Tim! What's wrong with you? Why did you hit me?* But I was too frightened to say a word. We sat there in silence. I didn't dare look at Tim for fear he'd deck me again. I stared straight ahead, looking at a faraway light on the hill. I was afraid to move.

I started to cry.

"Shut up!" Tim roared.

I tried to obey but couldn't keep from sniffling. A few minutes later Tim suddenly raised the gun and shoved the barrel against the side of my head, mumbling something under his voice. Tim pushed on the gun, and I felt the pressure of the cold, hard gun barrel pressing against my skin and bone.

The events of the next two seconds seemed to move in slow motion.

I lifted up my left arm so it was between my body and Tim's arm while simultaneously turning my head to the right and back toward the seat. At the same time I heard a deafening loud *bang!* and saw a streak of fire burst past my face.

My left ear was ringing like a burglar alarm. My face burned from the gunpowder.

With adrenaline surging through my system, I grabbed Tim's arm with my left hand and pushed his arm away from my head and down toward the seat. I turned to look at him while grabbing his arm with my right hand. I raised up, then threw my entire body weight down on his arm, eventually working my hands down to the gun and pressing it to the seat.

"Tim, please don't shoot me!" I screamed over and over. This was crazy. What had I done? I had never had a cross word with Tim, and now he was trying to kill me? It didn't make any sense.

Tim finally relaxed his arm. In response, I slowly released my grip after he let go of the gun. With the gun lying on the front seat, I thought about grabbing it and running, but I was too scared.

I wouldn't have had time anyhow. Tim threw the car in gear and quickly backed out to the main road.

That's when I noticed the bullet hole in the top right corner of the windshield. The light from the streetlight on the hill created a weird kaleidoscope effect in the spider web of broken glass surrounding the hole in the windshield. It scared me to think that the bullet that had shattered the glass could have been in my head.

Tim sped down Highway 74, accelerating as fast as he could go, barely negotiating the winding road. Then, while the car was still going, he yanked down on the gear shift, slamming the Olds into reverse. The transmission screeched with a horrendous sound of metal against metal, grinding the gears so loudly I thought the engine was going to explode. Just as it seemed the car was about to shudder to a stop, Tim slammed the car back into drive and stomped down on the gas pedal again. He repeated this several more times; it was as though he was deliberately trying to destroy his dead dad's car—and maybe us too. The Olds was a warhorse, though, and kept going, so finally Tim turned left and headed back west on Highway 74.

He pulled into another driveway and stopped, but I was not going to give him a second chance to shoot me. As soon as the car stopped, I ripped open the door. The interior light came on, and Tim instinctively reached over and felt for the gun.

"I gotta pee!" I lied, as I jumped out of the car and started running. I had purposely left the car door open because I knew if the interior light was on, Tim couldn't see me but I could see him.

I ran as fast as I could, trying to get away from the car, glancing behind me every few seconds, looking back over my left shoulder to see if he was following me. I could still see him leaning across the front seat, trying to grab the passenger door handle to pull the door closed.

I kept running down the median of Highway 74. When I saw the headlights pan across the trees, I knew Tim was backing the car up and heading my way. I dove onto the ground in the high grass of the median as he passed by.

When I was certain the car had disappeared, I stood up and ran some more. Every time a car approached from either direction, I hit the dirt, diving again into the median. I wasn't taking any chances. After running several more miles, I finally made it to the convenience store near Sante Trailer Park. I ran to the phone booth and dialed the operator.

When a woman answered, I practically yelled into the phone, "Please, help me! My stepdad was trying to shoot me."

"Slow down, son," the woman said. "What's your name?"

"Jimmy! Jimmy Wayne Barber. And my stepdad's name is Tim. Tim Allen. Please! You gotta help me. He's gonna kill me."

The woman seemed unfazed. Instead of sending help, she peppered me with more questions. I tried answering as many as I could, but then I saw a car approaching. I hung up the phone and ran across the parking lot and up the street that led to our trailer. It seemed unusually dark; there were no lights on in the trailer, but when I crept up and tried the front door, I was relieved to find it was unlocked.

Tim's car wasn't in the driveway, but I couldn't tell whether he was inside or not. A fearful thought darted across my mind: *Maybe he parked up the street, and he's hiding inside, waiting to get me.* Despite my fears, I opened the front door and stepped inside. I turned on a light and yelled for Mama.

No answer.

I closed the door and stood in the living room with my back pressed up against the front door. "Mama?" I called again. "Mama! Are you here?" I waited for an answer, but none came.

I knew it was risky to stay in the trailer by myself, but I was so exhausted, my eyes were so heavy, and I just couldn't run anymore. All I wanted to do at that moment was to lie down. I locked the front door and dragged myself to my bedroom.

My legs were covered with scratches, and my skin burned and itched from rubbing up against the tall grass in the median. The blood from my nose that had poured down the front of my shirt and shorts had dried, leaving dark stains. I was too exhausted to care. I fell onto my bed and closed my eyes. I knew that if Tim found me before I woke up, I might awaken in heaven, but I just didn't care.

Seventeen

SANTE SHOOT-OUT

I'M NOT SURE HOW LONG I STAYED ASLEEP, OR IF I SLEPT AT all. But I was startled fully awake by a noise behind me, near the bedroom door. Lying on my stomach in bed, I quickly opened my eyes and flipped over on my right side.

It was morning, and a bleary-eyed Tim was standing in the sun-drenched doorway of my bedroom. He was a mess. His eyes were bloodshot. And he was holding the gun in his right hand.

I immediately sat up in my bed. My heart began pounding faster, loud enough that I could hear it.

Tim glared at me, but neither of us said a word.

My eyes darted back and forth, looking at the gun, then at his face, then back at the gun, and back to Tim's face. I could see rage building in Tim's bloodshot eyes. I didn't know what to do, but I knew I had to do something. I made a snap decision. I sprang from the bed like a cat and ran toward Tim full force, with both my arms extended forward. But as light-framed as I was, my effort only pushed him back slightly, toward the wall in the hallway. I could see the gun in his right hand, and it was aimed right at my heart.

I rolled left, away from Tim, out through the living room, and bolted out the front door, running with all my might toward Grandpa's trailer. I knew my life was completely out of my control now. There was no way Tim could miss if he decided to pull the trigger. *He's gonna shoot me in the back*, I thought, as I ran for Grandpa's front door. But for some reason, Tim didn't fire.

I burst into Grandpa's trailer and to my surprise discovered that Mama had spent the night there. When I saw her, I immediately began pouring out my story of the events from last night. "Mama, you won't believe it. Tim shot up Charlie Barber's trailer, and then he tried to shoot me!" I showed her the blood on my shirt from where he'd hit me in the nose.

Mama didn't seem angry; she didn't even appear concerned. She just nodded and acted like it was no big deal. "He'll calm down sooner or later," she said.

I waited at Grandpa's half the day before returning to our trailer later that afternoon. I hoped that by then Tim would have had enough time to sober up. Maybe he was back to being "good Tim"—at least, I prayed he would be.

I slowly opened the front door and stepped inside the trailer, careful not to make any noise. It was ominously quiet, so I tiptoed toward the bedrooms. I looked to the left and saw Tim's shoes hanging off the bed in the back bedroom. I moved farther down the hallway toward Mama's and Tim's bedroom. I flinched instinctively when I saw him, ready to run again if necessary, but then I saw he was asleep on his stomach, still wearing the same clothes he had been wearing the previous day. I quickly surveyed the room, looking for the gun, but I couldn't spot it.

On the dresser sat a box of bullets, surrounded by another handful of bullets strewn on the dresser, along with some change Tim had apparently been carrying.

I slipped into the bedroom and gathered up the bullets, being extra careful not to make any noise by dropping any bullets onto the dresser top. When I was sure I had them all, I toted the bullets to my bedroom, where I closed the door behind me. I got down on the floor and crawled on my stomach all the way under my bed and hid the bullets in the far right corner against the wall. I quietly crawled back out from under my bed and hurried outside.

By nightfall Mama went back to the trailer to reunite with Tim. When she didn't return to Grandpa's, I figured it was relatively safe to go home, so I followed behind her a few hours later.

She and Tim were in their bedroom having a conversation when I walked in. Neither Mama nor Tim said one word about the events that had taken place the night before, so I didn't either. It was as if nothing had even happened. It was totally weird.

I spent the rest of the evening in my bedroom, trying to figure out what was going on and what, if anything, I should do. I didn't really have a lot of options.

My choice was made by default later that night when I woke up to the sound of glass shattering in our trailer. Someone had thrown a rock through the living room window.

I glanced at a clock on the wall and noticed that it was close to 1:30 a.m. Whoever had broken our window hadn't done so by accident.

Then I heard Mama yelling out the front door, "Charlie, you need to leave now!"

At first I thought Mama was talking about Charles, Tim's son, but then I heard the voice of my older brother, Charlie Barber. "Come on outside, Tim," Charlie Barber taunted. "We'll see how tough you are."

By now Tim was awake and up. He ran down the hallway and burst into my bedroom. "Where's the bullets?" he snarled at me.

"I don't know," I said defensively.

"Don't mess with me, Jimmy," Tim yelled. "Give me the bullets—*now!*"

I got down on the floor and crawled under my bed and grabbed the box of bullets. As I did, I heard more glass breaking and men talking loudly outside.

Charlie called out condescendingly again. "Come on, Tim. Come outside, Tim."

Another window shattered. Suddenly, rocks rained in through every window in the trailer.

I slid out from under my bed with the bullets in my hand, stretching my arm toward Tim. He handed them back to me, along with the gun, and growled, "Load it!" A weird thought flitted through my mind; it occurred to me that maybe Tim didn't know how to load the gun himself.

But I knew he was serious, and something bad was getting ready to happen. My hands shook while I frantically loaded the gun. We were standing in the hallway under a small window. Mama was in the kitchen, yelling at Charlie, telling him to stop throwing rocks and to leave.

I was shaking so badly, I couldn't get the cylinder to close, so I handed the gun to Tim. He took a bullet out of the cylinder and reinserted it, and the cylinder snapped shut. Tim walked toward the kitchen with the gun in his right hand.

I heard a noise and looked toward the front of the trailer. From my position I could see that Charlie had climbed up onto the tongue housing the hitch of the trailer, and he was leaning forward, crawling through the broken kitchen window.

"Get down, or I'll shoot you in the top of the head!" Tim roared at Charlie.

Mama turned around and yelled, "Tim, please don't shoot him." Mama then turned back to her eldest son. "Leave, Charlie! Please, leave," she begged. But the tone in Mama's voice told everyone that she knew nobody was leaving anytime soon, and we may not leave alive.

Charlie retreated from the windowsill, so Tim turned and strode back down the hallway to where I was trying desperately to be brave. He crouched under the small hallway window, stuck the barrel of the revolver out the broken window, and bellowed, "You better get outta here."

Charlie yelled back from somewhere, now on the front side of the trailer, "Come outside, Tim. You ain't gonna come shoot up my house and git by with it. Come outside and let's handle this like men."

"Charlie, please! Let's go." I recognized the woman's voice outside; it was Cathy, my brother Charlie's wife. Cathy was a mousy woman who never dared to contradict her husband. What was she doing here with this bunch of thugs?

"Shut up!" Charlie railed in return.

Those were the last words I heard before Tim pulled the trigger. *Bam!* The shot reverberated through the entire trailer. But since it was almost the Fourth of July, and many people in the Carolinas enjoyed setting off fireworks at night, the crackling sound of gunfire probably went unnoticed by the neighbors.

Tim fired again and again. The first few shots didn't faze Charlie or his comrades; they continued throwing rocks into our trailer and cursing at Tim, demanding for him to come outside while Cathy begged, "Charlie, please, come on. Let's get out of here!"

Mama warned Charlie to leave too.

I heard people yelling and more glass breaking. Moments later Tim fired three more shots.

A horrible wailing sound pierced the night air in the trailer park.

The rabble-rousers stopped in their tracks, and everyone outside got extremely quiet—everyone except Cathy, that is, who had been sitting in the car, calling out to Charlie. Cathy continued screaming hysterically. It was a horrific sound, the most painful cry I'd ever heard.

Then Charlie yelled, "You shot my wife!" He punched the front door of our trailer one more time and ran to his car, where Cathy was lying on her side in the front seat. Charlie and his cohorts piled into the car and roared out of Sante Trailer Park. Tim kept watch out the window for a couple of hours, in case Charlie might return, but everything remained calm for the rest of the night.

IT WAS ALMOST DAYBREAK BEFORE MY HEART STOPPED RAC-ing. "Pack your things," Mama said. "We're getting out of here." I tossed some clothes and my prized possessions into two cardboard boxes. We immediately abandoned the trailer and fled to Tim's uncle's place in Crowders Mountain, where we waited for daylight.

We learned later that Tim's shots had missed Charlie and his friends but not Cathy, who had been sitting in the car directly in Tim's line of fire. Ever the meek wife, she had waited behind the wheel of the car, just as Charlie had instructed her. At least three of Tim's bullets ripped into Cathy's body. She was shot in the shoulder and neck, and she must have tried to reel away or had lunged forward because Tim also shot her in the back.

Although none of us were ever the same after that night, Cathy's life was irrevocably changed. She never walked again. Thanks to Charlie's and Tim's macho nonsense, Cathy was paralyzed from her waist down for the rest of her life.

Eighteen

ON THE RUN

THE FOLLOWING DAY, TIM WAS AGITATED. WITH EVERY CAR that passed by the trailer park, Tim's body tensed in anticipation of the police coming to arrest him for shooting Cathy.

I stood outside beside the Oldsmobile and watched Tim peel the broken windshield away from the black, sticky safety adhesive that was holding the shards of glass together. He spoke not a word the entire time he worked to replace the windshield. It was almost as though Tim were in a trance.

Still anticipating his arrest, Tim worked feverishly to put the new windshield in place. When he finished, Tim said simply, "We need to get out of here. We're leaving."

I sat in the car, and as Ms. Friday had taught me to do, I wrote in my notebook that I was using as a journal, "Tim just replaced the window in the car, and we're getting ready to run from the law."

We loaded up the car with some clothes and a little bit of food and headed west, traveling from North Carolina toward Oklahoma, where Tim said he had some relatives. We were like Bonnie and Clyde with a kid, living in that car along the way, sleeping at rest areas and dodging the law. A few days later we arrived in Del City, Oklahoma, at the home of Tim's relatives, whom Mama and I had never met. From the way they regarded Tim, I wasn't sure that he had ever met them before either. They were an elderly couple—very nice but cautious. Even I could tell they were afraid to have us in their home.

They allowed us to stay for a few days before telling us we had to leave. Tim didn't argue. We loaded up the car and headed south to Waco, Texas. We spent the next few weeks living out of the Oldsmobile, driving aimlessly from one town to another. Being cooped up in that car for weeks made everyone grouchy.

The Oldsmobile used almost as much oil as it did gas, so someplace along the highway in Waco, Tim pulled into a park and changed the oil on the ground while I took a long walk. I walked by the river, then visited a thrift store, where I bought a baby blue T-shirt with airplanes printed on the front. The shirt cost me twenty-five cents.

When I got back to the car, we drove to the Waco Salvation Army mission, where we checked in and spent the night. Mama went to the women's side of the facility while Tim and I stayed in the men's quarters. We were each given a Ziploc toiletry bag and escorted to our sleeping quarters to unpack, then to the chow hall. After having dinner with the other homeless men, we headed to the bedding area and prepared for a shower.

I stepped into the shower area alone, peeled off my clothes, and turned on the hot water. That's when I noticed a big man loitering nearby, leering at me. As far as I could tell, there were no other men in the shower area, just the big man and me. Instinctively, I covered myself with my hands. For a fleeting moment, I wished that Tim were nearby.

The big man edged closer and said, "I saw you sleeping on the ground, then on the hood of the car at the rest area the other night. Those fire ants are bad, aren't they?" He said that he was a truck driver and that he had parked his truck in the same rest area.

I didn't respond. But he was right about those ants. We had slept on the ground a few nights previously, and the ants were so bad, I crawled onto the enormous hood of the Olds 88 and slept there. But I wasn't about to engage in a conversation with him. He finally left the dressing area, and I took a shower. The entire time I was under the warm water, I feared that the man was going to come back into the shower area before I finished. I quickly scrubbed, rinsed, and dried off. It felt so good to be clean.

I crawled into a bunk bed, surrounded by homeless men in other bunks. I didn't know where Tim was, so I lay quietly, trying not to be noticed with the sheet and blanket tucked under me on both sides. Although being wrapped up like a mummy made me hot and sweaty again, I felt safer and eventually fell asleep.

Early the next morning, the Salvation Army staff rushed everyone out of the mission. They weren't being rude; they had to prepare for the next batch of vagrants who would soon arrive. Tim and I reunited with Mama, and I was so glad to see her. We stashed our belongings in the backseat of the car, and I shaped them into a little cubby where I could sleep.

We drove eastward all that day and on into the evening. Mama and Tim weren't getting along well and were barely talking to each other. I couldn't tell if they were mad at me, angry with each other, scared, or simply in deep thought. When they did speak, they seemed to be scheming, talking in low tones, making me even more uncomfortable.

I nestled into the safety of the cubby I'd made from dirty clothes in the backseat, and wind streamed in through the open windows as the big orange sun set in the Texas evening sky. Occasionally our headlights caught the eyes of a deer grazing alongside a long, lonely back road. Music played at low volume on the car radio. Had it not been for the extreme tension, we made for a tranquil scene.

Mama heard something on the radio that piqued her interest. She leaned over and turned up the volume louder and louder. A song called "Venus" was playing on the radio, and Mama started singing along really loud, "I'm your Venus," clapping her hands and moving her shoulders. To my surprise, Tim joined in singing, swaying his upper body from side to side as he drove.

I scooted up to the edge of the backseat, put my elbows on top of the front bench seat, and bobbed my head to the beat of the song. The three of us sang and danced the entire song. It was the most exciting three minutes we'd had in more than a month out there on the road.

But as abruptly as the fun began, it stopped. When the song ended, Tim reached over and slapped off the radio. He stared straight ahead. I quickly sat back in the cubby in the backseat, and Mama went back to staring out the passenger side window. For nearly three minutes, we were a happy family, enjoying the music. Then it was over.

We drove late into the night until we found another rest area, where we could sleep. The following day was business as usual but at a different rest area. We were getting short on money, so Mama stuffed clothes under her shirt and pretended to be pregnant. Tim popped the hood and pretended to work on the engine, complaining about the car to anyone who passed by at the rest area. "What's wrong with your car?" someone always asked. He told people passing by that we were having car trouble and that his wife was pregnant and we needed food and fuel.

Inevitably, before long some kindhearted Good Samaritan took the bait. Seeing Mama in the front seat with her big belly, the benevolent soul believed she was pregnant. And seeing me in the backseat, looking mournful and sullen, sealed the deal.

Sometimes Tim and Mama worked the shtick several times at the same rest area. Compassionate, sympathetic people gave them money every time.

Sometimes we stopped at churches along the way, and Mama and Tim put on their show. Some churches had rules for what they could do to help passersby. Many didn't and simply gave us food out of their food pantry or benevolence ministries. We never attended these churches' services, but we took advantage of their kindness.

On more than a few occasions when we stopped for gas at a country gas station, Tim instructed me to fill the gas tank while he sat behind the wheel. The moment the tank was full, I slipped back into my cubby, and rather than going into the gas station to pay, Tim floored it. Taking money from generous strangers, begging for food from compassionate churches, and driving off from gas stations without paying for the fuel—it was just another day of life on the lam.

I HAD FALLEN ASLEEP AS WE DROVE BUT SENSED THAT IT was dark and late at night when I felt someone shaking me. "Wake up," a voice said gruffly.

I opened my eyes and saw Tim staring at me.

"Get out of the car and get your clothes," he ordered.

I had no idea where we were. Originally we had started out from North Carolina, heading west to Oklahoma. Then we had turned back southeast, driving through Texas. When I had fallen asleep that night, we were in Texas, heading east toward Florida. I crawled out of the backseat and stood up in a dark parking lot. Looking around, I saw a neon sign on the building: *Bus*. A billboard near the building read *Trailways*.

I rubbed the sleep from my eyes and noticed for the first time that Mama was standing behind the car, leaning against the trunk. I realized that she was crying, so I asked, "Mama, what's wrong?"

When she saw me, she opened the trunk. "You need to get your things out of the car," she said.

I didn't know what was going on, but I obeyed. I nervously walked around to the back of the car and pulled out my two small boxes that were tied together with a string. In addition to my clothes, inside the boxes were my most precious possessions, some of my drawings, some poems I had written, and most precious of all, my letters from Mama while she had been in prison.

"Do you have any money, Jimmy?" Mama asked.

She knew I always had money. I had worked to earn survival money from the time I was ten years old. As a kid, I went door to door in town, asking folks, "Is there anything around your house that you need done? Any work that I can do?" Sometimes I did the same with stores or businesses. So I always found odd jobs around town, whether it was cleaning up trash, mowing grass, or any dirty jobs they needed done. I saved my money because I never knew when Patricia or I might need to buy food or have a few dollars for emergencies.

"Yes, Mama," I told her naively. I looked in a leather pouch that Mama's former husband Robert Davis had given to me. He had told me that he'd made the pouch when he was in a mental hospital. It never struck me at the time that he and Mama may have spent time together in the psychiatric hospital.

"I have seventy-nine dollars and twenty-five cents."

"Good," Mama said. "We're in Pensacola, Florida. You'll need to buy yourself a bus ticket and head back to North Carolina. Find Patricia and tell her you need to stay with her until I return."

What? I heard what Mama was saying, but her statements made no sense to me. *What do you mean, go buy a bus ticket? Try to find my sister?*

Mama got back in the car and looked up at me from the passenger side of the Oldsmobile. She was crying and waving good-bye to me.

I was crying hard, too, but I managed to return her wave. As Tim drove away, I saw Mama turning around, looking back at me. Mama's face was wet with tears, and the look in her eyes said she didn't want to leave me. But she did.

I walked into the Trailways bus station and told the clerk where I needed to go. He took my money—all seventy-nine dollars, allowing me to keep my twenty-five cents—and gave me a one-way bus ticket from Pensacola, Florida, where I now was, to Gastonia, North Carolina, the area where Patricia lived with her husband, Steven. I walked back outside and sat on a bench while I waited for the bus.

Around three in the morning, a large Trailways bus pulled in to the station. I cautiously stepped up on the bus, walked down the long, narrow aisle, and found a window seat on my right. I put my boxes in the overhead rack and sat down. I sat alone in the middle of the night, with the left side of my face pressed against the bus window, as I looked out in the direction that the Oldsmobile had disappeared into the night, carrying Mama away from me. An awful sense of abandonment and rejection swept over me. I was thirteen years old, and I was alone in the world—again.

THE BUS WAS FULL BEFORE WE PULLED OUT. NOBODY wanted to sit next to me since I was filthy and smelled so badly. I was scuzzy and dirty from living in the car; it had been several weeks since I'd last had a shower at the Salvation Army, so my adolescent body odor was noticeably strong.

The bus pulled away from the station, and soon we were on the interstate to Atlanta, Georgia. With several stops in Alabama along the way, it was midmorning when the bus arrived in Atlanta. I was scheduled to transfer buses there, but I was clueless how to find the other bus and didn't discover it in time before it left the station without me. I asked someone for information and was directed to a waiting area.

Hours passed, and I was tired and hungry. I hadn't eaten or drunk any water since the previous day. I saw a popcorn machine that read "25 cents per bag," and it reminded me of the quarter I still had in that leather pouch. I dug out my last quarter and dropped it in the popcorn machine.

It was a small bag of popcorn—even in the late 1980s, you couldn't buy much for a quarter—but I sat in the chair and ate every kernel in the bag, even the unpopped corn kernels. The popcorn was extremely salty, and my lips were burning, but I was too afraid to leave the area to search for a water fountain. I didn't want to risk the chance of missing the last bus to Gastonia that day.

It finally arrived midafternoon. When I boarded the crowded bus, again the expressions on people's faces let me know they didn't want me sitting near them. I found a seat with space above to put my boxes, so I sat there, alone.

Late that evening we were still a long way from Gastonia when the bus driver announced over the intercom, "We're about thirty minutes early, so I'm going to pull into Wendy's. Please feel free to get off the bus and go get yourself something to eat. But stay close to the bus and don't wander off since we won't be here long."

One by one the passengers unloaded. I was the only one who stayed on the bus. I didn't get off because I didn't have any money. A number of passengers bought food and drinks and stood outside the bus, talking, laughing, and eating. I sat there, staring out the window, watching them eating and drinking cold drinks, my stomach growling. It had been more than twenty-four hours since I had eaten anything other than my small bag of popcorn, nor had I drunk anything. I simply turned my head and stared at the back of the seat in front of me.

The passengers loaded shortly afterward, and we continued on to another bus station, where I transferred again. I found the bus going to Gastonia, walked down the aisle and put my boxes in the overhead bin, and took a seat, just as I had previously. The bus sat idling as the driver waited on the boarding passengers.

A tall, skinny white guy with a flaming red Afro haircut stepped up on the bus. Adding to his odd appearance, the skinny young man was wearing a blazer and carrying a briefcase. He walked past empty seats directly toward me.

I sat staring straight ahead, trying not to make eye contact with him, hoping he wouldn't sit near me. But sure enough, the red Afro sat down in the seat right beside me. He jostled around, getting comfortable, and placed the briefcase in his lap.

I didn't say a word to him, pretending to ignore him. I thought, *It's strange he'd bypass all the empty seats to sit beside me, a kid! He has to be up to no good.* His unusual appearance and demeanor made me nervous, and I worried that he might be a pedophile.

The bus steered away from the station. We hadn't gone far when the weird-looking guy turned to me and asked, "Hey, kid; are you hungry?"

I looked at him cautiously, wondering what he had in mind. I paused, then said, "Yeah, I am."

The red Afro nodded in understanding. He slid two buttons on his briefcase to the right and left with his thumbs. The latches popped up, and he slowly opened the top as though he were opening a briefcase loaded with cash.

But what I saw was better than money! His briefcase was filled with crackers and all kinds of other snacks. He nodded toward the snacks and said, "Go ahead, eat whatever you want."

I could barely believe my eyes or ears, but I didn't want to be greedy. I took a pack of crackers and gobbled them down.

Meanwhile, he pulled a marijuana cigarette out of a little hiding place inside the briefcase. "I'll be back," he said. The red-haired guy stood up, sat the open briefcase in his seat in case I wanted something else, and walked to the lavatory at the rear of the bus.

A minute later I could smell the marijuana cigarette, its aroma wafting through the back of the bus. But before the driver noticed, "Red" stepped out of the lavatory and returned to his seat. I must have been looking at him quizzically because he said, "Man, this is what I do. I smoke, eat, and ride."

All I could think about was how glad I was that he sat beside me! I couldn't imagine an angel wearing a red Afro and smoking marijuana, but the guy was an angel to me that night.

It was well past midnight when the bus pulled into the Trailways bus station in downtown Gastonia. "This is where I get off," I told Red. I took my boxes down from the overhead bin and walked to the front of the bus. As I started down the steps, I turned and took one last look at my new friend. I waved at him, and he waved back at me with what looked like an expression of empathy. Despite our differences, we were kindred spirits. I smiled and stepped off the bus.

THE BUS STATION WAS CLOSED, WITH THE DOORS LOCKED and lights out. Nobody knew I was coming, so I wasn't surprised that no one was there to pick me up. Not even my sister, Patricia. She was fourteen, she and Steven married less than a year. I didn't know how they would respond to my intruding in their lives, but I had nowhere else to go.

I stood at the front of the bus station and looked up and down Franklin Boulevard, about a mile from Vance Street. There was no traffic anywhere, and it was dead quiet.

I pondered lying down in front of the bus station on the concrete, but I was too afraid to do that, considering that someone might attack me in my sleep. I walked around to the back of the bus station, searching for a spot on the ground, where I could sleep till morning. I found a dark area next to the back wall of the bus station, tucked away from the glare of any streetlights. I plopped down on the ground and cuddled with my boxes. I closed my heavy eyelids and drifted toward sleep.

But I had barely gotten comfortable on the ground when I heard something nearby that sounded like someone crinkling plastic. My eyes flashed open, and I was immediately on alert, my eyes darting every direction in the darkness. I saw what appeared to be cats walking around the bottom of a garbage can a few yards away. But then I noticed that these cats had long, skinny tails. I sat up to get a better look. That's when I realized they weren't cats; they were enormous rats.

I jumped up, snatched my boxes, and ran around to the front of the bus station. Just then I saw the blue flashing lights of a police patrol car reflecting off the brick buildings. An officer had pulled someone over.

I waited on the side of the bus station until the policeman finished dealing with the person he'd pulled over. Then I carefully approached him and said, "Hey, sir, can you take me to my sister's house?"

Startled, the officer asked, "Who are you, and what are you doing here?"

I guess he wasn't expecting a filthy thirteen-year-old kid carrying small boxes tied together to come walking out from the dark shadows, asking for a ride to his sister's house.

"What's your name? And why are you out at this time of night?" the officer wanted to know.

I told him that I had just gotten off the bus, but I didn't want to give him too much information because I didn't want him to know where Mama was. Mama had just recently gotten out of prison, and I was aware enough to know that her running off on her thirteen-year-old child would not go over well with her parole officer. They might ship her right back to prison. So I tried to protect her by saying as little as possible about Mama. I honestly had no idea of her whereabouts by now, anyhow.

The officer gave me a look somewhere between suspicion and pity.

"Get in the car," he said. "I'll take you to your sister's." He opened the trunk and told me to put my boxes in there. I started to get in the front seat when he stopped me. "No, get in the backseat."

He opened the back door, and I got in the backseat, a heavy wire screen separating us. I sat back in the seat. But when the officer pulled out, he drove in the opposite direction of where I told him my sister lived. He didn't say much until we arrived at the police station. Then he looked at me and asked directly, "Are you a runaway?"

"No, sir," I said with every bit of sincerity I could muster, but I didn't give him any more information than that.

I waited inside the police station and after more cross-examination and paperwork, the officer finally drove me to where he had located my sister's address, off Old Stanley Highway.

We arrived at her trailer around three o'clock in the morning, so the police officer got out of the patrol car and knocked on her door while I waited in the backseat. Steven answered the door. He and the police officer stood on the porch and talked for several minutes. I could tell by the look on Steven's face that he wasn't thrilled to see me.

Finally the officer walked back to the patrol car and opened the back door. I got out, and he retrieved my boxes from the trunk. He said good-bye, I thanked him, and I walked inside Steven's and Patricia's trailer.

Patricia was standing in the living room, dressed in her pajamas. She hugged me, then stepped back to look at me. "Are you hungry, Jimmy?" She knew I was famished, so she made me a bologna and cheese sandwich. As she stood there, watching me devour that sandwich as if I hadn't eaten in years, tears trickled down her face. "Do you want another one?" she asked before I even finished with the first sandwich.

Patricia was wise beyond her years. She knew that Mama had abandoned me.

After I had eaten, Patricia and I talked for a little while before she said, "You need to get to bed. We'll be getting up again in less than four hours. We'll need to enroll you in school today."

I washed up, and Patricia settled me into a bed. It felt fantastic. I was glad to be "home." It seemed I had barely gotten to sleep when she was gently shaking me awake again. I was still tired, but I got up and dug through my small cardboard boxes and picked out a pair of pants and a shirt that I'd worn to school last year. The clothes weren't new, and they certainly weren't clean. Nor did they fit well, but they were the best I had for my first day in junior high at a new school.

Nineteen

FACING THE BULLIES

A LOT OF TEENAGE KIDS CAN BE CRUEL, BUT JUNIOR HIGH kids can be downright vicious.

It was tough enough being the new kid at W. C. Friday Junior High School in Dallas, North Carolina, the school closest to Patricia's home. The trailer park where Patricia and Steven lived was a dump, with enough space for about five or six old trailers. I had spent most of my life in trailer parks, but this place was so rundown, even *I* was embarrassed for any of my classmates to know that I lived there.

While waiting for the bus, I stood across the road from the trailer park in a driveway that led to a nice house on a hill. When I got off the bus in the afternoons, I waited by that same driveway till the bus drove out of sight before I crossed the road and went back to the trailer park.

One day as I was preparing to get off the bus, a smart-alecky junior high kid asked loudly enough for everyone on board the bus to hear, "Why do you get off at that house? You don't live there."

I didn't respond and just stepped off the bus. But I knew that he knew. And now so did all the other kids on the bus. Of course, it was hard to fool anyone when I wore the same clothes to school every day.

About three months later Mama and Tim returned to North Carolina after being on the run from the law. Charlie and Cathy may have dropped the charges, or maybe because of their own issues, they never pressed charges, but Tim was never arrested for shooting Cathy. He and Mama moved in with Tim's sister, Kay, in a two-bedroom mill house in Belmont, North Carolina, right behind Stowe Mill. I had been living with Patricia and Steven during Mama's spree, but when Mama said it was okay for me to join them, I was elated.

Steven did not want me living with them, anyhow, and I knew it. Patricia and I were only a year apart in age, so like many siblings, we were prone to arguing with each other. But from Steven's perspective, I was a homeless kid they were helping out, and now I was fighting with his wife. So when the opportunity came for me to move in with Mama again, Steven sure didn't beg me to stay.

There wasn't much space in Kay's house, but I was happy to be back with Mama, even if it meant sleeping on the living room floor beside the gas heater. Mama or Tim never offered an explanation for why they abandoned me at the bus station in Pensacola, and I didn't want to destroy their newfound goodwill by asking.

Living at Kay's meant that I had to switch schools, changing this time to Belmont Junior High School. I was the new kid once again, so I was a target, a punching bag for almost every bully in the school.

The badgering intensified when I ignored a pretty girl who liked me. I wasn't rude; I simply wouldn't talk to her. Butch, a guy nearly twice my size, one of the more notorious school thugs, thought I was acting arrogantly, snubbing one of the local sweethearts.

"Do you think you're too good to talk to my buddy's sister?" Butch asked.

"No," I responded, "that's not it at all. You're out of your mind." Truth is I didn't want to be around *any* girl. I had to wear the same clothes to school every day. I was just too embarrassed to be *near* a girl. I had zero self-esteem.

Butch was a pack leader, a bully who lived in the same neighborhood as I did. He led a group of boys who took fistfighting seriously. The kids on Vance Street and in the trailer parks fought, too, but Belmont was a new world to me. These kids wanted to fight over almost anything.

Since Butch thought I was stuck up, he initiated the first fight with me at the bus stop, and from that point on, I fought someone different every day. Butch and his sidekick—a loudmouthed runt reminiscent of the punk in the movie *A Christmas Story* who wouldn't have dared say a word had it not been for Butch—stalked me every day when I got off the school bus. Fear built inside of me every afternoon as the bus approached our stop. Seeing Butch and his cohorts waiting for me was worse than my fear of snakes.

I knew that once I stepped off that bus and it drove away, I'd better run, or I was going to get beat up. But I didn't run; I never ran. I was too stubborn and prideful to run. I'd rather be laughed at for getting beat up than for being a coward.

Sure enough, Butch and his buddy ganged up on me again. They both punched me in the face and head with their fists. Butch held my arms like Mama did when she'd whip me, and his runt hit me again in the head. Pain seared through my head, and it seemed they had no intention of letting up, so I finally reached into my pants pocket and pulled out a knife.

When I flashed the knife, Butch and his friend backed up. They finally left me alone and ran home. I picked myself up, dusted off, and walked home as well. I was angry at myself for not fighting back. I could have easily beaten Butch's runt, who was my size, and I knew I could be just as mean as Butch, but I hadn't done much to defend myself.

Still brooding, I walked inside Kay's house and stood beside the heater, staring at the floor and thinking about what had just happened. I still had the pocketknife in my hand when Tim walked into the living room.

"Whatcha got there?" he asked, when he saw the knife. "Let me see it." He stretched out his hand.

I thought he wanted to see the knife and maybe have a fatherly heart-to-heart talk about dealing with bullies. Instead, when I handed him the knife, he threw it in the corner of the living room and, in one sweeping motion, turned back around. Catching me completely off guard, he punched me full force in the face on the side of my head. He grabbed me by my hair and pulled me around the living room, over to the couch, where he slammed my head down onto the furniture's wooden arm.

Between blows, I could see Mama standing in the kitchen, watching. "Mama!" I screamed. "Make him stop!"

But rather than stopping Tim or trying to calm him down, she stepped out of view, and Tim continued choking me and pummeling me with his fists.

His sister ran into the living room, yelling, "Leave him alone!" Grabbing onto Tim, Kay forced him to stop and release me.

I wiggled free and ran into Kay's bedroom and waited. A few seconds later Tim stormed into her room and headed toward me with his fist balled up. Then without saying a word, he stopped short, turned around, and walked out. I flopped down on the bed and nursed my wounds. I was bruised and scratched from my encounter with the bus stop boys, and now my head felt as though it were swelling up to the size of a basketball.

At school the next day the kids laughed at me, talking about the marks on my face and neck that Butch and his friends put there. Actually, the marks were caused by Tim's hands.

The abuse at school continued, so I decided I had to stand up to those bullies and physically fight back. I filled a two-liter plastic soda bottle with sand, tied a clothes hanger around the top of the bottle, forming a makeshift punching bag, and hung it from a tree limb in the backyard. I spent hours each day punching that bottle with my fists and kicking it, karate style.

I had watched David Carradine on television and figured if I could learn one of those karate kicks, I could win a fight. It wasn't long before I had my chance.

Carlos—a big, West Coast Hispanic tough guy, who was trying to gain respect from the East Coast rednecks—approached me in the school hallway outside the gymnasium. Carlos and I had never met, but he wanted to make an impression on Butch, the ringleader of the bullies. He walked toward me with his fist balled up, and almost instantly a group of kids surrounded us, anticipating a bloody spectacle—composed mostly of my blood.

I had no quarrel with Carlos, but I knew that if I was ever going to put a stop to the bullies picking on me, now was the time. As I stared at Carlos, his face morphed into a sand-filled, two-liter soda bottle right before my eyes. I knew what I had to do. The moment Carlos moved in on me, I jumped up in the air, spun my left leg around as hard and fast as I could, and smashed Carlos smack in the face with the side of my foot. *Just like David Carradine taught me.*

It was a lucky stroke, but it was perfect luck. A loud *pop!* reverberated throughout the hallway as my shoe connected with Carlos's face. Carlos never knew what hit him; he dropped straight to the floor with a splat.

The crowd of onlookers let out a collective gasp, "Oooh!"

Carlos lay moaning on the floor, with a foot-sized red welt rising on the side of his face. Word spread quickly throughout the school that little Jimmy Barber had knocked out tough-guy Carlos.

For some kids, this news was hard to believe. So, not surprisingly, another challenge followed quickly on the heels of my lucky kick. The next day another tall boy approached me in the bathroom, crouching toward me in a threatening manner with his fists balled up, ready to fight.

I didn't wait for him to throw the first punch but jumped up and kicked him in the forearm. "Owww!" he hollered, holding his arm to his chest. His arm swelled up immediately, and the look on his face was like that of a little boy who wanted his mommy. He grabbed his arm and held it, desperately fighting back the tears and trying not to cry in front of me.

I never found out if I had broken his arm, but no one else at Belmont Junior High, including Butch, messed with me ever again. In the bullies' minds, I had been transformed from "Little Jimmy Barber" to "Jimmy Wayne Barber, ninja warrior!"

Twenty

FAITH FARM

THE MORNING OF MARCH 18, 1987, MAMA SAID, "JIMMY, you're not going to school today. We're going down to the Gastonia courthouse."

"Why, Mama? What's going on?"

"We're going to see about getting your daddy to take care of you."

"What? Why?"

"Well, Jimmy, I've been taking care of you all these years, so it's time for your dad to take care of you for a while."

Her words hit me like a sucker-punch to the gut. I didn't understand why Mama wanted me to be with my biological father all of a sudden. I didn't even know the guy. He'd never been a part of my life, so why now?

We went to the courthouse and walked into an office, where Deputy Superior Court Clerk Sharon Hawkins was sitting in a chair behind a large desk. She had a serious look on her face.

"Please sit down, Jimmy," she said kindly, but by the way she said it, I could tell it was not an optional matter. I sat. "Do you know why you are here?" the woman asked me.

"Yeah, Mama said we were coming to see about my daddy taking care of me for a while," I responded naively.

Deputy Hawkins looked sternly at Mama and asked, "Is that what you told him?"

Mama hedged. "We had to tell him that or he'd run away," Mama lied.

"Wha . . . ?" I was confused and looked at Mama and Tim and then back at the woman.

She looked me right in the eyes and said, "Jimmy, you are here because your mother and stepfather have filed a court petition on you, claiming that you have been skipping school, fighting, breaking the neighbors' windows, and fighting your stepdad."

I let out a loud, "Huh?"

"You've been belligerent, and you've been suspended from school . . ." the woman read from a paper.

"That's not true!" I interrupted. I was shocked that Mama would tell such lies about me. I simply could not believe what I was hearing.

I quickly attempted to inform Ms. Hawkins that Tim had beaten me up. I admitted to her that I had skipped school one time, when I was scared of getting beat up again at school. But other than that, I was there.

She listened but remained unconvinced. Nothing I said mattered. The woman moved a few pieces of paper around on her desk, marked on some others, and then handed Mama a piece of paper. I later learned that the paper had my court date on it—for the next day!

We left the courthouse and drove back to Kay's house. It was an awkward drive, to say the least. No one spoke. Mama stared out the passenger window, just as she had done that evening in Texas. I sat in the backseat, as I had for most of the trip until the night Tim pulled up to the bus station in Pensacola. I felt hurt and betrayed by Mama for lying about me and especially for not defending me against Tim's accusations. But I didn't say a word for fear that Tim would knock my teeth out.

The next morning at 9:00 a.m., we arrived at the Gaston County Courthouse and proceeded to the assigned courtroom. The judge soon entered, dressed in a black robe, and took his seat behind a raised bench. Tim stood behind a table and told why he filed the petition against me. The petition said I had threatened my stepfather with bodily harm.

The judge then asked me to step forward and share my side of the story. I stood in front of the judge and, pointing at Tim, everything spewed out, like the burst of a geyser. "He gave me a gun to load," I said, "and then he shot my brother's wife. He's the one who's been beating me. He beat me up in the living room the other day for no reason!" I didn't even want to pause to breathe for fear the judge would stop me, so I kept talking as fast as I could. "I don't break people's windows in the neighborhood. I've never been expelled or suspended from school; you can see my school records."

"He's lyin'," Tim interjected. "He lies all the time."

The judge simply stared at me as though he thought I was lying or on drugs or something, but I wasn't.

After a few minutes the judge and Deputy Hawkins signed and exchanged some papers. He put down his pen, looked up at the group in his courtroom, and read, "On Jimmy's behalf, for his safety, the State of North Carolina is going to remove Jimmy Wayne Barber from the home due to his abusive situation and place him in the custody of Gaston County Department of Social Services."

Sadness covered me like a heavy blanket. I looked over at Mama, sitting with Tim. She turned her head away from me. I could not believe that she was allowing this to happen. *Why won't she stand up and tell the truth?*

Adding to the weirdness of the scene, Tim, Mama, and I left the courtroom together that morning and went back to Kay's house. For the next two weeks Mama and Tim and I actually got along. Mama treated me well, and things felt comfortable, almost like what I thought a normal home life might be. It wasn't an over-the-top love fest, but at least Tim wasn't hitting me, and Mama wasn't screaming at me.

I thought, *Hey, maybe Mama has changed her mind!*

She hadn't.

One day Mama told me, "Jimmy, a social worker will be coming to pick you up tomorrow and will take you away, so you need to have all your things packed and ready to leave."

No! I wanted to scream, but of course, I didn't. I was so confused. I

thought we had gone to court so we could get on track. I didn't understand that I was being sent away to another home. Or maybe a part of
me did know that I was being sent off to live somewhere else. I just didn't
want to accept it. I was only fourteen years old; I didn't want to be separated from my family again.

Being sent away was almost worse than the feelings I had experienced
after the bus station incident, where Mama had left me in the parking lot.
We had been reunited, and I thought she wanted me around. But now
it was clear that nothing had changed. At the same time, I was hopeful.
Maybe this was the escape route I'd been searching for. Even if it meant
going to a group home, it was worth it to get away from Tim.

On March 31, 1987, a white vehicle, bearing the
North Carolina state insignia, showed up in front of Kay's house. An
older woman came to the door, talked briefly with Mama, then told me
to gather up my belongings and put them in the car. "It's time to go," she
said. I had no idea where we were going, but I loaded up all my clothes,
drawings, and poems and put them in the back of the state car. Mama
never said good-bye or "I love you" or "I'll miss you." Nothing.

I walked around to the back of the house to take a last look. I couldn't
help noticing the beat-up, sand-filled plastic soda bottle still hanging on
the tree. It looked like I felt inside. I walked back around to the front of
the house and got in the car.

The social worker cranked up the motor, looked over at me, and
said, "My name is Kathy Flowers." I realized that she was merely doing
her job, and she appeared to be a nice enough person—but at that point,
she could have been Mother Teresa, and I still would have hated her. I
grunted something that sounded like hello.

Ms. Flowers drove me to a place called Faith Farm, a foster system group home operated by Lutheran Family Services and situated off
Dallas Stanley Highway. I was surprised when Tim and Mama followed
behind us in his car.

We pulled into the driveway that led to a simple but attractive two-story white farmhouse. I got out of the car and looked around at the scenery with large, lush, green oak trees. It looked like a postcard. It was an old house, but it appeared to be in great condition, with a well-maintained yard and nicely manicured bushes and flower gardens. *Wow, I've never been in such a rich house as this!* I thought. Of course, by most standards, it was a typical Victorian-style old house, but to me, it was a mansion.

I followed Kathy Flowers around to the front of the house, up onto a wide, gray-painted concrete porch complete with concrete pillars topped by wooden posts. I stepped through the front door, where I was warmly greeted in the living room by the staff. "Hi, Jimmy. Welcome. We're glad you're here."

I was pleasantly surprised that they knew my name, but then I realized I was alone in the house. The other residents—four boys at the time of my arrival—were in school. Nevertheless, the personal greeting made me feel special, and that was a new experience for me.

After brief introductions they gave me a tour of the home and then showed me to my bedroom. Downstairs, Mama and Tim put on a show, pretending to be the best parents ever, so grieved to have to leave their son. Upstairs, I unpacked my bag while Mama and Tim watched from the doorway. Neither of them said a word to me the entire time.

When it came time to say good-bye, I walked over and hugged Mama and even hugged Tim. "I love you," I said to both of them. The moment the words escaped my lips, I realized how strange they sounded. But if there was one chance left for them to change their minds about leaving me there, this could be it. No such luck. They turned and followed Kathy down the steps. They gave me no indication that I'd ever see them again. No "I'll miss you" or "I'll see you next week." Nothing.

From my upstairs window I watched Mama and Tim get in their car and drive away, just as they had that night in Pensacola. I didn't cry as much this time. Not because it didn't hurt and not simply because I was growing older, but more because I was getting used to Mama's leaving me.

I SAT ALONE IN MY ROOM, DOODLING ON SOME PAPER. Drawing pictures had become a ready therapeutic release for me, and when I wasn't writing poems, I loved sketching, even though some of my drawings were so dark and morbid, they nearly frightened me. I dreaded meeting the other boys who lived at Faith Farm because I'd heard about the kind of boys who lived in these types of places. *Will they be like Butch, and will I have to fight them every day?* I worried. *Will they try to rape me?* A thousand fearful thoughts flooded my mind.

Soon my questions were answered as a group of boys burst through the front door. They were happy, loud, and excited, having just gotten home from school.

Ben Foster and Tommy Brown immediately ran upstairs to my room and introduced themselves. They were nothing like the boys I had imagined. They were my age and more like nerds, but I didn't mind that. In fact, it was almost a refreshing change of pace compared to the tough guys I had endured at Belmont Junior High School. Marcus Ray and Antoine Daniels, two African-American boys, were a bit standoffish at first, but they soon warmed up. I was still hurt and angry on the inside, but at least I felt somewhat safe at Faith Farm, and I slowly dropped my guard.

The residents were all neglected, troubled boys. Some of them had parents who had died; others had been rejected by their parents or had gotten in some sort of trouble, or they were simply unwanted. All of us had done some bad things, but nothing worthy of jail. Nevertheless, we had all been ordered to Faith Farm by the courts.

The staff was kind but firm, with a no-nonsense approach to the rules. Their emphasis was on helping us put some order into our lives and preventing a free fall into trouble. They didn't threaten us, but we all understood that if we messed up and got thrown out of Faith Farm, our next stop would include a room with bars on the windows.

The group home was highly structured. We got up at specific times and went to bed at designated times. We had assigned chores inside the house and outside on the property, and we were paid a few cents for each task completed. The work could not be slipshod; it had to be done correctly. Our rooms had to be clean with our beds made every day. We were required to keep the rest of the house spotlessly clean too.

As time progressed, we became a close family rather than a disjointed group of fatherless boys. Tommy and I listened to music together. He shared Iron Maiden's *Live After Death* album with me for the first time. I loved it so much that Tommy gave me his Iron Maiden T-shirt. I soon began liking heavy metal music.

Ben was a good listener and a good friend, but I soon learned that getting close to anyone in a group home was unwise. Individuals could get ripped out of your life overnight. I came home from school one afternoon and learned that Ben had been transferred to another facility on the other side of North Carolina, closer to his sister who was deaf. I never saw Ben again. It tore me up that I didn't even get to say good-bye to my friend, but now I understood why the staff didn't want us to get too attached to one another.

Ben was soon replaced by Jett Roster, a cocky kid from Gastonia. "Hey, man! I'm Jett," he said, striding across the room and grabbing my hand. His handshake was strong, and I could tell Jett was going to be an instant friend. But my experience with Ben reinforced one of the most basic lessons of life in the system: don't get too close to anybody because he or she may not be here tomorrow.

THE STAFF DID ITS BEST TO PROVIDE US WITH A WIDE VARIETY of activities meant to simulate those of a normal family. We ate our meals together around a large dining room table. We went somewhere fun every weekend: bowling, skating, swimming at the lake, and even an overnight camping trip to Myrtle Beach. We went to church every Sunday morning, the church of choice of the staff member on duty. Sometimes a staff member might take us to a church of our choice, if we had one. To expand our perspectives and to provide us with a wider worldview, we watched the television program *60 Minutes* every Sunday evening. It was not optional.

A local JC Penney store was wonderfully kind to the residents of Faith Farm, giving us vouchers that could be spent at their store. I spent mine on a can opener for Patricia. I wasn't the only one who used the vouchers for someone else; almost all the residents did the same. The giving of gifts was not just to be nice; the gifts were our way of subtly crying out, "Will you please accept me?"

If there was any downside to my being at Faith Farm, it was the ridiculous counseling sessions the state required me to attend with mental health professionals at a hospital. I didn't mind the counselors' questions, but I took offense at the silly hand puppets they used in trying to get me to talk. The puppet would ask me questions, and I was supposed to talk to the puppet on the counselor's hand.

"I am fourteen, man. I don't need you talking to me with puppets on your hands."

"Oh, you are hostile."

"No, I don't talk to puppets."

"Oh, you're getting sassy. That's your problem. Just put the puppet on your hand and talk through the puppet."

"How are you doing, Jimmy?" the puppet across the table said to me.

"Fine," I said through my puppet.

"No, you have to make the mouth move."

"I'm not talking to some stupid puppet," I recoiled. I threw the puppet down on the table and got up, ready to leave. The counselor wrote down on his report: *Passive-Aggressive.*

I guess I was.

ALTHOUGH THE STAFF UNDERSTOOD THAT ALL THE BOYS AT Faith Farm came from backgrounds where we were accustomed to doing whatever it took to survive, stealing of any kind was not tolerated, no matter how petty or seemingly insignificant the theft. One night shortly after my arrival at the home, Tommy Brown noticed the office door was ajar after hours. Tommy had been at the home long enough to know where the staff kept their personal supply of miniature Snickers bars.

He slipped into the office and grabbed the entire bag. He ran upstairs and handed out candy bars to all the other boys, including me. "Hey, man, do you want some candy?" he asked.

"Sure do," I responded. "Thanks, Tommy. Hey, where did you get this candy, anyhow?"

Tommy told me. Since I was new to Faith Farm's strict discipline, I didn't think much about it when he told me where he'd gotten the candy. I figured the staff wouldn't care since they were only miniature candy bars, the size that is usually given away, anyhow.

I was wrong, very wrong.

When we got home from school the following afternoon, a staff member yelled, "Group!" which was the signal to assemble in the living room for a group meeting. We all ran downstairs and plopped down on the couch and chairs.

The entire staff stood in the center of the room, and Vanessa, a senior female staffer, said, "While you were at school, we inspected each of your rooms and found these." She held up a couple of candy bar wrappers. "Someone has gone into our office and taken a bag of candy bars from our safe. We checked everyone's room and found wrappers in all your trash cans, so therefore you're all guilty."

Vanessa walked over to me and stood in front of me. "Did you enjoy those candy bars, Jimmy?"

"Yes, ma'am," I replied spritely. "They were great!"

"Good, I'm glad you enjoyed them," she replied sarcastically. She turned back to the other four boys.

"You're going to have a lot of time to think about what you have done. Since we can't trust you, you're going to spend the next two weeks in this living room under close observation. In the evenings you'll be escorted upstairs to get your mattresses, and you will bring them down to the living room, where you will all sleep in the same room.

"You'll then take your mattresses back to your rooms in the morning and make your beds before school. And since we can't trust you to walk alone through the house, you'll even be escorted to the bathroom to take your showers and brush your teeth.

"Oh, one more thing: for two solid weeks, you will not be permitted to talk to one another. Period. No talking for the entire two weeks. If you need to talk to a staff person, you will raise your hand and wait for one of us to give you permission to ask your questions."

At first I thought they were joking, but I soon found out that the staff was dead serious. For two weeks we maintained absolute silence in the house. Saturdays and Sundays were the worst since we had no school and were home all day. We had to get up early, carry our mattresses one by one up the stairs, make our beds, and immediately come back down to the living room, where we sat the entire day on the couch without saying a word. Imagine five fourteen-year-olds going out of their minds in silence. If we fudged or flubbed up or purposely violated the silence, the staff added an extra day. Those were the longest days of my life.

After two weeks the staff allowed us to bring a workout bench into the living room and lift weights to occupy our time. But one of the guys got impatient and tried to jump in line. "Hey, it's my turn!" one of the boys protested.

"Put it up!" a staff member called out. "You're done." The workout bench was removed, and we were back to boring silence and inactivity.

Little by little, the staff reinstituted our privileges until we were allowed to have full access to the entire house again. But I never wanted to see another Snickers bar in my life.

Twenty-one

DOCTOR DEATH

THE STAFF AT FAITH FARM SERVED AS SURROGATE PARENTS for me, so when I complained of a nagging toothache, a female staff member took me to the dentist. After an exam, the dentist told the staff member I needed a root canal.

The two of them walked around the corner, and I overheard the staff member tell the dentist that I was living in a group home.

"Oh," the dentist responded. "He's one of *them*?"

"Yes, sir. We don't have dental insurance for our residents."

"Then I'll have to pull the tooth," the dentist replied. His words ripped through me, not because I was afraid of getting a tooth pulled. The real pain came from the knowledge that he didn't regard me as a normal kid with a toothache. The Novocain numbed the pain when he pulled my tooth, but it did nothing to numb the pain in my heart.

I RECEIVED A FEW LETTERS FROM MAMA WHILE I WAS AT Faith Farm, but none of them read like the ones she wrote to me when she was in prison. Now her letters were very generic.

Jimmy,

Sorry I haven't been able to send you anything. I'll try to see you soon.

Love,

Mom

I never asked her for a dime. The group home allowed us to earn a small amount of money for doing our chores—ten cents for vacuuming the downstairs, twenty cents for washing dishes—and occasionally a staff member might even pay me to wash his vehicle. So I didn't need any money from Mama. I did hope she might come for a visit, but for several weeks, she never did.

I rode an emotional roller coaster at Faith Farm. Some days were great, and I was up; others were terrible, and I was way down. I had always enjoyed drawing, and my sketches often depicted what I felt on the inside—drawing and coloring pictures of flowers and butterflies, with captions like "Love is very sweet," in my preteen years, to pictures of "Doctor Death" with the caption, "Born to run, bound to die" as a teenager. Many of my drawings before and during my stay at Faith Farm included horrifying monsters and devils. I produced more than one drawing with images of me at the bottom of the page, with slogans such as "In memory of Jimmy" and "Jimmy—gone but not forgotten."

Many of my drawings depicted demonic characters I imagined or copied from Iron Maiden albums. Yet at the same time I drew several beautiful pieces of Jesus, both as the suffering servant and as the returning Lord. Then I followed those drawings with more images from AC/DC and Iron Maiden.

On February 2, 1987, prior to going to Faith Farm, I wrote poems such as "Doctor Death":

I am a doctor, I have a cure
That will make you feel well.

I am a doctor, I have a cure,

That will send you to hell.

I wrote longer poems around that same time, with titles such as "Hell's Not Cold," "Fast Death," and "The Time Is Near." While living with Tim and Mama and attending Belmont Junior High, I had begun experimenting with self-harm, and that got worse when I moved to Faith Farm. I sat for long stretches of time, scratching my arm with my fingernails until it bled, which momentarily refocused my interior pain on some exterior point on my body. I also started listening to some really dark music and writing even darker poems. I was close to suicide several times while at Faith Farm. So the pain from self-applying tattoos on my body was merely a precursor to death. I put one tattoo on my leg, using an art kit that had ink I sometimes used in my drawings.

Using this method, I sat in my room one afternoon at Faith Farm with a needle and a jar of ink. I wrapped thread around the tip of the needle and dabbed it into the jar of ink. I began sticking the needle into my chest on my left breast. Dot by dot, I pricked my skin. I wiped the blood and ink off with tissue paper. The initials *FTW* were now tattooed on my skin, and I meant everything those initials implied.

MOTHER'S DAY WAS APPROACHING, AND THE STAFF AT FAITH Farm told me that Mama wanted me to spend the holiday with her. I was so excited. I hadn't seen or heard from her since the first day I arrived in the group home, a month earlier. Around the same time, the staff also informed me that the plan was to move me to a long-term facility at Elida, and I would not return home on a permanent basis. That infuriated me, and I threatened to kill myself or our staff person, Kathy, or both of us if I did not get to return home.

One evening shortly before my scheduled visit with Mama, I had a strong disagreement with one of the staff. I dismissed myself from the dinner table, ran upstairs to my room, and found a knife I had hidden, in case Antoine Daniels decided he wanted to sneak into my room while I was in bed.

Antoine had slipped into my room once before in the middle of the night. I was nearly asleep, but I felt him lie down on my bed beside me.

Startled, I yelled, "You better get out of here, now!"

Antoine laughed uproariously, as if he was just joking around, and he ran out of the bedroom.

Maybe so, but I wanted to make sure that the next time he decided to joke around, I'd be prepared. The following day, while I was in the office, I spied a pocketknife in a toolbox. I nonchalantly knelt down, and without drawing attention to myself, I casually wrapped my hand around the knife and shoved it in my pocket. I ran straight back to my room and hid the knife in a place where I could get to it—just in case.

Now, a few days before Mother's Day, I came running back down the stairs to the dining room, wielding the pocketknife and yelling, "You're not stopping me from going home!"

The staff and the residents sat frozen at the wooden dining table, not certain of what I planned to do. I wasn't sure myself, so I ran outside into the front yard, where I stood and yelled some more. Cheryl, one of the lead staff members, followed me outside and attempted to calm me down as I held the knife in front of me.

When Cheryl stepped toward me, I pressed the knife's point against my stomach, threatening to kill myself. I knew I wasn't going to stab myself, but she didn't. Cheryl finally talked me into giving her the knife, and we went back inside the house.

My outburst could have destroyed any opportunity to go home for a visit with Mama, but the staff recognized that I was operating out of deep anger. I'd had numerous sessions with my counselors and the entire group about better ways of handling anger. I apologized to everyone, and the incident, although noted in my records, was not held against me.

On Mother's Day I could barely contain my excitement when I saw Mama pull up in the driveway. I ran out to her car and hugged her. We were excited to see each other. Once we left the property, Mama asked me if there was anything I needed.

"Yes," I told her. "I'd like to have a fan for my bedroom." We went to a store, and she bought me a small fan that clipped onto the headboard of my bed. She also purchased a green apple, a bag of Funyuns, and a Mountain Dew. We then headed to the trailer, where she and Tim now lived.

As soon as he saw me walk in the door, Tim left without even acknowledging me.

"What's wrong with him?" I asked Mama.

"Oh, he's mad. Don't worry about it. He's probably jealous that you are here."

Mama and I spent the entire day together, and that evening she took me back to Faith Farm. I sure hated to see her drive away. I spent the remainder of the night in my room.

The next morning one of the staff members said, "Jimmy, we're not taking you to school today; you need to go to the hospital."

"Why? I feel fine," I said.

"You'll understand when we get there."

They wouldn't tell me what was going on, but I knew instinctively that Tim had done something to hurt Mama. We arrived at the hospital and went to the section used as a battered women's shelter. When we walked in, I saw Mama sitting in a chair with her head down. At first, I wasn't even sure it was her. Her face was swollen and marbled in black, purple, and yellow bruises. Her hands were sliced and covered in dried blood, as though she had tried to grab a knife and the blade had slid through her fingers.

I ran to her. "Mama, what happened? Mama, tell me! What happened? Did Tim do this to you?" I asked.

"Yes," she said quietly through her swollen and parched lips. "I was in the bed asleep when Tim came into the bedroom drunk and started hitting me while I was still under the covers," she said. She tried to fight him off, but Tim had stabbed her in the stomach with a pocketknife that Mama kept on the side of the bed. Mama stumbled out of the house and made it to the neighbors', who called an ambulance.

I felt furious and helpless at the same time. "Mama, do you need anything?"

"I need something for this headache," she answered.

I had a few dollars in my pocket, so I told her I'd be back shortly. Although her doctor could have prescribed something to ease Mama's pain, I felt it was my responsibility to do something. After all, Tim had probably beaten the daylights out of her because of my visit. I ran across the road to the convenience store at the bottom of the hill and purchased a box of BC Headache Powder and took it back to Mama.

Mama told me that this beating was the final straw, that she was going to divorce Tim and she wanted me to come back home to live with her. Before she left the hospital, the DSS began working on the transition, and I began mentally preparing to leave Faith Farm.

I WAS DOING MY BEST TO WALK THE LINE AND STAY OUT OF trouble, so I could go home and look after Mama. That's why I freaked out when on June 16, 1987, I heard that two new residents, Jack and Dillan, had stolen some money out of the staff's office and were planning on running away. My first thought was, *Oh no, guys! Please don't do it. We'll all be sitting in the living room for another two weeks.*

I called both of them into my room and told them about the stolen Snickers candy bars. I begged them to put the money back.

Dillan went downstairs, slipped into the office, and placed the money back into the safe. Shortly afterward the staff on duty yelled, "Group!"

I knew what was about to happen. We all filed into the living room, and the staff person said, "Someone has been in the safe, and we want to know who it was. We'll sit here until someone owns up."

I wasn't about to snitch on Jack or Dillan, but I gave them a look that let them know they'd better speak up. The silence in the room was thick. Finally one of them quietly said, "I took the money, but Jimmy talked us into putting it back."

I hadn't expected that sort of honesty and was probably more shocked than the staff!

The staff dismissed everyone except Jack and Dillan. They spent the rest of the night in the staff office getting lectured about stealing.

The next day at school I heard my name on the intercom; I was being called to the front office. When I walked into the principal's office, I was surprised to see one of the staff members from Faith Farm sitting there. She said, "I'm checking you out of school early today, Jimmy, because you and I are going to the mall."

"Why?" I asked.

"I'm taking you to the mall, and you can buy anything of your choice for as much as fifty dollars, as a reward for talking Dillan and Jack into returning the money they stole last night."

"Oh, you don't have to do that," I said, thinking that not having to sit in the living room for two weeks was reward enough for me.

"No, we want to reward your good choice," she explained. So we went to the mall, where I picked out a pair of cool blue-and-gold Quiksilver swim trunks. I was thrilled because Faith Farm had a beach trip scheduled, and I didn't own a swimsuit. Now I did.

THE STAFF AT FAITH FARM REQUIRED THAT WE COMPLETE daily evaluations, along with the staff's daily reviews replete with their comments about our day, reprimands, evaluation of our progress in working toward our goals, and encouragements to do better. As I'd done since sixth grade, I continued to write in my journal as often as possible. My journal entries while at Faith Farm were much more positive than what they used to be. Where I had written before in my journal: "I was abused today" or "I hate living," my Faith Farm entries now read:

May 1, 1987: I went to my first jr. high prom with Tina Miller at W.C. Friday. Well, it was her prom, and she invited me. [I was so unsophisticated; I called her corsage a croissant. I didn't know any better.]

May 18, 1987: I wore an EKG machine to monitor my heartbeat. I have an irregular heartbeat, but I think it is cool.

June 6, 1987: I went to the lake with the group. That was so much fun.

July 4, 1987: Kathy made me listen to Jimmy Buffett on the way to Myrtle Beach, SC. The pavilion was one of the greatest places I've ever been. But I'm mighty sunburned.

One of the most foolish practices of Faith Farm (or any group home) was bringing teenage girls to live in the same home as teenage boys. Tia, the oldest in our home, was seventeen. A second girl, Somer, was fourteen. The boys and girls had their own facilities, and we were to live as "brothers and sisters;" but many of the boys and girls were already sexually active. Those who weren't likely would be before they left the home. Once Chris, our live-in staff person, went to bed, we had the run of the house. Did they really think that a fourteen-year-old boy wouldn't be attracted to a fourteen-year-old girl? Or a seventeen-year-old girl wouldn't have sex with a sixteen-year-old boy just because the rules said not to do that? The co-ed living situation was an irresponsible accident waiting to happen, and many did. Worse yet, there were emotionally fragile, needy, or damaged kids who were sometimes needlessly placed in vulnerable, compromising positions. But as a teenage boy, discovering how wonderfully different girls were from boys, I didn't complain.

Prior to moving into the group home, I kept all my personal belongings in two cardboard boxes. But at Faith Farm someone on staff gave me an old suitcase with discolored copper latches. That old suitcase became my own personal treasure chest in which I kept my most cherished items. I used the suitcase to store letters from Mama, my early report cards, some of my artwork, and many of my poems. I also kept the receipt from the Trailways bus station and other special receipts.

Overall, living at Faith Farm changed my life for the better. Although it wasn't an authentic family situation, living at the group home showed me what a normal household could be like. I learned structure and discipline that influence me to this day. I stayed at Faith Farm for almost four months, and they were the best four consecutive months of my childhood.

Twenty-two

DIDN'T SHE ALWAYS
COME BACK?

My last day at Faith Farm Group Home, July 15, 1987, was bittersweet. Mama had left Tim and wanted me to come home; that was the good news. The bad news, of course, was that I was leaving my closest relationships in the world again. I knew I would miss the kids, but I had also come to appreciate the staff at Faith Farm, recognizing that some of them genuinely cared for me and had poured their lives into trying to help me survive for the past four months.

The day of my departure, the entire staff and all the kids gathered around the wooden dining table to share ice cream and apple pie. We laughed about our experiences and took Polaroid pictures.

Mama was present, along with Penny, a dyed-blonde, older teenager Mama introduced as the niece of a friend. I'd never before met Penny, but she was cute so that was enough of an explanation for me. Besides, I was focused on saying my final good-byes to everyone.

There were lots of hugs and even a few tears at my "victory" party. I had lived at Faith Farm for fifteen weeks and a day. Although it had taken me a while to adapt, I'd grown to love Faith Farm. I recognized that it was going to be difficult to make the transition back to life outside, especially since I still had a lot of trust and anger issues toward Mama percolating within me. But I loved her, and love gave me hope that some-day she might change. Unfortunately, my love for her also enabled her to mistreat me.

MAMA, PENNY, AND I DROVE AWAY FROM THE PEACE AND order of Faith Farm to a small house in a gully on Maine Street in Bessemer City, where Mama introduced me to her new boyfriend, Harvey. I wasn't surprised that she had already hooked up with another man. Mama always had to have a man.

Harvey seemed to be a nice guy, but I had thought Tim was pretty nice, too, when I first met him. I could not have dreamed of the poten-tial evil within Tim. Now I could, so I was cautious around Harvey.

I settled into the back bedroom in the far corner of the small house. Later that night I realized why Penny was staying the night. Mama intended her to be a sort of welcome-home-gift to me.

Anytime Mama had been released from prison, the first thing she did was find herself a man. Since Mama perceived me as being a prisoner who had just been released, she assumed I needed sex. It was a long night with a very short ending. I didn't even know Penny's last name.

The transition back to Mama's lifestyle was tougher than I thought it would be. I had no plans, no dreams, goals, or purpose. I spent every day trying to figure out what I should do next. There were no week-end trips to the beach or going to church and watching *60 Minutes* every Sunday night, as I'd done at Faith Farm. Although I probably wouldn't have admitted it—and may not even have realized it yet—what I missed most was the structure in my life that Faith Farm had helped me establish. I missed someone holding me accountable for my actions. I missed group meetings and Inspection Day, when we cleaned the entire house, all the way down to wiping the baseboards and vacuuming under the couch.

In some ways I did feel like a prisoner, recently released from prison, who didn't know how to function in a society that had no structure. The prisoner then becomes depressed and, all too often, finds a way to get back behind those walls, where he feels safe.

I had nothing to do, nowhere to go, and no discernable reason to be alive. So I plunged into a deep depression. Fortunately, Harvey owned a lawn mower, and he allowed me to use it. I kept busy trying to earn some money by mowing lawns.

On the evening of August 8, 1987, I returned home after working in the neighborhood all day, mowing lawns. I rolled the push-mower down the hill of our yard and parked it under the porch, as I always did.

Just then Mama rushed out the front door, carrying a large bundle of her clothes in her arms. I could tell by the look on her face that something was wrong. It was the same look she had the night she left Carroll.

"Mama, where ya going?" I asked.

"I don't have to tell you where I'm going," she snapped, as she headed up the hill toward an old Ford Galaxy she had picked up somewhere. Mama tossed all her clothes in the backseat and slid behind the wheel of the car.

I ran up the hill, reaching the driver's side window just as she turned the ignition key, frantically asking her again, "Mama, where ya going?" She didn't reply; she stomped down on the gas pedal and the car roared away.

I ran back to the house, calling out for Harvey. He wasn't there, but he returned home shortly afterward. I could see the sadness in his eyes when I told him about the way Mama left. He was determined to find her.

Harvey and I got in his car and headed to Belmont, a short drive away, to where Mama and I had been living prior to my going to Faith Farm. He seemed to know exactly where he was going. Harvey turned by the Stowe textile mill and slowly drove down Belmont Avenue toward the house of Tim Allen's sister, Kay.

Mama was standing in the yard with Tim. *Oh no!* I thought. *Not again.* Sure enough, just as I had suspected, Mama had gone back to Tim.

Harvey stopped the car in the middle of the street, stared at Mama and Tim for a few seconds, and then slammed the car in reverse. He knew. He backed up, turned the car around, and without saying a word to Mama or Tim, he drove to Gastonia and pulled into a parking lot with a phone booth on the corner. He parked the car beside the phone booth, handed me a quarter, and asked me to call Mama.

I had no idea what I might say to her, but I stepped inside the grimy metal-and-glass phone booth, put Harvey's quarter in the slot, and dialed Kay's number.

A male voice answered, "Hello?" It was Tim.

"Is Mama there?" I asked.

"She doesn't want to talk to you," he said, then hung up the phone.

Probably to discourage me from calling back, Tim picked up the receiver again and laid it on the coffee table beside the phone. He didn't realize I was still on the line; I had not disconnected, so I could still hear Tim and Mama talking and laughing in the background. I stood in that phone booth and listened. I screamed again and again for Mama to pick up the phone, but she never did. I knew what that meant.

For a long moment I couldn't move. Cars whizzed past as I stood in the filthy phone booth, staring through the hazy glass, smeared with fingerprints, spit, and tobacco juice. Thoughts of Mama having fun with Tim tormented me. I wondered if she knew I was on the phone, listening to her giddy behavior and raunchy talk.

When I could no longer endure listening to them, with tears streaming down my face, I hung up the receiver, yanked open the rickety folding door, walked out of the phone booth, and flopped down in the front seat of the car.

"Did you talk to her?" Harvey asked. I told Harvey what had happened, and he asked no more questions. He merely shook his head sadly, cranked up the car, and drove back to Bessemer City.

A week went by, and Mama still hadn't returned. Other kids and their families were getting ready for schools to open soon, buying new clothes, getting their backpacks stocked and ready, but I had nowhere to go. I was lonely and depressed, and part of me even began envying the kids in Grace Group Home, a foster care home one block away and across the street. I could see its back door and the kids going in and out of the house.

Some friends of mine from Faith Farm, Tia and Raymond, had been transferred to Grace, so I stopped over to visit them. Seeing them reminded me of all that I was missing. I never thought that I'd want to go back to a group home, but anywhere was better than being abandoned.

But Mama would be back soon, I felt sure. She always came back. Then she'd leave again or dump me off with somebody. But she always came back.

Not this time. After a few weeks it became increasingly obvious that Mama wasn't coming back, so Harvey decided to move on with his life. Nevertheless, he was concerned about me and wanted to make sure I had a place to live before he moved away from Bessemer City. Ironically, a man I had known only a short time, who had been shacking up with my mother when I met him, was more concerned about my well-being than my mom. Despite his faults, Harvey was a good man.

One afternoon he said to me, "My sister would like to meet you." Harvey's sister was older than him, in her midsixties. We went to her house in south Gastonia, and I spent the entire day with Harvey's sister and her husband. It was an awkward visit and felt more like a job interview.

When Harvey had said, "My sister wants to meet you," he had conveniently omitted, "to see if she and her husband like you." But I understood. I had read somewhere that back in the 1880s, immigrant orphans were loaded on trains in New York City and transported west. The train stopped at depots in small towns along the way. At every stop the orphans stood outside by the train as ranchers sized them up, pinching their arms and checking their teeth to see if they were healthy enough to work on the farms. When a rancher found an orphan to his liking, he gave the child a home in exchange for work.

One of those orphan train kids, a fair-haired, blue-eyed boy named William Bonnie, became one of America's most notorious frontier outlaws, known as Billy the Kid. Legend has it that Billy was a mere fifteen years old when he shot his first victim. I could understand that.

I moved in with Harvey's sister, her husband, and their grandson a few days later, but my stay was short. The adults were kind, but I didn't fit in.

Harvey's relatives hinted to me that I could stay with them only until I found someplace else to go. A few days passed before they told me that their grandson's mother, who lived in another state, was coming to North Carolina and needed my room.

I really didn't want to leave—where was I to go? So I pretended that I didn't understand what they were implying. I went on to school as if everything was all right.

I was sitting in class when a woman's voice came over the intercom, requesting that my teacher send me to the office—with my books.

I knew what that meant.

For a brief moment I considered running out the back door of the school. But, resigned to my fate, I reluctantly walked toward the school office. Sure enough, when I looked through the office windows, I could see Kathy Flowers sitting in the office waiting area. I walked in, and in an emotionless, matter-of-fact voice, Kathy told me why she was there. "I've come to take you to the Dallas receiving home, Jimmy."

I felt weak and betrayed. I'm not sure why, but that rejection hurt more than most. Harvey's relatives had been so nice to me; they had convinced me I was welcome to stay in their home. But now they were asking me to leave. Actually, they weren't asking.

I turned over my books to the school secretary and trudged to the DSS hatchback vehicle parked out back beside the school cafeteria. As Kathy and I walked past the long line of kids standing outside, waiting to go into the cafeteria, I noticed several of them pointing and laughing at a pair of white underwear pressed against the window in the white DSS car.

The underwear was mine, and I was totally embarrassed.

When we got to the car, I found my other clothes, strewn on the floor and up under the hatchback window as though they had been hastily thrown into the backseat of the car. Another woman was seated in the front passenger seat, so I slid in the back and tried to collect my clothes.

I turned to Kathy and asked, "Where's my twenty dollars?" She didn't know what I was talking about. I explained to her that I had hidden twenty dollars in the drawer under some clothes.

Silence. Kathy wasn't about to return to the house for my twenty bucks. In fact, as we headed down the road, Kathy looked at me in the rearview mirror and said, "This is my last day at the DSS, so this is Carla Moore, your new case worker."

Carla looked not much older than a kid herself, around twenty-two years old, I guessed. "Hello, Jimmy," she offered a smile. "I'm looking forward to working with you."

"Hello, Carla." I didn't say anything else to either of them. I sat in the backseat, seething about how Harvey's relatives had done this, not to mention my hard-earned, missing twenty bucks.

Looking idly out the back window, I suddenly realized Kathy was driving in the same direction in which Harvey's relatives lived, the same folks who had just evicted me from their home. As we approached the road that led to their house, a crazy thought occurred to me: I decided to visit them one last time before being sent back to a group home. With the car still moving, I opened the back passenger-side door and jumped out. I hit the ground and rolled to break the blow of striking the surface.

I heard Kathy slam on the brakes, the car sliding to a stop. She and Carla quickly got out, and Kathy yelled, "Jimmy! Jimmy, get back here. Get back here right now!"

I brushed myself off and stood up straight. I cursed them and held up my middle finger as I walked backward and away from them. They continued to yell for me, demanding that I get back in the car.

I turned and ran toward Harvey's relatives' home. When I glanced over my shoulder, I saw Kathy and Carla getting back into the car and driving away. I slowed to a brisk walk, continued down the street, up to the door, and rang the doorbell. Harvey's older sister opened the front door, but when she realized it was me standing there, she quickly slammed the door closed. I heard her yell, "Call the cops!" and then the old man began yelling, too, telling me I'd better leave.

I stood on their front porch and cried. I cried so hard I could barely breathe. No one came back to the door, so after a few minutes, I walked off their steps, still crying.

The next-door neighbors heard me and called me into their home. We sat in the kitchen, and they talked to me and helped me calm down. Since I had nowhere else to go, they notified the police and told them where I could be found. Shortly afterward the same white DSS car pulled up in the driveway. Kathy and Carla picked me up and took me to the receiving home in Dallas, North Carolina, a home designed for about ten kids in transition. All the kids would be placed in another home within thirty days.

ONCE I GOT CHECKED IN AT THE RECEIVING HOME, I WAS happy to see Marcus Ray. I hadn't seen him since Faith Farm. But Marcus now acted very differently than he had when I first met him; he seemed much angrier. A black guy shared a room with Marcus.

One night shortly after I arrived, Marcus planned an escape. He had taken a butter knife and had rigged the alarm system over the back door so the alarm wouldn't go off when he opened the door to escape. In the middle of the night, I heard a loud scream from across the hall. It was Marcus's roommate, crying out that Marcus had stabbed him with a dart. He kept yelling and crying until the staff arrived at their room. Marcus claimed it was an accident, and the staff permitted him to remain in the receiving home. His roommate's outburst apparently scuttled Marcus's escape plans for the time being, but I was too scared to sleep the rest of the night, knowing there was a chance Marcus might stab me too. He just was not the same Marcus I'd met at Faith Farm.

The next day I contacted JR Wilson, the man who moved Mama, Patricia, and me out of Reed's Trailer Park and into Sante Trailer Park. I had kept JR's phone number on a three-by-five-inch card in my wallet. About forty handwritten phone numbers were on this card—contact numbers as diverse as Faith Farm's to the number of the local hospital. I kept the card with me for years (and still have it).

I told JR that I was at the Dallas receiving home and asked him if he would come pick up all my belongings. I didn't tell JR, but I knew I was going to run away, and I didn't want to leave my drawings and poems and letters behind because I feared I would never see them again. JR arrived that afternoon and loaded my things into his vehicle. "I'll keep them for you in my lawn mower shed," he promised, "until you find out where you're going." I had no way of knowing at the time how significant JR's simple act of kindness would be in my life. (Had he not preserved my belongings, many of the notes and resources for this book would have been lost.)

That evening, September 4, 1987, I slipped out the front door of the receiving home, ran away, and never went back. It was colder outside than I anticipated, so after walking a while, I found a pay phone and called JR again. He met me at a store up on the hill and took me to his home in Bessemer City. As we were riding down the long dirt road, I saw a Gaston County patrol car sitting in JR's driveway. I guessed that the police might already be looking for me. "Please, JR, don't stop. Please. Just drive to the bottom of the road and let me out at Reed's Trailer Park."

JR reluctantly complied. As soon as he stopped the car, I got out, fled into the woods, and hid.

Twenty-three

MY WORST BIRTHDAY EVER

LATER THAT NIGHT I WALKED BACK TO JR'S HOUSE, WHERE he and his wife, Jean, allowed me to stay the night. And the next night. And the next. I stayed with them for nearly a month, sleeping on their couch.

I was unsure what I was going to do with my life or where I could go. I was fourteen. I was now officially a runaway. I hadn't been to school in weeks. I became depressed, so depressed that at one point, I didn't even talk to JR or Jean for a solid week.

JR got up each morning and went to work. Jean went out somewhere, so I mindlessly sat in their house the entire day, doing nothing, not even watching television. As far as I was concerned, my life was over. I felt useless and figured I'd never amount to anything. I hated living, and more and more, I just wanted to die.

One day I asked JR if he'd take me to Patricia's trailer, off Airport Road in Gastonia. "I'll be glad to take you," JR said. He took me to Patricia and Steven's place and dropped me off, but when I called him to come pick me up, he didn't answer.

I visited with Patricia all day. When Steven returned home from work, I left Patricia's and started walking down the road, hitchhiking to anywhere. An old man picked me up and took me to the corner of

Airport Road and New Hope Road. I glanced at the road sign with a sarcastic laugh. If there was ever anyone who needed new hope, it was me.

I continued walking in the cold, not sure where I could go. By nightfall I had made my way to Uncle Austin's house in Crowders Mountain. Five years older than my mom, Uncle Austin was a crusty codger cut out of the same mold as Grandpa. But he was Mama's brother, and besides my mom and sister, he was my closest kin. He lived on the mountainside with his wife, Diane; his daughter, April; and his son, Chad. I knocked on his door and told Austin I needed a place to stay. He refused to let me stay with them, but he told me that I could stay in Grandpa's old, abandoned trailer, still on the hillside.

Grandpa's trashed trailer didn't have heat, water, or electricity. It had been a wreck when Grandpa had lived in it, and now that he was in an old folks' home and it hadn't been used or kept up in the years since he left, the trailer had deteriorated even more. Austin told me to dig through the pile of junk in his backyard. "There's a cot in there somewhere," he groused, "and you can use that to sleep on." I rummaged through the junk until I found the cot. Austin laid a piece of spun glass wall insulation on the cot and covered it with plastic. He wrapped the cot with string to hold the plastic and the insulation together, forming a makeshift bed.

"The weather's gonna turn nasty cold," Austin warned, "so don't sleep in your clothes, or you'll be cold throughout the day." He even gave me an old Sears and Roebuck coat. The coat was big enough for two people my size, but it helped keep me warm. (More than twenty years later, I wore that oversized coat in a music video for a song I wrote called "Paper Angels.")

Although it wasn't exactly southern hospitality, I appreciated Austin's kindness in allowing me to stay there. I stayed in that freezing cold, run-down trailer for two weeks.

To help stave off the bitter cold, I bought a blue sleeping bag for $18.38 on October 17, 1987. (I still have the receipt and the sleeping bag.) It wasn't much of a sleeping bag, but it kept me from freezing in that trailer. It was so cold that I could see my breath at night by a trace of light streaming in the window from the pole in the churchyard down the hill and across the road. I often would lie there at night, shivering and thinking about my life. Sometimes I wondered where Mama was . . . and I'd get angry, very angry.

In the morning, just after dawn, I awakened to the sound of Austin banging on the side of the trailer with his hand. That was my alarm clock. I got up, put on my thermal underwear, and went outside to feed the goat and chickens. That was part of the deal in exchange for my use of Uncle Austin's luxurious accommodations.

After I fed the animals, Austin sometimes invited me inside to eat breakfast, complete with eggs and tomatoes. Following breakfast, he always had a chore for me to do. I didn't mind. I was accustomed to work, and I was glad for the food.

Austin owned a lot of land, so we'd drive a few miles over the border to South Carolina and work all day, cutting trees and chopping firewood. My job was to clear out the brush from around the bottom of each tree with a heavy ax so Austin could get to the bottom with a chain saw.

One day I grabbed a thick vine and started to chop it in half, but as I swung the ax downward, I missed, and the blade went through my knuckle on my left hand, nearly chopping off my index finger. Pain seared through me and blood spurted in every direction. Austin wrapped an old rag around my finger and pressed the knuckle back together. "Keep this rag on there till the bleeding stops," he instructed.

An injured finger didn't get me out of work. Although chopping vines was impossible, I spent the next week working in Austin's backyard. One day Austin gave me a small steel brush and told me to sand all the rust off the bed of his pickup truck.

At first I thought he was kidding. But he wasn't.

I spent the entire day scraping rust off the truck bed. It was a difficult job, done nowadays mostly by electric-powered sanders. The following morning Austin woke me up, yelling obscenities, beating the side of the trailer, cursing me and asking me why I hadn't sanded down his truck as he had ordered.

This guy must be nuts! I thought. Austin had watched me sand his truck bed the day before, but this was exactly how he treated his son, Chad, as well. He'd find a reason to get mad, and then he'd start an argument.

Since we hadn't painted or sealed the freshly scraped truck bed, the moisture had settled in it overnight, causing the bed to oxidize again. Austin probably knew that, but he just wanted to fight.

I was not about to put up with him cursing me, and I sure wasn't going to fight him. He was three times my size, and the Sears and Roebuck coat he gave me reminded me just how long his reach was. I had to fold the cuffs back twice.

Instead of arguing with Austin, I quietly gathered up my things, put them in my backpack, and walked out of his yard, down to the dam in the creek, where I used to fish as a little boy. I wasn't sure where I was going or how I might get there. I couldn't do anything else—so I walked. I was wearing jeans and Austin's coat. It was so cold the only thing I could think about was getting warm.

I found a small cave, hollowed out in the rock, so I huddled in close to the stone for shelter. I remembered a pack of matches in my backpack and took them out; there were only three matches in the pack. I gathered some leaves and attempted to light them to make a fire.

The first and second match went out as soon as I struck them. With only one match remaining, I knew I needed to do something differently. In my bag I had a small bottle of Stetson cologne that had once belonged to Tim Allen's dad. I removed the cap and carefully drizzled cologne all over the leaves. Trying to keep from shivering, I struck the last match. *Poof!* The spark caught the alcohol in the cologne, and I had a fire at last. The leaves began burning, and I added more twigs and brush to my campfire. As I basked in the fire's warmth, I realized the date. It was October 23, 1987—the morning of my fifteenth birthday.

PHILLIP, ONE OF MY BEST CHILDHOOD FRIENDS, STILL lived on the mountain with his mom and dad, Duty and Lawrence Spicer. Occasionally, on nights when I couldn't sleep, I sneaked up the hill through the woods to see Phillip and get some food. That morning I realized I couldn't stay in the cave by the creek forever, so I crept up through the woods so nobody would notice me and knocked on Phillip's trailer door. His dad let me in, and I told him what happened. Lawrence probably knew that I was on the run, but he was kind to me. "Are you hungry, Jimmy?"

"Yes, sir," I answered honestly, still rubbing my hands to get warm.

Lawrence grilled some cheeseburgers for his family, and a big one for me, and we all sat in the living room to eat together. I was famished, so I chomped right into the cheeseburger. It was delicious! I gobbled down two big bites, and was about to take my third when I heard a knock on their front door and the squawk of a radio, like the ones used in a police car.

Lawrence answered the door, and there stood Larry Hamerick, a Gaston County police officer. "Sorry to bother you folks," the officer said, "but I have a pick up order for a runaway that you might know, Jimmy Barber. His uncle says you might know where he is." Lawrence stepped out on the porch, and I could hear him talking to the policeman. I thought of running, but I was so exhausted and emotionally drained, I simply froze in my chair.

After a while Lawrence and the officer came inside, and Officer Hamerick explained that he had come to pick me up and take me to the county detention center. Phillip sat pouting, and Phillip's mom started boo-hooing, so Lawrence wrapped her in his arms, trying to calm her. "Can he finish eating?" Lawrence asked.

The officer noticed the burgers and glanced at me sitting on the living room couch. "Sure, go ahead, Jimmy," Officer Hamerick said kindly. "Finish eating your sandwich before we go." I looked at my cheeseburger, but my stomach was whirling so badly, I couldn't even eat any more. I put down the sandwich.

"Okay, then, are you ready to go?"

"Yes, sir," I said. "But let me go out back and get my backpack." I fully intended to run for the hills, but the officer was no fool. The policeman followed me around to the back of the trailer, where my backpack was leaning against the porch, and then he escorted me to the squad car. He put my backpack in the trunk then told me to put my hands behind my back. "I'm sorry," he said, "but I have to put handcuffs on you." He snapped the cold steel handcuffs onto my wrists, and as he did, I heard Phillip's mom burst into tears.

Officer Hamerick helped me inside the backseat of the squad car, pushing my head down to avoid hitting the car's roof. I looked out the window at Phillip, Lawrence, and Duty. They were standing on their front porch, and Duty was bawling.

As Officer Hamerick drove down the hill, I saw Uncle Austin and his son, Chad, in the yard. Uncle Austin looked at me and laughed.

On the way I stared out the window, and Officer Hamerick talked. But he spoke about only one subject: Jesus. "You know that Jesus loves you, Jimmy," he said. The officer didn't try to ram his faith down my throat, but he knew he had a captive audience, so he shared freely about God's unconditional love for me. "No matter what we've done, He loves us," Officer Hamerick said. "There's nothing you have done or ever could do that would keep God from loving you, Jimmy."

I wasn't convinced. "If He loved me, I wouldn't be sitting in your squad car right now," I replied caustically.

Officer Hamerick drove to the Gaston County Detention Center in Dallas, North Carolina. He helped me out of the car and into the facility. He unfastened the handcuffs, checked me in, and said good-bye.

In complete contrast to Officer Hamerick's kind professionalism—Officer Hamerick later went on to become a psychotherapist, a clergyman, and a military chaplain—the officer on duty at the detention center was an older man, overweight, and unnecessarily mean. "Get in here, boy," the officer growled at me. I stepped into the processing area he had indicated.

"How many tattoos and scars do you have, kid?" he asked, as he moved around me, writing notes on a clipboard. He noted the gash on my finger where I'd hit myself with the ax. The cut had gotten infected, and my finger looked awful. The officer scribbled more notes. "Strip," he said.

I looked at him in confusion.

"Take your clothes off, all of them," the officer roared.

I hesitated, "Huh?"

"Take your clothes off," he yelled, "or I'll take them off for you."

"I don't think you will," I said under my breath.

The officer stood up, looming largely over me, and looked as though he was about to move across the room toward me.

Oh, crap! I said to myself and pulled off my shirt. The officer glared at me as I removed the rest of my clothes. I stood there in front of him, naked and humiliated.

He curled his lip and rubbed his nose, sniffing. "Boy, how long has it been since you've taken a bath?"

"Two weeks," I answered sincerely, thinking he really wanted to know.

"Bend over, spread your cheeks, and squat," he ordered. This crass, demeaning technique was intended to reveal or loosen any contraband I may have tried to conceal before entering the facility. To me, it simply decimated what little dignity I had remaining.

The officer slowly walked around my naked body. Satisfied that I had nothing to hide, he ordered me to go over and stand in the shower but not to turn it on. I obeyed and tried not to cower as he walked toward me holding a bottle of disinfectant. Without warning, he sprayed it all over my body then poured some other substance, I assumed to be lice-killing shampoo, on my long hair. Once I was lathered up, he turned on a water hose and doused me again from across the room.

I felt like one of those men I had seen in civil rights films being hosed down with fire hoses by police officers. Any resident racism I may have had remaining from my KKK-surrounded childhood went down the drain along with the suds from the disinfectant.

The officer then ordered me to take a shower under the shower heads, and he watched me the entire time. Despite the horrendous humiliation, the hot water felt wonderful on my body.

"That's enough," the officer called.

I dried off with a towel he handed me and put on some clean, prison-issued clothes, including a pair of pants, a T-shirt, and a pair of pink socks. Inmates were not allowed to wear shoes inside the facility, so I was issued rubber sandals, similar to shower shoes, instead.

I was then led to the dayroom, where all the other boys were detained till bedtime. These were the bad boys, not the Faith Farm boys. In that room were kids who had killed their parents; others were in for committing rape, and still others had pending drug charges.

I, on the other hand, was a runaway—a small, skinny kid runaway—and I was scared to death.

In the dayroom I sat at a table and ate the peanut butter crackers the detention staff had given me, topped off by a glass of milk. About ten other boys were in there, watching television. I spoke to no one and tried to avoid making eye contact with anyone. I was nervous, but it was warm in the room, and I was thrilled to have the crackers and milk and a television.

At bedtime I was led down the hall to my cell, the last door on the right, and was glad to discover that each boy was housed in a separate cell. The cell was sparse, with nothing but a bed bolted to the floor, a pillow, a wool blanket, and a small pocket Bible lying on the bed. The windows were barred and screened. Oddly enough, once the solid steel door slammed behind me, I felt much safer than I had in the dayroom among the general population.

Periodically throughout the night the officer on duty raised the flap covering the window on the cell door. He looked in, checking to make sure I was doing what I was supposed to be doing, made a few rude, salacious comments, and then let the window flap loudly slap shut, smacking against the door as he walked on to the next cell.

I shut my eyes and tried to sleep. *Happy birthday, Jimmy!* I said to myself. It was definitely a birthday I would never forget.

Twenty-four

BUMPING INTO ANGELS

Around midmorning, October 27, 1987, a uniformed detention center staff member came to my cell. "Come with me," he ordered, and I quickly complied. By that time I was convinced that some of the staff members were angels, and some were devils—and it seemed that the devils had the angels outnumbered. I had been repeatedly cussed out and referred to by every derogatory name I had ever heard and some that I didn't even know the meaning of. Granted, there were several dangerous characters passing through the detention center on their way to more secure facilities, so I understood why the staff couldn't be buddies with the boys. But why did they have to demean and denigrate everyone merely to keep order? Why did they purposely attempt to make everyone feel like trash, simply so they could maintain some sort of mental or emotional leverage? Most of the boys in detention weren't hardened criminals—yet. But if they were moving in that direction, little about the detention experience would stop or prevent them from spiraling downward. *There has to be a better way*, I thought.

The staff member escorted me to the front office, where I saw Lawrence Spicer sitting in a chair beside his brother-in-law, Maurice Edwards. Was I ever glad to see them! The surprise got better. Lawrence explained that they had come to get me out of the detention center and planned to take me to live with his family until Maurice and his wife, May, could be certified as foster parents. I would then go to live with Maurice, May, and their son, who was close to my age.

I didn't know the Edwards family, and I had no idea how they arranged these details so quickly, but I was ecstatic and tremendously grateful when we walked out of the detention center and went to Lawrence's trailer. I stayed with the Spicer family, they enrolled me in school, and we planned for me to eventually move in with Maurice and May.

My hopes soared. The Edwards family lived in a nice house in Chapel Grove, a quiet, suburban neighborhood. It was unlike anything I had ever experienced. I was finally going to have a real family. Throughout the month, as Maurice and May prepared to become official foster parents, I visited with them in their home, spending lots of time with them and their son.

Imagine my disappointment when I learned that after my few visits with the Edwards family, they decided not to follow through and become foster parents. The official reason given had something to do with Maurice's health. Whether it had to do with me personally, the family situation, or something within the system, I never knew for sure. But I couldn't help thinking it must be some defect in me.

I couldn't blame the family. They didn't know me; they were simply operating on Lawrence's recommendation, so their willingness to try taking me in was commendable. Compatibility between foster parents and foster kids, as in any relationship, depends a lot on chemistry; sure, it can be developed, and the Bible says "love covers over a multitude of sins" (1 Peter 4:8), but it helps if you have some things in common. Moreover, you can't "try on a kid" to see if he will fit with your family, as you might try on a pair of shoes to see if you like them.

That's why it takes a special person to be a great foster parent, someone who realizes that the child he or she is receiving isn't perfect and probably is carrying a lot of heavy emotional baggage and bad habits.

But that understanding and acceptance are essential if foster parents truly hope to bring any sense of normalcy to the child living with them in their home. The rest is all uphill from there.

Regardless of the reason, on December 7, 1987, my new DSS case worker, Carla Moore, arrived at my friend Phillip Spicer's grandmother's house, located across the dirt road from Lawrence and Duty Spicer's trailer, where Phillip and I had been hanging out and goofing off. I recognized the young case worker and understood the implications of her showing up. My spirits plummeted immediately.

"Hello, Jimmy," Carla greeted me kindly. "I've come to take you back to the receiving home."

"Hi, Carla," I answered despondently. I had no beef with her; she was a good person trying to do a difficult job. But seeing her reminded me of everything that was wrong in my life, and depression swept over me. We were standing in the living room, and I told her I needed to use the bathroom before we left.

I was extremely saddened and angered by the news that I had to leave. Maybe something deep inside me hoped that even if I couldn't live with Maurice and May, at least I could stay with my friend Phillip and his family. I was tired of being tossed from one place to another. I was mad, and I was depressed. More than that, I was done.

When I walked into Mrs. Spicer's bathroom, I opened the medicine cabinet and grabbed the first bottle of pills I saw. I stared into the mirror. *Good-bye, Jimmy Wayne Barber.* I opened the bottle of pills and swallowed every last one of them. I closed the bottle, placed it back in the cabinet, and returned to the living room. I got in the white DSS vehicle, and Carla drove me back toward the receiving home in Dallas, North Carolina.

I stared out the passenger window and waited to die. We finally arrived at the receiving home, and I began unloading my belongings. I kept thinking to myself, *Any minute now, I should pass out, start bleeding out the mouth, or something.*

Nothing. Not even a headache.

About that time the Spicers frantically called Carla. "We think Jimmy has taken a bottle of pills!" Carla raced back to the receiving home and found me.

"Jimmy, did you take a bunch of pills when you went to the bathroom at Grandma Spicer's?"

"Yeah, I did," I replied, embarrassed that she had found out before I was dead. "But they haven't seemed to work yet. I feel fine."

"Oh, Jimmy!" she groaned. "Come on, we need to get you to the hospital right away."

"Why? I'm okay. Really, I am."

"Do you know what you took?"

"No . . ."

"Neither do I," Carla said. "Come on, get in the car."

Carla raced to the hospital and guided me into the emergency room. Meanwhile, the Spicers gathered up all of Grandma Spicer's medication bottles and brought them to the hospital. The doctors examined me inside and out.

After a few hours an emergency room doctor returned with his report. "There were a lot of dangerous medications in Mrs. Spicer's cabinet, Jimmy," he said with an ominous tone in his voice. "At least ten different pills in that cabinet are lethal in large dosages." The doctor paused and glanced down at his chart on which he had some notes. "But fortunately for you, and all of us, you grabbed the one bottle filled with antibiotics. The medications you ingested are not lethal."

"Does that mean I'm going to live?" I asked.

"Yes," the doctor replied. "You're going to live. In fact, you're going to be fine. Since you took a bunch of antibiotics, you're going to pee an awful lot tonight because we need to flush your system, but you are going to be perfectly well. You were lucky this time. Please, don't let me see you in here for this reason ever again."

While Carla and the Spicers were elated that I was going to live,

I was furious. *God! You've got to be kidding me. Why are You doing this? I don't want to live like this anymore. I hate my life. Please stop this madness.*

I was such a loser. I couldn't even kill myself right.

I LIVED AT THE RECEIVING HOME THROUGHOUT THE MONTH of December, but I told Carla, "I can't do this anymore. I'm not going to stay here. I don't want to be here. I'm gonna run. You know that."

Carla nodded. She understood. "Let me see what I can do, Jimmy." Carla made some overtures to Patricia, asking her if I could live with her and Steven for a while. "You don't want your brother living in a home, do you?" Patricia was more than willing to have me close because, although I didn't know it at the time, her husband had been abusing her and knocking her around.

The DSS found an address for my mother, so it seemed natural that they would approach her, too, letting her know that I needed a place to stay. But although Mama was living only a few miles away, she made no effort to get me out of the receiving home. Finally, after sixteen days, Carla worked out an arrangement with the county and with Patricia and Steven for me to stay with them for a while. Two days before Christmas 1987, Carla picked me up at the receiving home and took me to Patricia and Steven's trailer in Gastonia. Although it wasn't the best environment for me, it was better than being illegally on the run.

ALTHOUGH I DIDN'T KNOW IT, CARLA HAD SIGNED ME UP for the Salvation Army Angel Tree, a program that gives Christmas presents to needy children. Before leaving Patricia's, Carla presented me with a special gift from the Salvation Army. It was a guitar! I was ecstatic. I'd had a toy guitar as a five-year-old, but this guitar actually played. It was small and inexpensive, made of reddish-brown wood, with white keys and a black pick guard. The action was set high, almost like a dobro, and it was almost impossible to accurately tune it, but I didn't care. It was a guitar, my first guitar!

Carla started to get in her car to leave, but I asked her to wait a few minutes. "I'll be right back," I promised. I ran inside the trailer and wrapped a small gift for her. I hurried outside and sheepishly handed it to her.

"You're probably going to laugh when you open it," I said.

She did. The look on her face was priceless. She laughed first, and then to my surprise, tears trickled down her face as she thanked me over and over for the gift.

It was a bottle of men's cologne—used, and only half full—but it was all I had to give her. Carla knew that, and she kindly and appreciatively accepted my gift.

CARLA GENUINELY CARED ABOUT ME, AND IT SHOWED BY the attitude with which she did her job. She worked tirelessly, trying to secure a better living arrangement for me. Although she wasn't happy to hear it, she believed me when I told her that I would resist any further efforts to place me in another family within the foster system. "Wherever they put me, I'm gonna run," I told her. I had no clue where I would go or what I would do; I was just tired of being a ward of the state.

Carla could tell I was serious, so rather than wasting time trying to get me placed with another family, she worked to formalize a relationship with Patricia and Steven in which they might be able to receive a few dollars from the Gaston County Department of Social Services for keeping me. For that to happen, Patricia and Steven had to have full custody of me, though, so that's where Carla directed her efforts—no small challenge, considering that Patricia was only a year older than I was. The program, Aid to Families with Dependent Children, was similar to those found within most state or county foster care systems. The foster parents won't get rich, but hopefully, they will receive a small amount of money for food and other essentials to help care for the child living with them. Most counties are willing to do this because, in the long run, it is much less expensive than housing, feeding, and caring for a child in a group home.

On April 6, 1988, the Gaston County DSS vacated my custody indefinitely. That meant I was out of their system—they no longer took any responsibility for me. I was still six months away from turning sixteen, so until then my sister and her husband would be my legal guardians.

But not for long.

Twenty-five

FAMILY AFFAIRS

FROM THE TIME I WAS A LITTLE BOY, VISUAL ART—SKETCHING, drawing with colored pencils, or painting with watercolors—had always been my way of escaping reality. Even when circumstances were horrible, living with Mama and Tim, with noise and nonsense swirling all around me, I often sat at the kitchen table and immersed myself in my artwork. Writing poems was a similar outlet for me. But now, with a guitar, I found another doorway into the artistic world. Although I was an awful guitar player, I enjoyed playing, and the music became a heartfelt means of expressing my inner thoughts and feelings.

My brother-in-law, Steven, was an amateur guitar player, too, but rather than being a point of connection between us, the guitar became a point of contention. I wasn't good, but I learned everything he knew on guitar within the first week of having my own. That's not saying much because Steven never excelled past "The House of the Rising Sun" and the introduction to "Smoke on the Water."

When Steven heard me playing those songs, he walked from the living room into my bedroom and told me to stop strumming the guitar because it was too loud.

Okay, I thought, *maybe I'm making too much noise.* After all, trailer walls are mighty thin.

I strummed the guitar lightly so Steven wouldn't hear me, but within minutes he was back in my room. "I told you to cut it out," he said.

"Sorry," I answered. "I didn't mean to bug you."

When Steven left the room again, I continued practicing but without strumming the guitar; I simply laid my fingers on the strings, forming various chords from songs. Steven must have been listening with super-sonic, high-powered antennae or something because he heard even those muted sounds of my fingers on the strings and the occasional squeak of my hand changing chords. Within seconds he was back in my bedroom doorway; he stood there glaring at me angrily.

I stopped playing the guitar altogether whenever Steven was at home. It was strange. I sometimes stayed in my room and simply stared at the guitar lying on the bed beside me. I wanted so badly to pick it up, to touch it, to play it, but I knew that would just cause trouble.

We moved four times within eight months. During one of those moves, mostly done by pickup truck, my guitar fell off the back of the truck and was crushed. At least, that's what Steven told me.

AS MUCH AS I HATED JUNIOR HIGH, IT WAS STILL BETTER than going home and being around Steven. In school my favorite class was art. One day, while working with watercolors, the teacher instructed the class to paint the picture he had displayed in front of us. Once I finished the painting, the teacher surprised me. "Now, turn the canvas upside down," he said.

When I turned the canvas from top to bottom, I discovered that I had painted an awesome picture of the Outer Banks of North Carolina, complete with a beach with white sand dunes, blue water, and a clear blue sky. Although I couldn't take any real credit for it—all I had done was follow my teacher's instructions—the painting was *beautiful*.

That painting somehow gave me a glimmer of hope when so many things in my life were upside down. *Maybe one day*, I thought, *it will all turn around and become a beautiful picture as well.*

STEVEN WORKED AS A GRUNT ON A CONSTRUCTION JOB, AND Patricia worked in a textile mill on the other side of Gastonia. Home life was stressful with the limited space and resources. Adding to the tension, Patricia and I, like many teenage siblings, sometimes argued with each other or said things we didn't really mean. We weathered most of those storms and laughed about them later. Conditions often got volatile when I saw or heard Steven mistreating my sister. "Leave her alone," I would say, ready to fight.

"Look! She's my wife. If you don't like it, get out."

"Don't tell my brother to get out!" Patricia would jump between us.

"Yeah, if you don't like it, you can get out too," Steven would rail at her.

Then one day, while standing at the kitchen sink, Patricia looked at me pensively and said, "Jimmy, I'm pregnant." She was seventeen, wise for her age, but not much more than a child herself.

I didn't know whether to celebrate or to cry. I could tell she was nervous, and I was anxious for her as well. Her life with Steven was a living hell, and now she was about to bring a child into it.

During the next eight and a half months as she carried her baby, she continued working at the textile mill. I'd hear her vomiting in the bathroom every morning, then getting into an old, burgundy Ford truck she drove to Saunders Thread mill, where she stood on her feet all day long to earn $3.75 per hour. She came home late every evening, wrung out and exhausted. Steven still expected her to cook, do laundry, clean house, and keep up with all the other domestic chores, so I tried to pitch in even more to take any strain off her that I could. Still, there were many prenatal issues about which I knew nothing, and Mama never showed up to help Patricia through her pregnancy. But Patricia and I went through it all together.

When Patricia stopped working, the finances got even tighter. We moved back to Holland Memorial Church Road (known locally as Bell Road) in Bessemer City, where Steven's mother, Ruth, a sweet woman, allowed us to live with her. Steven told me I had to get a full-time job and start paying rent, so I finished the ninth grade, but I had no intention of going back to school.

I probably would have dropped out of school immediately, had it not been for Cindy Ballard, a guidance counselor at Highland Junior High, where I was now attending. I walked into Ms. Ballard's office, told her I was quitting school because I had to get a job, and I handed her my books.

"Oh, no, Jimmy, you can't do that," she said. I had known Ms. Ballard since I was thirteen, meeting her shortly after I had returned to North Carolina on the bus from Pensacola. She wasn't about to let me quit school.

She marched me over to the office of Lee Dedmon, the principal. Mr. Dedmon was a giant of a man, six-foot-eleven inches tall, but he was no match for the godly, gutsy Ms. Ballard. She explained my circumstances to the principal and said, "Jimmy is not going to quit school, but he has to get a job, so he needs some special consideration and help with his homework."

Although Ms. Ballard lived in Lincolnton, North Carolina, she drove forty-five minutes out of her way, all the way to Bessemer City, to pick me up and take me to school every morning. She knew that I could refuse to get on the bus, but if she came to get me, I couldn't blow off going to school so easily—especially when I knew how far out of her way she drove to pick me up. If she could get me into class, I had a chance to learn. After school I rode the bus home, but the next morning Ms. Ballard was right back to pick me up again.

"Jimmy, you must finish school," Ms. Ballard continually emphasized to me. I wasn't a good student, and worse than that, prior to Ms. Ballard's taxi service, I skipped school so frequently I received several suspensions. Even when I showed up for school, I was a perpetual discipline problem for my teachers. But Cindy Ballard went to bat for me over and over again. When it became obvious that my grades were a disaster and my attendance and behavior at school were not pluses, Ms. Ballard arranged for me to take some classes and tests that summer to make up for my poor grades, and she drove me to the remedial classes. She simply refused to give up on me. Thanks to Ms. Ballard, I didn't quit school.

As soon as school was out for the summer, I began working full-time at Hardee's fast food restaurant as a cook. When I got paid, Steven demanded that I turn over my entire check to him. When I balked about giving him every penny I earned, he countered, "Either that or leave." Later that summer I quit my job at Hardee's and picked up another job sweeping floors at Walt Gilreath's machine shop, near where Steven's mother's house was located.

PATRICIA GAVE BIRTH TO A BABY BOY ON JANUARY 15, 1989. They named my new nephew Brian. Patricia was elated, and even Steven was affected by the birth. When he came home from the hospital after seeing his newborn son, Steven said happily, "That will change your life." Unfortunately, Steven's upbeat attitude didn't remain for long.

Despite doing my best to pay my way, Steven told me I had to leave. I understood and didn't blame him. He and Patricia were struggling as it was, we were living with his mom, and having a teenager living with them boosted their expenses and imposed on their privacy. They received only thirty-nine dollars per week in assistance from the state toward my support, so I was an extra burden Steven didn't want to carry.

I had been in contact with Mama occasionally over the past few months, and I had found out that she was living back in Reed's Trailer Park, sharing a trailer with friends. In my naive sixteen-year-old mind, it made sense that since Steven had asked me to leave, the most logical location for me to live would be back with my mom. I knocked on the door of trailer number 5. Mama came to the door, and after a brief conversation I asked if I could move in with her.

Mama wasn't too sure she liked that idea.

"I've got a job sweeping floors over at Walt's machine shop," I said, nodding toward the building across the way, right behind Ruth's house, where Patricia, Steven, and the baby lived. "I can help out with the rent and groceries," I offered.

That was the clincher. When Mama heard that I had money, she allowed me to move in with her and her friends.

I had "borrowed" a bicycle—I planned to return it . . . someday—and that was my means of getting back and forth to work. Walt came by every morning to pick me up at Mama's, and I put my bicycle in the back of his truck so I could ride home by myself each evening. After work I could walk out the back door of the machine shop and go over to Ruth's house to see Patricia and my nephew, Brian.

I loved playing with baby Brian and holding him close to my heart. Sometimes I'd run over during my breaks at the machine shop just to spend a few minutes with him. I helped Patricia care for him, cuddling him, feeding him, napping with him; I almost enjoyed changing Brian's diapers! Something about seeing Brian and the miracle of new life touched me deeply. Being an uncle was the best gift I had ever received.

SUMMER WAS JUST GETTING STARTED. I WAS SIXTEEN AND had no clue where I was going to live that winter. I knew that living at Mama's was temporary. It always was; something always caused her to blow up or get off track somehow. Sure enough, after about a month, I came home from work one early summer evening, walked into the bedroom, and noticed a letter from Mama lying on my bed.

I picked up the letter, dated June 28, 1989, and discovered that, as she so often did, Mama saw herself as a victim. She wrote:

Jimmy,

I know in my heart that you don't care anything for me, and you know that you and I can't get along. So just get your s*** and get out. I have been hearing the things you said about me and anyway, you can't stay here if you ain't going to help me out. And you told Bill you was not going to do anything else for me.

But that doesn't matter to me. I can make it without you. So just do what you said, and get the h*** out. And I'm not mad. . . . I want you to know that I do thank you for what little you have done.

Get out!

Mama had allowed a man and a woman to move in with her. None of them had jobs; I was the youngest person living in the trailer and the only one of the four of us who was working. But the three adults shared the same bed, and on more than a few nights, I could hear the three of them having sex.

Finally, I couldn't take it anymore and confronted my mom. "Mama, please make them leave."

"No, I'm not making them leave. They're my friends." The discussion grew more heated, and I probably said some things I shouldn't have, but the situation was ridiculous.

"Well, Mama, I'm not going to pay any more rent if you are going to let your friends live here for free."

The letter on the bed was Mama's response.

Oddly enough, I didn't even hurt when I read it. I was already numb from years of her neglect. Still, I was afraid. I had nowhere to go. I packed up my few belongings, including Mama's letter, and left Mama's trailer.

MAKING MATTERS WORSE, I GOT HURT AT THE MACHINE shop when a shaving of metal ricocheted off the milling machine and lodged in my eye. Walt took me to the hospital, and the doctors were able to remove the fragment, but afterward Walt was nervous that I might be a liability. "Jimmy, I don't really need you here at the shop anymore." He let me go.

Things were looking bleaker by the moment. I couldn't go back to Patricia's, Mama had thrown me out, and I had lost my job. I had no place to live, so I slept wherever I could at night, couch-surfing from one place to another, eating wherever I could find food, staying with anyone who would allow me to spend the night. During the day I canvassed the area, looking for work. I was a long-haired, dirty, scruffy, homeless kid, so employers were not exactly lining up to give me a job. I was desperate. I had to get some money—soon—and I needed something far more than an income. I needed a home.

In the spotlight at Madison Square Garden, gazing out at 18,000 screaming fans, all I could see were the exit lights, as pivotal events of my life flashed through my mind.

Carroll Collins, Mama, Patricia, and me. Carroll treated Mama like a queen.

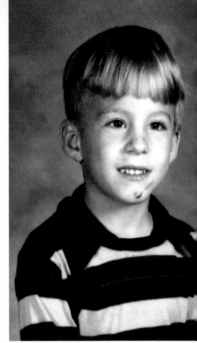

Picture day, and I fell chin-first on a huge rock in the front yard while waiting for the bus to arrive.

Our first and last Merry Christmas living with Carroll in Johnsonville, SC.

I was only seven years old when I experienced the horrors of Vance Street.

Patricia *(right)* and I were like sister and brother to our foster sister, Tina Miller *(left)*.

One of the many receipts for money orders I sent to Mama while she was behind bars.

10-A—THE GASTONIA GAZETTE, Monday, Aug. 26, 1985

Puppy fluff

These fluffy female 6-month-old puppies have nowhere to go. They're waiting at the Matthews Animal Shelter on the Dallas-Cherryville Highway for someone to pick them out of the crowd. If you are interested in a new pet, visit the shelter between 9 a.m. and 5 p.m. weekdays and 10 a.m. to 2 p.m. Saturday and ask for tag number 362 or her sister.

Living with Grandpa when Mama was gone, Patricia often played the role of parent.

After Sparkles died, J.R. took her pups to the pound and brought back this newspaper clipping for me.

—Jimmy

ESSEMER CITY CENTRAL SCHOOL

This report is to keep you informed of your child's work. This report, the interim, or progress report will go home every Wednesday. So expect something from school every Wednesday. If you do not get it, find out from your child why.

Please sign and return to your child's teacher.

Report Period 1, 2, 3, ④   Date 4-29/5-3

Student   _Jimmy Barber_

Teacher   _Friday_

☐ Has completed all work assigned
☑ Has not completed all work   _Make up work_

    ☑ Reading/Writing   ☐ Science
    ☐ Spelling   ☐ Health
    ☐ Math   ☐ Social Studies

Needs extra help in _all subject areas_

I included my sixth grade progress report in my first CD liner notes.

Ms. Friday *(top row, center)* was my sixth-grade teacher—twice. With the help of her leather strap, she taught me discipline. She also taught me to journal.

At my debut CD release party, I saw Ms. Friday for the first time since sixth grade. She stood in line for two hours to surprise me.

As soon as I saw Ms. Friday, I gave her a big hug. She is not merely a teacher; she is an educator. She still keeps in touch with me to this day.

Tim, Mama, me, and Grandpa. I was thirteen in this photo, just before Mama and Tim abandoned me at the Pensacola bus station parking lot in the middle of the night and drove away.

The Trailways bus station parking lot. After I bought this bus ticket, I had twenty-five cents left in my pocket.

I lived at Faith Farm fifteen weeks and a day. I really didn't want to leave. Mama came to my "victory party" and took me back but abandoned me again. This receipt is for the sleeping bag I purchased when I lived in an old house trailer that had no heat, electricity, or water.

I followed my art teacher's instructions to paint this piece "upside down." When I turned it "right side up," I discovered a beautiful painting of the Outer Banks, which gave me hope that one day my life might turn around and become a beautiful picture too.

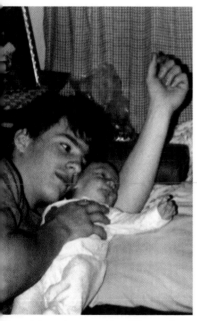

I was sixteen when my nephew Brian was born.

Brian came along as a support vehicle driver during my walk halfway across America.

My niece, Charleigh, and I enjoyed a day in Malibu.

By age three Charleigh had already been in three foster homes. Patricia and her husband, Tim Looper, adopted her and became her Bea and Russell.

This is foster care that has come full circle. Charleigh is all about the curls and pearls; she's a girly girl!

Bea and Russell Costner, the elderly couple who invited me to move in with them as a sixteen-year-old homeless boy. They changed every cell in my body.

Bea and Russell's house, where I lived for six years.

Bea attended all of my shows—this picture was taken at my first paid event.

A pianist and poet, Bea always encouraged me to pursue my dreams of becoming a musician, but she didn't live long enough to hear me on the radio or to see me perform on the Grand Ole Opry.

After Russell died, Bea would sit every day in these green chairs facing their woodshop—the chairs are in my home today.

My junior high guidance counselor, Cindy Ballard, refused to give up on me.

After moving in with Bea and Russell, I had perfect attendance for three straight years.

Thanks to Cindy, I graduated, class of '92.

In 1994, I earned an associate degree in criminal justice . . . because I knew a lot about it.

Working as an officer for the North Carolina Department of Corrections, I saw many of the kids I grew up with in the system, including DD, one of my best friends.

This was where my music career really started: Fantasyche. *(left to right)* Me, Rob Daniels, Chad Houser, Richard Calhoun, and Eric Pruitt.

The guy who brought me to Nashville and signed me to Opryland Music Group, Mike Whelan, also introduced me to the Blue Bird Café, Music City's legendary songwriters' venue.

People 2003 "Sexiest Man Alive" issue—obviously they needed a page filler!

Signing my first recording contract with Dreamworks— I felt as though I had just won the lottery!

Photo by Vickie Ferrante

Rob Daniels and me, on stage together again. Nineteen years earlier, on the Osage Mill shipping dock in Bessemer City, we had dreamed of this moment.

Photo by Lillie Pawluk

Crowd surfing and trusting fans not to drop me—they never let me down.

Photo by Vickie Ferrante

On the road with Brad Paisley's American Saturday Night tour, playing my black Takamine guitar, singing "Sara Smile," the song that got me my record deal.

Posing with my four band members—we did it! We had just performed at one of the most famous venues in the world!

January 1, 2010, in below-zero wind chill, I began walking halfway across America to raise awareness for at-risk youth aging out of foster care.

I found Ruby in White Deer, Texas. She had been in a kill shelter, so I adopted her and brought her to Nashville.

Six months after leaving Nashville, I finally arrived in Arizona. It would be another month before Ruby and I reached Phoenix.

Photo by Chris Baldwin

During Meet Me Halfway, Dr. Brian Allen read a *People* article with this photo. When I broke my foot, he opened his office on a weekend to help me. I couldn't have finished the walk without all the good people who supported me every step of the way.

Kids at HomeBase Youth Service in Phoenix, waiting for me to cross the finish line. They understood and appreciated my walking 1,700 miles. I was nearly overwhelmed with emotion. This was what I was born to do.

Being presented a bill signed by Tennessee Governor Bill Haslam, extending foster care to age twenty-one—a major victory and worth every step! *(left to right)* Grand Ole Opry General Manager Pete Fisher, State Representative Mark White, me, State Senator Doug Overbey, and State Treasurer David H. Lillard Jr.

Don't walk only when it is convenient; don't merely walk till you get tired; keep walking through it all. Walk to Beautiful.

Part Three

SAVED BY LOVE

Twenty-six

THE MOST BEAUTIFUL
WOMAN IN THE WORLD

EVERY DAY WAS A CHALLENGE, NOT TO SUCCEED BUT TO survive. Nobody wanted me around; I smelled badly because I hadn't taken a bath in days. I had few job skills, so no one would hire me for serious employment; people didn't even look me in the eye when they passed me on the street. I took any odd job I could get and was glad to do whatever work was necessary to earn enough money to buy some food. Fortunately, summer evenings in North Carolina are pleasant, and sleeping outside on the ground was something people actually did for fun. For me, it was a necessity.

One day I was riding down Highway 274 on my borrowed bike, looking for any work somebody might pay me to do, when I passed S&W Woodworks, a mom-and-pop woodshop. The shop had formerly served as a fueling station back in the 1940s. It was the place everyone in the surrounding area went to buy gas for their cars or some milk and bread for dinner. The owners had bought one of the first televisions in town and set it up in the shop, so the store became a popular gathering place.

As I was about to ride past, I noticed that the garage bay door was open. In years gone by, cars entered those doors and were hoisted up on the hydraulic lift over the work bay so the mechanic could change the oil. Now it seemed that the work bay had been covered over with flooring.

I looked in and saw an old man standing at a large band saw. He was cutting dashers to be inserted in decorative butter churns he was making.

A voice inside me said, *Go in and ask that old man if he has any work you can do.* I had experienced that voice speaking to me several times in my life, and I had learned to recognize the importance of paying attention to it.

I turned my bike around and headed back across the sawdust-covered parking lot toward the bay door with the paint peeled off. I pulled up close, leaned the bike against the white brick building, and walked inside.

The old man must have known I was there, but he didn't even look up from his work. He didn't acknowledge my presence in any way.

"Sir, do you have any work I can do?" I asked tentatively.

Still without looking up, the old man said, "Ask the boss," and nodded toward a white-haired woman in the back who was manhandling a powerful, loud, radial arm saw. When she saw me, she hit the off switch and walked over to where I was standing.

She wore a cotton dress coated in sawdust, an apron, and goggles. Her white hair had sawdust blown all through it, and her arms were covered with sawdust as well. I repeated my question, asking if she had any work I could do.

She slowly looked me up and down, and despite my ratty-looking long hair and faded tattoos, she said, "Come back this afternoon and cut our grass. He's Russell, honey, and I'm Beatrice Costner, but I'd just as soon you call me Bea."

"Okay! Thank you, ma'am, er, I mean, Bea. What time would you like me to be here?" She gave me a time, and I continued down the road, but not too far away.

I showed up on time and followed the old woman down to a storage shed beside her house. "The yard work is getting too much for Russell," she said as we walked. Understandably so. I rolled the heavy Snapper riding mower down the two parallel ramps made of boards, checked the oil, and filled the gas tank. The property was large; even with the riding mower, I could tell that it would take me several hours to mow the entire yard. I got busy.

About midway through the job, I saw Bea walk out the front door of her house, carrying a Coca-Cola and a doughnut. She waved me down, and I drove the mower up the field toward her house and parked under an old apple tree so heavy with apples and the lack of pruning that it looked like an umbrella. A rusty fence ran right through the apple tree, where the tree had grown around each rusty wire over the years.

Bea handed me the Coca-Cola and doughnut over the fence, and we talked briefly. Actually, she talked, and I listened. She had much to share. And she had such a positive attitude about everything. She even complimented me about the way I was mowing the yard. I wasn't used to such encouragement, but I appreciated her kind words.

I finished cutting the grass and did the trim work, which entailed quite a bit of effort since the Costners had a stand-alone swing, several lawn chairs, a birdbath, and nearly every piece of outdoor ceramics known to man. When I finished trimming, I put away the tools and rolled the mower backward, up the boards and into the shed, steering it by the white handlebars. I could see how this might have been a difficult chore for Russell. It wasn't easy for me.

Once everything was put away, Bea handed me a twenty-dollar bill. My eyes opened wide. I couldn't believe that she gave me that much money to cut her grass, especially since I had used her mower and her fuel. I could eat all week long on twenty dollars!

The old woman looked at me intently. "Can you come back next week and cut the grass again?"

"Yes, ma'am," I said. "Absolutely!"

I cut the Costners' grass every week for the remainder of the summer. Toward the end of August, the grass wasn't growing as fast, and the
yard work was slowing down. Thinking ahead, I worried about where
I was going to work through the winter and how I was going to buy
food. That week, when I mowed the Costners' yard, Bea met me during
my break, outside under the apple tree, as she had done every week. As
always, she handed me a Coca-Cola and a doughnut, and I thanked her
sincerely.

I expected Bea to tell me what a lovely day it was or to make other
small talk, but she didn't. Instead, she asked, "Jimmy, where do you live?"

Her question took me by surprise. *Oh, no!* I thought. I didn't want
to tell her that I was homeless, sleeping wherever I could find a bed or
outside on the ground when I couldn't find a friend willing to take me
in. I didn't want to let her know that the twenty dollars she paid me each
week was the major portion of my income, with which I purchased necessary items from one week to another. I felt sure that if she knew I was
homeless, she and Russell wouldn't want me to come around anymore.
But looking at her beautiful, beaming face and her bright, honest eyes, I
knew I couldn't lie to her. So I gave her the most general answer I could
think of in the moment.

"Oh, up the road," I replied.

Bea nodded slightly. "Well, Russell and I have been talking, and we
want to know if you'd be interested in moving into our home. We have
a spare bedroom you could use."

My first thoughts were not positive. *Yeah, sure*, I thought. *I'll move
in, and they'll make me leave within a week or a short time after. That's
what everybody else has done.*

My second thought was, *Yes, but at least it's a place to sleep tonight,
and maybe they'll let me wash my clothes and take a shower and eat.*

"Okay," I said. It was as simple as that. The transaction—the invitation and the acceptance of the invitation—that would change my life
forever didn't involve a lease, a contract, or even a handshake. It was a

done deal with just Bea's word. I was moving in with the Costners. I was sixteen; Russell was seventy-nine, and Bea was seventy-five. We had absolutely nothing in common—or so I thought.

LATER THAT EVENING, I STOOD AT THE DOOR AND RANG the doorbell to Bea and Russell's house. Bea answered with a big smile. She opened the glass storm door and invited me inside.

Carrying a plastic bag filled with my dirty clothes, I followed her to a bedroom. The area had formerly been a two-car garage, but it had been completely renovated, converting it into a large bedroom. They had planned to use the room for Bea's aunt, but the elderly woman had passed away before she ever really got a chance to enjoy it.

I could not believe my eyes. The room had new carpet, a brand-new bed, a new nightstand with a clock, and a piano against the wall.

"This will be your room," Bea said.

I looked at the room and furniture in awe. *There's no way this old lady and man are going to let me stay here for long*, I thought. I set my bag of clothes in the corner but didn't unpack it. Through my experience in the foster care system, I had learned that not unpacking was a common trait among foster kids. They knew there was a high probability that they would be asked to leave, so why bother to unpack? Even many who stayed did not unpack for several months.

Four days passed, and I was still there, but I knew that any minute now, the Costners were going to tell me to leave. I just knew it. Bea was wonderful to me those first few days, but Russell barely spoke a word to me. That fourth day, Russell passed me in the hallway, put his hand on my shoulder, and stopped me.

I cringed. I wasn't accustomed to having a man touch me. I'd been beaten and abused by Tim Allen, and I'd never known the gentle touch of a father. To me, when a man put his hand on me, that was a threat. I didn't trust any man. What was Russell going to do?

"I need to talk to you," Russell said.

I knew it! I thought. *They've found out about my background. Now he's going to tell me that I have to leave.*

The same gut-wrenching feeling I had felt so many times before filled me again, leaving no room inside, not even to breathe; it felt like emotional asphyxiation.

Russell was a hard-nosed veteran of World War II. He had been wounded in battle and had earned a Purple Heart; he was about as tough and stern a man as I had ever met. The best way to describe Russell is to imagine combining Andy Griffith with Clint Eastwood's character in the movie *Gran Torino*, absent the profanity.

Russell wasn't the type to say a lot, but when he did speak, it was impossible to misunderstand him. For example, he once told me, "Jimmy, if you blow grass in my tulips again, I'm going to fire your ass."

So when Russell said he wanted to talk with me, I knew this conversation wasn't going to last very long.

"Sit down in that chair," he ordered, pointing toward his recliner. I complied and sat in Russell's chair while he sat in a chair across the room, next to the front door.

Russell held up three fingers and said to me in very a firm tone, "There's two things you've *got* to do if you're going to live in my house."

I wanted to correct him and tell him that he was holding up three fingers instead of two, but something told me that this was one of those times when I needed to keep my mouth shut and listen.

"The first thing you've *got* to do is . . ." Russell paused briefly to make sure he had my attention. Believe me, he had it. "Cut off all your hair. It has to be cut just like mine." He lowered one finger, and I quickly stole a glance at Russell's military haircut, straight out of 1945. *Oh, boy!*

"Second, we want you to go to church." Russell lowered the second finger. "And if you don't do those two things, you've got to leave now," Russell said, with great emphasis on the word *now* as he lowered the third finger.

"Yes, I'll do that," I heard myself saying out loud. *What? Did I say that?* Yes, I did!

I figured that Russell would let the haircut slide for a while, but Russell was a very smart man and always thinking strategically. He nodded and said, "Then get in my truck, now."

I dutifully went out to his green Dodge farm truck, and the two of us drove to Dixie Village Shopping Center, where we walked into the barbershop—not the hair-styling salon. We went to a *barbershop*.

"Hello, Mr. Cole," Russell greeted the barber.

"Hello, Mr. Costner," the barber said. "What can I do for you?" The barber looked at Russell's hair. He clearly did not need another wisp of hair cut off.

"This boy needs a haircut," Russell replied, nodding in my direction. There was no debate about how I'd like my hair styled. It was definitely a one-style-fits-all sort of shop.

"Get up here, boy!" the barber said in a tone of voice that made no attempt to conceal how eager he was to plunge those clippers into my long hair.

I sat down in the large barber's chair facing an enormous mirror, and the barber wrapped a cape around my neck.

"How's business, Mr. Costner?" he asked.

"Fine, sir," said Russell.

The next sound I heard was the buzzing of clippers zipping around my head. Long hair piled up on the floor all around that chair; undoubtedly, it was more hair than Mr. Cole had cut the entire week. Within twenty seconds I was nearly bald. I looked in the same mirror, where my image had been a few seconds earlier, and I now saw some kid with a military haircut. My head without hair resembled a cheap baby doll. I looked like Mr. Peanut.

Russell paid the barber five dollars and thanked Mr. Cole for his fine work. As we walked outside, I headed toward the farm truck, but Russell veered to the right.

"Where ya going?" Russell asked in his usual drill sergeant tone. I stopped short, and Russell nodded toward a department store. "We're going in here to get some school clothes," he said.

At the front of the truck, I turned around and followed Russell into the store.

"Pick out some pants," Russell said.

I stood motionless for several moments. "I don't know how. I've never done this before," I replied.

"What size do you wear?" he asked.

"I'm not sure," I said. I wasn't joking. In sixteen years of life I had never shopped for new clothes. I simply wore whatever I had or whatever somebody gave to me. I didn't even know where to start.

Russell asked the clerk, a young woman, to assist me in finding the right size school clothes, and she was kind and patient, almost stylish in her selections for me. Russell paid for the clothes, and we headed home with my new look.

One day I called my former guidance counselor, Cindy Ballard. I hadn't seen her or talked with her in months, not since Mama had kicked me out. I excitedly told her, "Ms. Ballard, I have good news. I have a new place to live."

She had good news for me as well. "Jimmy, you passed your summer courses and got good scores on your tests. We need to get you back in school."

I enrolled as a sophomore in Bessemer City High School on the first day of the new school year. From the day I set foot in Bea and Russell's home, I never missed another day of school. I even went to school on Senior Skip Day.

On September 21, 1989, Hurricane Hugo hit the East Coast, making landfall at Charleston, South Carolina, with sustained winds of more than 135 miles per hour. The gigantic storm moved north at nearly 30 miles per hour, creating havoc all the way up through Charlotte and into West Virginia and Pennsylvania. Damages were estimated at seven billion dollars! The category 4 hurricane roared directly over Bea and Russell's house. We all gathered in the basement for hours, waiting and praying for the hurricane to pass. *Thank God for this couple,* I kept thinking. *Just a few weeks ago, I was living outside.*

That next Sunday I didn't need Russell to encourage me to go to church. Church attendance was a regular thing for the Costners. Bea was a musician; she played piano for services at Regan Mill Baptist Church, even though she and Russell had literally built the church on Holland Memorial Church Road. But she felt needed at Regan Mill, so that's where we attended.

WITHIN TWO MONTHS OF MY MOVING IN WITH THE Costners, Russell was diagnosed with terminal cancer. Neither he nor Bea seemed shaken by the news. They had absolute faith that the moment Russell took his last breath here on earth, he would be with Jesus in heaven, so there was no weepy sentimentality surrounding his illness. He was a soldier awaiting his next assignment.

Even on good days, Russell never said much to me; he'd just stare at me. Sometimes he stared at me so much that it made me nervous. What was he looking at? What did he expect to see? What was he searching for? His eyes seared into me and pierced me right to the heart. I could feel him scanning every centimeter of my soul.

He wasn't trying to intimidate me. I think he was staring at me because he wanted to be absolutely sure that Bea was going to be okay after he was gone.

One time Russell stared at me so long, I sketched a picture of him. When I showed it to him several hours later, he asked if he could take it to church. I said, "Sure, I drew it for you. You can do whatever you want with it." Russell showed that drawing to all his friends and bragged on me in front of them. That was the first time in my life that a man acted as though he was proud of me.

I was accustomed to men who were abusive, so my guard was up constantly. Combine that fear with the arrogance and insecurities of a normal teenager, and it makes for a volatile mix. Russell probably sensed that about me at first and wasn't about to let some punk street kid get by with anything in his home.

Although I was only sixteen, I had lived a lot of life in those years. I wasn't about to let another man put me in my place, so there was bound to be some tension. That drawing changed everything between Russell and me. I didn't know how to respond to his praise other than try to make him proud of me again. Unfortunately, I didn't have many more opportunities.

THE CANCER SPREAD QUICKLY, GOBBLING UP THE LAST healthy cells in Russell's body. His health declined rapidly, and on November 6, 1989, Russell Costner, the strong American soldier and an even stronger soldier in the army of the Lord, was promoted to glory.

I like to imagine that when Russell met Jesus, He said, "Russell, there are two things you've got to do if you're going to stay here in my home. First, you've got to go to church. The second thing is, you've got to grow your hair out long, just like Mine."

Bea was sad but not inconsolable. She knew Russell was ready to go, and she knew she would see him again. She missed him terribly, but she understood that she still had some work to do. I didn't know it at the time, but part of her remaining work involved me.

Twenty-seven

MY FIRST BAND

I DIDN'T THINK I WOULD BE ABLE TO CONTINUE LIVING AT Bea's after Russell's death. If for no other reason than appearances, I felt sure Bea might prefer that I move on. Imagine my surprise when within hours after Russell's funeral service, Bea met me in the front yard by the apple tree. All her family members were inside, congregating in the living room and kitchen the way people do after a funeral.

Bea said, "Jimmy, I believe you were sent here, and I want you to stay if you want to."

I was surprised but relieved. "Yes, ma'am, I do. I will. I would like to stay, Bea."

Several months went by, and Bea asked me to move into the bedroom that was next to hers. I assumed having me closer made her feel safer, but looking back, I think she may have had another reason. Every night I could hear Bea through the wall, talking aloud to Jesus. I could hear her bones cracking and the bed springs squeaking as she leaned on the bed to get down on her knees to pray and then slowly pulled herself back up, sometimes as long as an hour later. She prayed for her relatives and a lot of people whose names I didn't recognize, and every night I heard her praying for me.

Bea still went to the woodshop every day. She kept the business going by herself for the next two years. For her, it wasn't about making money, but Bea spent the majority of her time inside the woodshop making butter churns and weaving baskets.

Her daughter, Sandie, and her husband, James Conrad, lived next door with their son, Josh, who became my best friend all through high school. Josh and I did everything together, and Sandie and James always included me in family activities, even taking me along with them on vacation to the mountains, during my sophomore and junior years in school.

Meanwhile, Bea continued working, and the family's concerns grew. We were all afraid that Bea was going to accidentally injure herself. Her concentration seemed lacking since Russell had passed, and we felt it was only a matter of time before she pulled that whirring radial arm saw across her hand.

But any time someone suggested to Bea that it might be time to close doors on the woodshop, she'd bristle. "No!" she'd insist.

The woodshop was where she and Russell had spent their life together and where she still felt close to him. Closing the door on the shop would be like saying a final good-bye—and after more than sixty years with him, she still wasn't ready to say those words.

One morning I walked into the living room, and there she stood, facing Russell's and her fiftieth wedding anniversary picture. She was stroking it softly with her hand and telling Russell how much she missed him and loved him. Not wanting to intrude, I slipped away quietly, and she never even knew I was there.

Bea continued working Mondays through Fridays. Every morning she walked out her front door, across Sandie's yard, and into the woodshop. By noon, a glow of sawdust was hovering in the air outside the bay door.

Bea was also a pretty good musician, and she especially enjoyed gospel music. Some mornings Bea turned on the record player, loaded up a bunch of 33 1/3 rpm gospel albums, and sang every word along with the artists on those vinyl records. One after another, the albums played for hours. And Bea sang. Did she ever sing! She'd reach for those high notes and hold them like an opera singer. Her beautiful vibrato filled the house. Sometimes I couldn't help but sing along with her.

The smell of air freshener let me know that it was Saturday. I'd hear the long spray from the can of air freshener and Bea's pet black mynah bird say, "Hello, hello." Bea answered, "Hello," and the bird repeated her words. Bea carried on a conversation with that bird while she laid clean newspapers in the bottom of its cage. Then came more air freshener. When the house smelled like potpourri and everything was exactly the way Bea liked it, then came rehearsal.

Bea would sit down at the piano and practice each hymn she planned to play at church the following morning. It was her Saturday morning routine, and she did it every week.

Bea's love of music and poetry was infectious. She encouraged me to pursue writing poems, and when an opportunity came for me to join a band—even though it was a rock band—Bea was supportive.

To help Bea, and to have a bit of spending money of my own while in high school, I got a part-time job at the Osage textile mill in Bessemer City. One day while taking a break, I overheard two fellow high school students, Rob Daniels and Chad McAllister, talking about music. "I'm looking for a singer to join my rock band," Rob said. "If you hear of anyone, let me know."

"I sing!" I blurted out.

"Really?" Rob asked, running his hand through his long, curly, blond hair. "Well, come over around five o'clock this afternoon, and I'll give you a few songs to learn."

I showed up at his house on time and met with the other band members: Richard Calhoun, who played drums, and Eric Pruitt, the bass player. Rob played lead guitar and was the leader of the band. Although the band did not yet have a name, he was very serious about it.

Rob gave me a cassette tape, and I headed back to Bea's to begin learning the songs. Because I was totally inexperienced, I didn't realize that the two songs on the tape—"Piece of Mind," by the band Boston, and "Modern Day Cowboy," by the group Tesla—were incredibly difficult songs to sing, even for seasoned professionals. I worked on them, nonetheless, and several days later I went back to Rob's house to audition.

I was nervous because this was the first time I'd ever sung into a microphone. I was clueless about everything related to music performance. I just knew I had a love for it and dreamed of standing on stage one day, singing to an arena filled with fans.

Unfortunately, the audition did not go well. The songs were pitched in the same keys that the artists had recorded them. I could barely hit the high notes, so I was turned down for the gig.

The next day at work I explained to Rob, "Hardly anyone can sing those songs in their original keys. Why don't you give me one more shot singing something that you've written?"

"Okay," Rob said, "come by the house again and get a copy of two songs I wrote." I showed up at Rob's house, just like before. The band members didn't say much and gave the impression that Rob was wasting their time by giving me two of his songs to learn.

I took the songs back to Bea's house and spent every waking moment working on them until I felt as though I could sing them with my eyes closed.

Rob saw me at the Osage mill and said, "Rehearsal is Thursday night." "I'll be there," I assured him.

When I showed up for practice again, none of the band members said much. Their attitude was, "We'll tolerate this guy's audition, but we know he isn't ever going to be a singer."

Rob plugged in his white Flying V guitar and began warming up along with Richard and Eric. After a few minutes Rob looked at me and asked, "Are you ready?"

It was time to show them what I'd come up with. I sang my heart out, and although the rehearsal didn't go as well as I had hoped, I got the gig! I was now the lead singer in a rock-and-roll band.

I couldn't wait to share this news with Lynn, my first serious girlfriend. I had met Lynn at school in cabinet-making class, and later we went to work at the same textile factory. Lynn and I had established a fun relationship, but for some reason, Bea wasn't impressed with her. She told me one day, "Jimmy, don't ever let a girl stand in your way."

"What do you mean, Bea?"

"Just make sure she's right; make sure the relationship is right." Bea's comment almost offended me because I sincerely cared for Lynn. I was in love—as much as I knew of it—and I had even thought that someday we might get married. Before long I was spending half of my time with the band and the other half with Lynn, school, and work. The band rehearsed three to four times each week for several hours at every session, so there wasn't a lot of extra time for a dating relationship.

Bea's intuition and misgivings about Lynn proved accurate. One day I walked into the textile factory and saw her kissing another guy in the nook, where she and I often took our breaks. That ended my relationship with Lynn, but it didn't end the hurt in my heart.

I realized that Bea was right; she wasn't trying to deprive me of a good relationship. But she had a spiritual perception and discernment, and I learned to trust her opinions.

WITH LYNN OUT OF MY LIFE, I POURED MYSELF INTO THE band. One day Rob and I were together when he said, "I came up with a name for the band," as he was pumping gas into his white pickup truck.

"Really? What?"

"Fantasyche!" he said, as though it were the greatest name for a band since the Beatles.

"Fanta what?" I asked.

"Fantasyche, like Queensryche, and the fantasy of the mind," Rob explained.

"Oh, yeah, I get it," I replied, but I really didn't. I mulled over the words *fantasy of the mind* as I sat in the passenger seat. *I'm still not sure what it means, but it is a cool name for the band*, I thought.

My role with the band was that of lead vocalist, carrying all the loud, screaming lead lines. I didn't play any instruments, but I sang hard, nearly blowing my vocal cords out on the heavy metal sound we emulated. Most of our lyrics—if anyone could hear them—were about escapism.

I performed onstage in front of a live audience for the first time at Bessemer City Junior High School, playing for a job fair in the school. The enthusiastic response of the junior high girls, screaming and waving their hands high in the air as we played, was addictive, and I was instantly hooked.

We soon entered our first "battle of the bands," hosted by Yesterday's nightclub in Hickory, another small town nearby. Yesterday's was a popular rock-and-roll hot spot, so when the woman in charge of the band credentials handed me a laminate, enclosing my name tag, I was so excited I almost didn't notice the name Fantasyche right above my name. This was big time in a small town. I was so proud of that name tag; I even wore it to school the following week.

Fantasyche didn't win the battle of the bands that night, but we did place second, and that just made us hungrier. The band practiced more. We were featured on *Local Licks*, a radio show where local artists might have an opportunity to have one of their songs played on the station. That was the first time I heard myself on the radio.

The second battle of the bands was held at Casper's nightclub in Gastonia. The band played hard rock and roll, and I sang even harder. The competition was stiff, and I will never forget hearing the emcee's words, "And the first place winner is . . . Fantasyche!"

As part of our prize package, the band got to record a two-song demo in a professional recording studio in Charlotte. This was my first experience inside a recording studio. I was amazed and impressed by all the records hanging on the wall, and I was somewhat intimidated by the engineer. He'd been in the music business a long time and obviously knew far more than anyone in the room. Or at least he acted as if he did. I was clueless about the recording process, but I was excited to learn.

ROB WAS IN CHARGE OF EVERYTHING. A FEW WEEKS AFTER
we did our demo, he called a band meeting at his house in the basement, where we practiced. When we showed up, Rob handed each of us
a box of cassettes. On the cassette packaging in bold letters was the name
Fantasyche written on the front and back, along with the song titles
"Shoulda Known" and "Keep on Dreaming," two songs written by Rob.
We were as excited as little kids on Christmas morning.

Rob explained to the band that we needed to sell the cassettes for
five dollars each so we could pay back the loan his mom and dad had
given us to pay for manufacturing the product. We sold the cassettes at
school and at shows.

With our first two-song demo cassette, we dreamed of being rock
stars. I thought that wearing purple spandex shorts, a jean trench coat,
and sneakers was cool. When I walked onstage dressed like that at
Peppers, a popular local club, I quickly realized that the audience was
comprised completely of truckers, bikers, and rednecks—and they were
all men. There wasn't a woman in the room! There I stood, without a
shirt on, and nearly got booed off the stage. I was glad to get out of that
place with my life!

Fantasyche had a good run; we stayed together as a band for more than
a year and a half, not bad for high school kids. But by the time I reached
my senior year, things were changing in the band. Parents got involved,
reality set in, and the band members began changing their minds about
any long-term commitments. But unlike the other band members, I didn't
have anything or anyone to fall back on if this band didn't work. It was the
only thing I really had going on.

Performing music was my dream. Yet when I looked at the band
realistically, I realized that heavy metal "hair" bands were on the decline.
I knew in my heart that our band wasn't going to make it. Any other
conclusion was only wishful thinking. I folded up my microphone stand,
packed up my Shure SM57 microphone, wrapped up my cord, and said
good-bye to Fantasyche.

SHORTLY AFTER THAT ROB MOVED TO VIRGINIA TO continue pursuing music. I didn't know if music was even an option for me anymore. I loved music, but I knew there was no job security in the music business. I decided it would be smart to finish high school and go to college. I tried to put the dream on the back burner, but when you've been bitten by the music bug, that desire doesn't go away so easily.

Still, I might have found some form of inoculation if a criminal named Jody Lee Hager hadn't shown up at my high school.

Twenty-eight

IT'S NOT WHERE YOU'VE BEEN; IT'S WHERE YOU'RE GOIN'

From the back of the auditorium in Bessemer City High School, I listened in awe to Jody Lee Hager as he stood onstage, shared his story, and performed a few original songs on a cheap, brown, dreadnought guitar—a guitar stamped with prison unit number 4515.

Jody was an incredible motivator. His performance moved an entire auditorium filled with high school students, teachers, and administrators. Adding to the uniqueness of Jody's performance was the fact that he was a current inmate at the Dallas Correctional Facility and was participating in Think Smart, a program that allowed prisoners to leave the facility under strict supervision to share their stories with schools, churches, and civic groups. The goal was to inspire others to "think smart" and avoid criminal activity.

Despite Jody telling the students, "Guys, think smart; don't do drugs, don't get in trouble, and don't be like me," as I listened to him, I thought, *I want to be* just *like him!* Not Jody the criminal, but Jody the musician and storyteller.

Oddly enough, one of the most poignant songs Jody performed

was a Christmas song, "For Days Like This," a song he had written describing the loneliness he felt in prison at Christmastime. I couldn't believe that he sang a Christmas song in the middle of spring, but Jody communicated the message so powerfully, it reached right into our hearts.

I had performed with Fantasyche and had even sung at a few weddings, but Jody's performance inspired me. From that moment forward I knew exactly what I wanted to do—I wanted to write songs by putting my poems to music, perform them on an acoustic guitar, and share my story. Maybe I could inspire someone the way Jody influenced me. It was just a kernel of an idea, but it was beginning to take root.

THE FOLLOWING WEEKEND, WHILE ON MY WAY TO WORK AT the textile mill, I spotted a small brown guitar leaning against a table at a yard sale in a gas station parking lot. The traffic light turned green as I slowly drove past the guitar. I alternated between watching the road ahead and glancing back to check out the guitar, all the while slowly changing gears on my pickup truck. I hadn't shifted past second gear before I turned the truck around and drove back to the yard sale. I got out of the truck, walked directly to the guitar, and picked it up.

It was a Harmony six-string guitar, an inexpensive instrument similar to the one I had while living with Patricia and Steven. I looked at the neck and the tuning keys, then flipped the guitar over and looked at the back. I examined it from every angle, as though I actually knew something about guitars, which of course, I didn't. "How much is it?" I asked the woman conducting the sale.

"Forty dollars," she replied, as though she were offering a special deal.

I pondered for a few minutes—forty dollars was a lot of money to me—before handing her two twenty-dollar bills.

I opened the driver's side door and gently laid the guitar on the bench seat as though I were placing a sleeping baby in a crib. I slid in beside the guitar and drove on toward the Osage mill, looking over at the guitar's reddish finish and black pick guard several times as I drove. When I arrived at the mill, I got out of the truck, looked back at the guitar one more time, and then closed and locked the truck door.

I walked through the gate and raced up the stairwell to the spinning room, where my best friend, Josh Conrad, and our boss, Posey Williams, were waiting on me.

"Where ya been?" Posey asked, looking at his watch.

I immediately shared with them the great news about the guitar and my dreams to become a country music singer.

Josh and Posey stood in the doorway of the spinning room and looked at me with a blank stare. Neither of them said much, but I could guess what they were thinking by the way they grinned.

"Okay, you'll see," I said with a grin to rival theirs.

For the next six hours, all I could think about was that guitar lying in the front seat of my truck. I didn't even know enough about guitars to realize that leaving a stringed instrument in a hot vehicle all day is not a good idea. I could already hear myself singing "Chasin' That Neon Rainbow," a song written and recorded by Alan Jackson.

As soon as I finished my shift, I ran back to my truck. There on the front seat of the pickup lay the guitar I had been daydreaming about for the past six hours. I couldn't wait to play it; except for the few songs I had learned at Patricia's, I didn't know where to start.

I drove to the Music Center in Gastonia and purchased a Mel Bay guitar chord lesson book, a well-known, simplistic instruction manual, then headed home. For several weeks I studied the chord book. I was making fairly good progress when I thought of an idea.

I APPROACHED MRS. LOVE, THE ATTRACTIVE, YOUNG GUID-ance counselor at Bessemer City High School, and told her how much Jody Lee Hager had inspired me during his Think Smart school assembly. I asked if she could arrange for me to meet Jody. My hope was that he could teach me a few things on the guitar and share a few tips about songwriting. Mrs. Love's father, Mr. Charles Mears, was the superintendent at the Dallas prison, where Jody was incarcerated.

Mrs. Love promised to ask her father about my request. A few weeks later correctional officers greeted Mrs. Love and me at Gate 1, patted us down, and then led us across the prison yard to a concrete picnic table between the lieutenant's office and the music room.

Minutes later Jody Hager walked across the graveled midyard, approaching the picnic table. He was wearing green pants, a white T-shirt, and black boots—mandatory prison garb for all inmates at Jody's honor grade level.

Jody sat down beside Mrs. Love and began making small talk at the table. She explained to him that I had come to ask him some questions about playing guitar. At the end of the visit, I told Jody that I hoped I could come to see him again. He agreed.

A second visit went much the same as the first. After that, I continued to visit Jody alone, without Mrs. Love. During the third visit, Jody actually spent time playing the guitar and discussing music with me. He taught me the guitar part to "Anymore," a popular song by country artist Travis Tritt. We spent a few more minutes practicing the song, and just before I left, he wrote down the lyrics on a piece of paper and handed them to me to learn.

I visited Jody one more time at the prison. During the visit, superintendent Charlie Mears approached me on the midyard. At first I thought he was going to tell me that I could not visit Jody anymore, but he didn't. Instead, Mr. Mears said, "I've been watching you out here on the prison yard, son. Call me when you graduate from college, and I'll give you a job."

That was the best news I'd heard since the Costners allowed me to move into their home. After working for more than two years in a textile mill, I was ready for another sort of employment. Of course, Mr. Mears may not have known I was still a high school student. It would be at least two more years before I could leave the textile mill.

I WAS SO EXCITED TO BE LEARNING GUITAR. I WANTED TO expand my repertoire of music and at the same time learn to sing better. As the lead singer with Fantasyche, I had basically been screaming on pitch—or close to it. But I was impressed with Jody's smooth vocals melding perfectly with his tasteful guitar licks. I said, "I want to learn how to sing like that!"

I couldn't find a voice teacher at school, so I sought out the best vocal coach I could find. Becky Hyde Smith was a part-time vocal teacher who had heard me on the Fantasyche demo cassette, and she was willing to help me. The first day I met with her, Becky asked me to sing along with her. She began playing the piano, and I started yelling in tune. She stopped playing and said, "Jimmy, please stop screaming at me!"

We started from scratch. We began by doing vocal warm-ups. Becky played scales over and over, and she made me match my voice to the notes up and down an octave. "La-la-la-la-la-la-la- laaaaa." She taught me about volume control and speech-level singing, and she introduced me to great vocalists, teaching me to emulate their diction and vocal control. Becky displayed tremendous patience with me, but she was also firm in her demands for perfection when it came to practicing my vocals. I am indebted to Becky to this day for teaching me to sing, not only with passion but proper diction and intonation.

I GRADUATED FROM BESSEMER CITY HIGH SCHOOL IN JUNE 1992. The school gave me a special award for three straight years of perfect attendance. Of course, Bea attended the ceremony, and I could tell that she was proud of me.

Mama was there too. She had bought me a new pair of shoes to wear to my high school graduation, and she purchased my class ring for me. I didn't expect her to do anything like that, and I appreciated her kindness.

Receiving my high school diploma was especially meaningful to me. It was more than a piece of parchment with some writing on it. The diploma symbolized all the achievements and positive changes that had taken place in my life since moving in with Bea and Russell three years earlier. The boy living in Uncle Austin's trailer couldn't have done that, nor could the kid who had been living from bed to bed, meal to meal. But thanks to Bea, I now believed I could do anything, simply because I had a place to live and some loving encouragement. And now I was even planning to go to college.

I enrolled at Gaston College, in Dallas, North Carolina, that fall. I decided to major in criminal justice—since I knew a lot about the subject.

Classes started in September, and I thoroughly enjoyed them. I had grown up around crime, so I related to many of the lessons taught. I continued practicing my guitar and working on my vocals. In December 1992, with Bea in mind, I wrote my first song, "My Only Friend," after a close friend's mom passed away. I wasn't good at expressing grief, so I gave him the song to help us both deal with his mom's passing.

One of my most memorable experiences during my education at Gaston College was a field trip. My criminal justice instructor, Don Lawrence, told the class to wear a collared shirt on Monday morning. We were going to visit the Dallas Detention Center. "This will give you a taste of the real thing," Professor Lawrence said, "taking criminal justice out of the textbook and letting you see it in real life."

I didn't need to visit the detention center to see what real life inside was like since that was the facility in which I was locked up on my fifteenth birthday. I didn't tell my professor or any of my fellow students that I knew more than I wanted to know about the detention center.

When we arrived, we were ushered to a side room to await the officer who would guide us through the facility. I felt uneasy as I stood in the back of that room, behind all the other students, with memories pummeling my mind. A heavyset officer walked through the double doors, and I recognized him immediately. I swallowed hard. It was the same officer who had checked me in the night of my fifteenth birthday.

He looked right at me, but he didn't recognize me. The last time he had seen me I had been wearing scruffy clothes, had filthy long hair, and was scared stiff—looking like a deer caught in the headlights. Now I looked much different, with clean clothes, a stylish haircut, and a confident look in my eyes. I stood quietly, my back against the wall, as the officer began his introduction.

"Good morning, and welcome to the Dallas Detention Center. In here we have all kinds of *trash.*" The officer practically spat the words from his mouth.

All kinds of trash? I couldn't believe what I had heard!

I wanted to say something to this man, but I was reluctant to speak up. I had not shared my story with anyone, not even the people closest to me. And no one knew my story, not Bea, not my girlfriend, not my best friend, Josh—no one. I thought people would judge me if they knew where I'd been or the lifestyle I had led.

But something was welling within me. I stood there fuming as the officer continued explaining to all the college students what the detention center was and how it operated. I had zoned out of his speech by this point, and all I could think about was this man calling the youth behind these walls *trash*. Finally I couldn't take it any longer; I knew I had to say something to the officer.

I was so nervous, my body was shaking. My mouth was dry, and I could hardly form a word, so I simply yelled out, "Sir!" Several of my fellow students whirled around in surprise at my outburst, but the officer was still spewing out his spiel.

I raised my hand and shouted loudly again, "Sir!" More students turned to look at me, and the officer heard me this time.

"You may not remember me," I said, "but the last door on the right was mine. And you were the officer who checked me in that night, on my fifteenth birthday."

I noticed the students' expressions suddenly change, as more of them turned and stared at me in disbelief. I could imagine them thinking, *How can a guy who looks like you say that you ever spent time in a place like this?* They knew me as Jimmy Barber, the quiet, studious guy with an Eastpak bag and a nice haircut. They didn't know the hurt little boy who lived deep inside me. They could not even imagine the heartache I had experienced. But I didn't have time to address all that.

I continued talking to the officer, speaking loudly enough for everyone in the room to hear. "I'll never forget what you said to me and the way you treated me that night, and I just want you know . . ." I could feel my voice cracking with emotion, so I took a quick breath and forced myself to keep going. "I just want you to know that some of these kids in here have been abandoned by their own families. We all make mistakes, but there's one thing we're not. We're *not trash!*"

The officer glared at me. For a long, awkward moment, nobody made a sound as the entire class stared at me. Then someone clapped, and in another second the whole class began applauding, including Mr. Lawrence, while the officer just stood there glowering at me.

The officer hastily concluded the tour. Afterward a number of my classmates approached me and wanted more details. "Were you really in this detention center, Jimmy?" I answered their questions as honestly as I could.

This was the first time I had ever shared any part of my past with anyone, but I knew I had to speak up because that officer said the same hurtful words to me the night he checked me in, making me show him all my scars and tattoos, making me strip naked. That was his normal routine.

I knew that if I didn't confront him, he would continue saying those hurtful words about other kids, and people who didn't know any better would believe him.

More than that, I knew that if I didn't raise my voice in those kids' defense, I couldn't live with myself.

When we returned to Gaston College, Mr. Lawrence called me into the hallway and asked more questions. He gave me an open invitation to share any relevant parts of my story during his class, at any time, depending on the topic he was teaching.

That was the day I decided that I would do whatever I could to help the youth living in various forms of government care, especially kids like me, who were bounced around through the foster care system.

Although I didn't know how I could make it happen, I made a promise to myself that I was going to move to Nashville, get a record deal, and write songs that speak up for the kids whom some people regard as trash. And I wanted to tell those kids, and anyone else who would listen, it's not where you've been, but it's where you're goin'; it's not who you were in the past, but it's who you are today—that's what really matters.

Twenty-nine

WORKING INSIDE

BESIDES BEING THE GUIDANCE COUNSELOR WHO SAVED MY education, Cindy Ballard was one of the earliest and most enthusiastic encouragers of my music. She was not bashful about recommending me for every sort of performance, whether for a wedding, karaoke fest, or backyard concert. I appreciated her confidence in me, especially since my guitar playing was still horrendously rough and I had written only a few songs of my own. Nevertheless, Cindy saw potential in me, or perhaps she realized that even if I could never turn my music into a career, it kept me motivated and out of trouble.

It was Ms. Ballard who recommended me to perform at an outdoor event in Gastonia, known as The Volunteer Roundup, where I sang some songs with karaoke machine backup music and some of my first original songs. Bea went along with me and sat in the front row.

The event took place August 25, 1993, with temperatures soaring to nearly one hundred degrees; everyone was dressed casually, so I performed in shorts and a tank top. There were a lot of distractions outdoors, and I worried that some of the adults and kids weren't really listening. But they were. Afterward one of the sponsors of the event, Anne Elam, sent me a card with a check for twenty-five dollars. In the memo line of her check, Ms. Elam had written, "Professional Entertainment." It was my first paid gig, and the organization for whom I performed was the Alliance for Children and Youth, a group that assisted at-risk kids.

I graduated from Gaston College in August 1994, with a degree in criminal justice. Bea was once again there for the ceremonies. The first call I made after graduation was to Charles Mears, the superintendent of the prison. I reminded him about his job offer he had mentioned several years earlier. True to his word, Mr. Mears recommended me for a job as a corrections officer—a prison guard—at the medium security prison in Shelby, North Carolina.

THE FIRST DAY ON THE JOB, THE SERGEANT ORDERED ME TO distribute the mail to the inmates. I began calling out the names on the envelopes.

"Speak up!" yelled one of the prisoners.

I increased my volume as I called out the names, but it still wasn't enough.

"Louder!" another inmate demanded. An officer standing nearby took the mail from me and loudly called out each name. He'd been in the military and had a drill-sergeant-type voice. He looked at me and said, "You ain't gonna last a week in here."

For the next two months I was locked in a cellblock with sixty inmates. I didn't realize how dangerous the conditions were and how alone I was until one night I was surrounded by a gang of inmates, and one of them threatened me. I looked around for backup from the relief officers, but they were nowhere in sight. I didn't have a radio or pepper spray. Fortunately the inmates merely harassed me, but it spelled the end of my time in that facility.

Within several months I was transferred to Dallas, unit 4515, the same unit in which Jody Hager had once been incarcerated.

Sergeant Jeff Newton was my commanding officer there. He was a no-nonsense sort of guy who had served in the air force. Sergeant Newton called me into his office the first night I was on duty. He sat at his desk while I stood in front of it. He didn't offer me a seat. "I've already received word from someone at the Shelby unit that you are no good as a corrections officer," he said flatly. I thought of protesting but held my tongue.

"But I'm going to give you a chance to prove them wrong," he said. "You have my support one hundred percent."

"Thank you, sir."

"Don't blow it."

"No, sir. I won't."

Sergeant Newton continued, "Just remember to always be firm, fair, and consistent."

"Yes, sir." I knew instinctively that I was working for one of the best bosses anyone could ever have.

Sergeant Newton's patience with me far surpassed anything I expected. Many times I deserved to have been fired from that job, but Sergeant Newton kept giving me chances to redeem myself. For instance, a few months after I started working for him, he got a tip that a convict was planning an escape. Sergeant Newton wanted *me* to be the officer who intervened and foiled the escape. He could then tell headquarters what a fine officer I had become, and of course, he'd get the credit for training me.

He planned the sting and told me to wait in a particular spot on the prison yard. "Watch that back door of the chow hall, and when you see the convict come out, bust him!"

The other officers were positioned and guarding other exits. Twenty minutes went by. It was deathly quiet when I put in an emergency call for help to Sergeant Newton on the walkie-talkie. Every officer involved in the operation could hear the communication.

"C-18 to C-10."

"C-10, go ahead 18."

"I sprayed myself with pepper spray, and I need help!"

"10-4, C-18."

Sergeant Newton wasn't surprised. Instead of bragging on me to headquarters, he had to write an incident report. The convict had gotten word that we were lying in wait for him, so he nixed his escape attempt. Everyone was safe, except me. My eyes stopped burning a few hours later. Sergeant Newton gave me a three-hour knee-buckling lecture, during which I had to stand at attention in his office while he droned on and on about the proper use of pepper spray and why it is unwise to jostle the container during a sting operation. I already knew that part.

IF YOU'VE NEVER WORKED WITHIN THE PRISON SYSTEM, you might think that a minimum custody prison isn't as dangerous as a maximum security prison. Certainly a minimum security facility houses more inmates convicted of misdemeanors, such as embezzlement or drunk driving. But it also houses rapists and murderers. A security level doesn't define the type of convict; it merely defines the type of prison. Once a prisoner has served most of his sentence, the state begins to prepare him for life on the outside by housing him in a prison with more freedoms. But a murderer in a super max facility is the same murderer in minimum security. It's still a very dangerous environment.

In prison all you have is your name and your word. This applies to both inmates and officers. If I told an inmate that I would give him a headache tablet at 11:30 p.m., I learned quickly that I better be giving him that tablet on time, or my word wouldn't be good. I knew that if my word wasn't good in prison, it could put my life in great danger.

More than any concern for my personal safety, seeing some of the same kids who had been with me in various county receiving homes was one of the most shocking aspects of working in the prison. I couldn't help thinking, *That easily could have been me, had it not been for Bea.* Some of the kids had aged-out of the foster care system at eighteen, but the day they walked out of group homes or foster care, many of them had few alternatives. With nowhere to go and few resources, their futures were almost predetermined.

Just as Ms. Friday had predicted, without an education they were destined for prison or the cemetery. I had heard horror stories of kids who left the foster care system at eighteen and had gotten in trouble with drugs, alcohol, prostitution, human trafficking, and all sorts of other evils. Some were homeless, living on the streets; some were in prison; some were dead.

One inmate I encountered in prison, Decarlos White, was a strong, black guy I had grown up with on Vance Street. Decarlos, known as DD, had made it quite clear to me that he hated white people. I was determined to change his mind about white people, especially me.

When I became commanding officer (CO) of the community work crew, Decarlos was one of the inmates who had earned enough trust inside to be permitted out to work on my road crew. For an incarcerated convict, to work outside the prison was a privilege.

One day we were in Kings Mountain, picking up trash on the side of Highway 216. DD was in the back of the line since he didn't like anyone standing behind him. The only person behind DD was me. DD stopped and turned around.

"CO," he said. It was the first time he had spoken to me since seeing him in prison.

"Yes, what's the matter, DD?"

DD nodded toward a house that sat about one hundred yards away. "That's where my mama lives."

"That's interesting," I replied, not catching his meaning.

"I ain't seen her in years. Can I go see her?" he asked.

"What? Mr. White," I said, trying to maintain a sense of decorum with my old acquaintance, "you know I can't do that. If I let you go see your mother, everyone on this chain gang is going to expect a favor from me."

DD simply stared at me.

I thought about his request. I understood what it was like for a person to be separated from his parents. This might be my chance to change DD's mind. It could also be risky. I could get fired for letting him out of my sight or assisting an escape. I was the officer in charge, and if DD fled or, worse yet, committed another crime, the burden of his actions would be my responsibility. As I pondered the possibilities, I decided the risk was worth it.

"Mr. White," I said slowly, "I'm going to let you go see your mother. But if you're not back in fifty-nine minutes, as far as I'm concerned, you will have escaped," I said. "And you know what that means."

DD nodded. He understood that if I reported him as an escapee, when the authorities tracked him down, they would either shoot him or send him back to a maximum security facility to do hard time.

DD ran as fast as he could across the field and up to the front door of his mother's house. I watched him and remembered a twelve-year-old boy running across a field in Reed's Trailer Park, hurrying to get to the phone to talk for a few minutes with his mother who was in prison.

I could see Mr. White's mother when she opened the door. She grabbed him and hugged him, and they disappeared into the house. Fifty-nine minutes later Mr. White came racing back across the field.

He was out of breath and said, "My mama was making me a shepherd's pie, but I ran out of time and couldn't eat it." He was trying to catch his breath and waiting on me to offer an invitation for her to bring it out to him. When I didn't respond, he asked, "Can my mama bring me that pie?" I could tell he was serious.

"Mr. White, you are really pushing it," I said quietly.

Again, he just stared at me.

I looked over at the house and saw his mother standing in the doorway. "Okay, she can bring it to you," I said.

Mr. White motioned for his mother. A frail, little black woman wearing a do-rag on her head, tied in the front, slowly walked across the field, carrying a pan with a dish towel under it. She handed Mr. White the pie, and they sat there on the side of the road as he ate and she cried.

The other convicts continued working and pretended they didn't see DD and his mama. It was an unwritten rule of prison life that male convicts dared not stare at another inmate's mother, sister, or girlfriend. A short time later we packed up and drove back to the prison.

Why would I take such a chance? Because Mr. White and I had grown up together on Vance Street and lived in the county group homes together. I remembered him, and he remembered me. I wanted to help him because that's what Bea did for me.

Several weeks went by, and Mr. White never even said thanks for sticking my neck out for him. Then, on an intensely hot summer day, my crew was in Dallas, working on another long, winding back road. As usual, I was at the back of the line, standing behind Mr. White.

"Don't go around that corner," DD said under his breath.

I thought I'd heard what he said, but I wasn't sure.

I asked him to tell me again, but he couldn't or other inmates would hear him. I realized he was giving me a warning. I waited a few minutes then yelled out to the convicts, "Gentlemen, it's extremely hot out here, and I'm not feeling well. Let's get inside the vehicle and cool off."

I didn't have to make that suggestion twice! The inmates piled into the state van—all except two white cons who had been lingering. They finally came and got into the van. I closed the door and immediately headed back to the prison.

I now knew why DD had warned me not to go around that bend in the road. Those two inmates had planned to jump me and then escape. DD had heard about their plan from other inmates, and that was his way of thanking me for allowing him to see his mother.

DD served his time and was released from prison on April 21, 1999. Long after we both left the prison system, we kept in touch, and today he is one of my best friends in the world.

Thirty

COUNTRY BUST

I WAS SITTING ON THE BEDROOM FLOOR AT BEA'S HOUSE IN 1994, when a man came on *Crook & Chase*, a popular country music television show hosted by Lorianne Crook and Charlie Chase. The musical guest that day wasn't a big name star, but he was one of the most successful songwriters in Nashville. Using only a guitar, he performed three hit songs that he had written—all of which I recognized were recorded by major country stars. I was so naive to the music business, I didn't know that many of music's greatest performers didn't write their own songs. At first I wondered, *What's this guy doing singing other people's hits?* The more I watched and listened, though, I began to let my dreams run wild. *I wonder what it would be like to write a song with that guy?*

When the songwriter completed his set, the hosts and audience applauded enthusiastically for Skip Ewing, one of Nashville's most prolific and most successful writers.

I had already been writing some songs and performing locally. Anytime I sang someplace, Bea always went along with me and sat in the front row. Funny, though, she hardly paid attention to my singing. She'd just sit in the front row and read her Bible throughout my performance.

The first time I performed without sound tracks in front of an audience was a disaster. My friend Lloyd Kelso married Debra Burns, an aspiring country singer. Debra enjoyed some success with a song called "Runaway Heart," so Lloyd's parents scheduled a concert in their backyard, and I asked him if I could sing a few songs to warm up the audience before Debra started. I usually sang using karaoke tapes for background music, but this was the first time I attempted to play my guitar and sing at the same time. I was horrible. I don't mean that I wasn't good. I mean I was absolutely awful! The audience was kind, but by the second song, Lloyd stood up and waved his arms and yelled to me, "Stop!"

"What?"

"That's enough." I felt as though someone had just reached out a long hook and pulled me off the stage.

I didn't learn my lesson, and a short time after that, I tried to do another performance without my karaoke background tapes. This time I attempted to perform "My Only Friend," the song I had written about my friend's mom, with Bea in mind.

I sat on stage at Highland Junior High and started noodling through it, but I couldn't do it. I tried several times but couldn't get my fingers and mouth to work together at the same time.

"Close the curtain," I said disgustedly.

"Come on, Jimmy!" people in the crowd called out. "Sing!" They had heard me sing at various functions around the area but always with backup music, never to my own accompaniment.

"I can't," I whined.

"Yes, you can. Come on, sing for us."

I muddled through the song, but it was terribly embarrassing, especially with my friends in the crowd and with Bea sitting on the front row.

I was so discouraged about my guitar playing that I almost gave it up. I enjoyed singing to the background tapes. Who needs a guitar, anyhow?

I did. Nashville is a guitar town. I knew if I were ever going to make it as a singer, I needed to be able to play guitar. I kept practicing, working harder to learn the guitar; I wanted to play so badly. When I first started playing, I practiced in the bathroom, sitting on the bathtub, facing the wall. I turned out the lights so I couldn't see my hands. Slowly but surely I got better and didn't have to stare at the strings as I played. So I am living proof that singing in the shower might help.

O NE OF THE MORE ROWDY VENUES WHERE I SANG—WITHOUT my guitar—was at a karaoke contest sponsored by WSOC radio station at Coyote Joe's, a popular bar and country dance club, with a large American flag hanging in the back of the room and a spacious dance floor. It had a small stage and a balcony, where people could sit and watch the performances. On weekends hot regional bands played at Coyote Joe's, but during the week, the owners kept the place busy with crowds of people coming to hear their friends singing karaoke. I entered the contest every Thursday night I could. A cash prize of seventy-five dollars was awarded to the winner, which was determined by audience response—how much noise the friends and fellow drinkers could make on behalf of their favorites. One of the songs I sang frequently was Garth Brooks's hit "The Thunder Rolls," written by another premier Nashville songwriter, Pat Alger, and the crowd always responded enthusiastically. I frequently came home from Coyote Joe's with an extra seventy-five dollars in my pocket.

My girlfriend, Tonia, went along with me and supported me. I had met Tonia at Ingles grocery store shortly after my heart had been broken by my former girlfriend. I was rather shy, so I didn't immediately go out and try to get another girlfriend. But when I walked in the grocery store and saw a young woman with bright green eyes, long blonde hair, and a vibrant smile working behind the cash register, I really wanted to meet her.

I made frequent trips to the store because I didn't have much money, and, especially while I was living with Bea, I didn't have a lot of space to store food. I simply bought what I needed or wanted for that day. I pretty much bought the same things every day—an apple, some bread, and maybe some sandwich meat.

After I had been in the store several times, Tina, one of the pretty girl's coworkers, approached me and gave me the new girl's name and phone number. "Don't say I told you so, but the cashier over there would like to get to know you." I was thrilled to have her number, but I was still too shy to call her.

A few days later I was in Ingles, standing in Tonia's line, waiting to check out. Her line had four guys in front of me. At another register a few aisles away, a less-attractive young woman had a totally empty lane.

"Aisle Four is open," she called out in a squeaky voice. "Aisle Four's open," she repeated, looking directly at the five of us guys in Tonia's line. Nobody moved. A rugged-looking guy in front of me turned around and nodded toward Aisle Four. "You can go over there."

"Nah, I think I'll wait right here."

"Me, too," he nodded. "She sure is pretty, isn't she?"

"That's *my* girl," I said impulsively.

The tough guy glanced at me, looked at the pretty girl behind the cash register, then back at me. He stepped out of line and moved over to Aisle Four, which was still empty.

When I finally got to the register and worked up enough nerve to talk to the pretty girl, I introduced myself. I fumbled through asking her if she wanted to go get some pizza after work. Surprisingly, she agreed. But when she met me for pizza, she brought along her sister. The sister was ultra-protective of Tonia, so I spent most of the time answering big-sister questions, trying to convince her I was safe, and hardly got a word in with Tonia.

The following day a woman I had known from Osage Mill textile factory asked if I would sing a few songs at a cookout. I said, "Sure. Is it okay if I bring along a friend?" Tonia went along with me, and I happily sang for hours, using karaoke background tapes. I sang every song directly to Tonia, whether she was looking at me or not. Tonia and I were a couple from that day forward.

Along with Bea, Tonia believed that I could make my dream happen; she had so much confidence in me that she was willing to go with me week after week to Coyote Joe's. Normally about twenty or thirty singers competed for the prize each week. Many of the singers were off-key drunks, but there were always several talented musicians as well. Nevertheless, I established a pretty good track record, winning the prize week after week. Since I was working and saving money, I took the bold step of moving out of Bea's house and into my own place, a ratty trailer near work that I rented for forty dollars a week. I got so accustomed to winning at Coyote Joe's that I counted on the extra seventy-five dollars every two weeks to help pay my rent.

One Thursday night I did my usual rendition of "The Thunder Rolls," and the sound guy did his part, adding a few effects with the sound and lights. I fully expected to pick up my seventy-five dollars at the end of the evening. But that night Johnny Johnson, a guy wearing a big black cowboy hat, got up and started playing the fiddle, and he was hot! The purple lights on the stage made the violin look as though it were smoking. The guy with the fiddle stole the show. He was incredible, speed-playing licks on the fiddle. The crowd started cheering for him; he was so good, I cheered for him as well.

I lost that night, and Johnny Johnson won. I didn't like losing, but I was very impressed with Johnny's talent. Years later I was on a show with Rascal Flatts. I was doing a sound check when a fiddle player started to tune up. I looked up and saw Johnny Johnson, now one of the hottest fiddle players in country music.

I REALLY DIDN'T KNOW ANYBODY IN THE MUSIC BUSINESS, but my friends Lloyd and Debra Kelso encouraged me to visit them in Nashville. Lloyd had a law firm on the corner of Chet Atkins Place and 18th Avenue, part of Nashville's famous Music Row.

In October 1996, I loaded my bicycle—I had not yet returned the borrowed bike that I had been riding the day I met Bea and Russell—in the bed of a 1984 brown Ford truck. I wanted to have the bike just in case the truck broke down on my way to Nashville.

I drove the longest trip I'd ever driven outside of Charlotte, nearly four hundred miles up Highway 74, across Interstate 40, westbound to exit 209B, Demonbreun Street, also known as Music Row. I spent three days observing and meeting with a few of Lloyd's friends whom he had met in the music business or represented as an attorney. I met with music legend Don Light, whose publishing fame rested on Jimmy Buffett's "Margaritaville," and I sang a few songs for him. I met Charlie Monk, another music publishing mogul, at the church Lloyd and Debra attended. I met with a few executives from music companies, and a few others. I was surprised at how nice these people were to me even though I was a nobody. I made several trips to Nashville over the next few months, just trying to get my foot in the door of the music business. But, although the doors opened with relative ease, nobody seemed interested in my songs or me as an artist, and nothing ever came of my visits.

I was still working full time at the prison. It was relatively easy to make trips to Nashville when Sergeant Newton was kind enough to arrange my schedule so I would have three days off in a row. I could make a hasty trip to Nashville and be back in time to work the third shift, from eleven at night to seven in the morning. But when I took the community work crew job, I had to plan my trips sparingly, using only my vacation days.

There's a saying in the music business: you must be present to win. In other words, I needed to move to Nashville before I could expect anyone to take me seriously. I understood that, but I was also wary enough to know that I better have a reason to move to Music City before giving up a real job to pursue what may turn out to be a pipe dream. One morning, after I had worked a long third shift at the prison, I was awakened from a deep sleep by somebody pounding on the side of my rented trailer, banging away right where my bedroom was located. In my pre-coffee condition, I could barely function, but I recognized

Tonia's voice outside the trailer, calling to me, "Jimmy! Get up! I have something to tell you."

I stumbled to the front door and invited Tonia inside. "Wha . . . What's the matter? What's going on?"

"Nothing's wrong, but you need to get cleaned up and put on some singin' clothes. We're going to Charlotte."

"What's in Charlotte? Tonia, what in the world are you talkin' about? I just got to bed a few hours ago. I'm not going anywhere."

"Yes, you are," Tonia insisted. "My friend Christy Williams gave me her ticket to the Opryland Theme Park auditions that are being held today at the Charlotte Convention Center."

"What? Why isn't Christy going? She really wants a shot as a female artist." Christy and I were friendly rivals on the local singers' circuit, which made me skeptical and quite reluctant to take the invitation seriously. It didn't make sense. Similar to the "tickets" awarded to contestants on modern-day television shows, such as *American Idol*, *The Voice*, and *The X Factor*, of the thousands of tryouts for Opryland, only a limited number of contestants actually receive an invitation to audition before the decision makers. Christy had received one of those tickets. So why would Christy give away her ticket—and her chance to possibly break into the music business—to me?

"I am not going to any audition," I said vehemently. I was convinced that the audition was probably a gimmick or maybe even a scam, trying to bilk money out of hopeful musicians, and I didn't want to let Christy "get one on me."

Tonia refused to take no for an answer. "Come on, Jimmy. Let's go."

"It's a scam, Tonia. Watch and see."

I must have said those words a hundred times as we drove the thirty minutes up I-85 toward Charlotte. Tonia didn't say a word the entire trip. She just kept driving.

We finally arrived at the Charlotte Convention Center, parked, and went inside the enormous building. I was overwhelmed and felt so out of place. I was a small-town, country guy; I wasn't used to the big city. Everything about it scared me.

Worse yet, we couldn't find the audition room in the huge convention center.

"See, I told you it was a scam," I complained to Tonia after we had walked into several empty rooms. "Let's go."

Tonia said, "Hold on. Let's try this room."

We had finally found room 213A, where a panel of old men— probably in their early forties or fifties, but they looked old to me—were sitting behind a long table. There were no other contestants, no piano, no microphone, nothing; just them. I knew we had the wrong room again, but from the doorway, Tonia ventured, "Is this the room where the Opryland Theme Park auditions are supposed—"

"Yeah," one of the grumpy old men interrupted before Tonia could finish her sentence. "Come down here and put your tape in that cassette player, press play, and sing. You're number 300 and the last one of the day," he said. He apparently thought Tonia was the contestant and seemed disappointed when I walked in front of the long table and put in my background track. Tonia stood behind me and waited.

The music came on, and I began singing "Love, Me," a huge hit song for Collin Raye, written by Max T. Barnes and Skip Ewing, the guy I had seen on *Crook & Chase.*

I barely had opened my mouth and hadn't even finished the first line of the song when the old man pressed the stop button on the tape player and said, "Okay." He told me to put the other tape in and press play. After listening to 299 other auditions, I guessed that he'd heard enough of "Love Me."

I started singing my second song, "Papa Loved Mama," and I was so flustered, I forgot the words to the song. The judge hit the stop button again, and said, "Okay, that's it."

"Huh?" I asked. *That's it?*

"That's it," he repeated loudly.

"Now we need to see you dance," one of the other men said.

"I can't dance," I said. "I don't dance."

"Well, try," he said emphatically.

Another judge took me to a side room where there was a video camera. "As soon as the song comes on," he instructed, "start dancing."

I looked ridiculous gyrating around the room in my tight jeans, a dingy white T-shirt, a vest that looked like a Turkish rug, my bargain Jesus Store boots, and my string-tie bolo, with a saddle clip that stuck me in the neck every time I moved. But they wanted me to dance, so I danced. And the judges got a good laugh out of it.

On the way home I was fuming. "I told you it was a scam!" I kept saying to Tonia over and over. "I can't believe I let you talk me into this, and now they have me on camera dancing, or whatever you want to call it."

Tonia just smiled and kept driving, occasionally snickering when I mentioned the dancing. Back home I didn't mention the botched audition to anyone, even if someone asked how it went. I changed the subject immediately. I tried my best to forget the whole ridiculous affair, and I almost did, until I got an unusual phone call.

Thirty-one

NASHVILLE NOVICE

I DIDN'T GET THE JOB AT OPRYLAND. SEVERAL MONTHS after the audition, though, I received a phone call. "Is this Jimmy Barber?" a man asked.

"Yeah, who's this?"

"My name is Mike Whelan from Opryland Music Group in Nashville, and I was one of the judges at the Opryland Theme Park audition. I got your name and number off your application."

"Uh-huh," I replied skeptically.

Mike said he wanted to get together to talk.

"Uh-huh, sure." I thought my friend David was prank-calling me. "C'mon, David," I said. "Stop playing games, or I'm going to hang up."

"Well, this is Mike Whelan; write this number down before you hang up the phone," Mike said. He rattled off a phone number.

I wrote the number but remained suspicious. We talked further, and I told Mike that I was planning another trip to Nashville in a few weeks. "I could come by your office while I'm in town."

"That would be great," the man replied.

Before we hung up, I asked him to repeat the phone number one more time. I wanted to make sure this wasn't David rambling off a fake phone number, and if he could remember it, then it might not be a prank call after all.

Mike Whelan immediately said the numbers again, exactly the same way he had said them five minutes earlier.

That was the moment when I thought for the first time, *This might really be a music executive from Nashville calling me.*

I ARRIVED IN NASHVILLE ON DECEMBER 16, 1996, A COLD, winter day, and checked in at the Best Western hotel near Music Circle, part of Music Row. I drove down the Row the evening before my appointment and found Opryland Music Group (OMG), a three-story, red-brick building with dark, tinted windows. I wanted to know where the company was located so I could be sure to get there on time.

The following morning, the closer it got to ten o'clock, the time I was scheduled to meet with Mike Whelan, the more nervous I became, pacing the hotel room floor and staring out the window.

I arrived at OMG on time, and the receptionist, Jamie Green, kindly instructed me to have a seat and said she would notify Mike. I was in awe of what appeared to me to be one of the most opulent office foyers I had ever seen and was blown away by the fancy surroundings and the magnificent marble floors. Shortly afterward, the receptionist told me to go on up to the third floor, where Mike would be waiting on me.

Once the elevator doors closed, I took a deep breath and said a prayer. I smiled and said, "God, I wish Bea could see this place." When the elevator doors opened on the third floor, I got another shock. On the walls in front of me were framed albums of songs that OMG had published, albums by stars such as Patsy Cline and Hank Williams. I even spotted "The Hokey Pokey." Seeing those iconic records on the walls made me even more nervous.

Mike Whelan met me in the hallway, firmly shook my hand, and invited me into his office. He was a stocky guy who looked more like a football player or a power lifter than a music guy, but we spent the next half hour or so discussing my music. He didn't ask me to sing a note; he simply wanted to talk with me. "Do you write your own songs?" Mike wanted to know.

"Well, yeah, I've written at least five or six songs," I answered naively.

A glint of a smile crossed Mike's face, but he didn't respond negatively. I didn't know that most successful songwriters have written literally hundreds of songs, not six. But I was so clueless about the music business that I didn't even understand the role of a music publishing company.

The meeting went okay, but nothing tangible was decided.

MIKE AND I KEPT IN TOUCH OVER THE NEXT FEW MONTHS. He called me one afternoon and said, "I'm going to send you some songs to learn, so you can come out here and record them during your next trip."

I didn't understand why he wanted me to record someone else's songs, but I agreed to do it. Every day for the next few weeks, I anxiously checked the mailbox, looking for the songs Mike said he would send.

Nothing. The box was empty. I called Mike dozens of times, and the receptionist told me, "He's in a meeting," a phrase I later learned was Nashville-nice for saying, "He doesn't want to talk to you right now."

Finally, several weeks later, I received a package from Opryland Music Group. Inside I found three songs, each one written by Skip Ewing. I dubbed those three songs over and over, filling an entire ninety-minute tape.

I listened to those songs constantly, day and night. I wore earphones to bed with the songs playing softly in my ears as I fell asleep. I listened to the songs while working out on the road with the prison work crew as I kept watch over DD White and the other convicts. Every time the ninety-minute tape stopped, I flipped it over and pressed play again. I learned those songs backward and forward.

On May 15, 1997, I was back in Nashville, at the Opryland Music Group Publishing Company. Mike Whelan welcomed me, and we walked down to the studio, where he introduced me to the engineer, Bill Harris. "Call me when you guys have finished recording the three songs," Mike told Bill, "and I'll come down to listen to them." He looked at me and said, "Jimmy, I'll see you later this evening." Mike waved good-bye and closed the heavy studio door.

Bill Harris was a kind, patient, old-school Nashville engineer. He had recorded hit songs for all sorts of artists. He positioned me inside a studio vocal booth and went back into the control room. Once Bill got the equalization and volume levels set on the microphone, he asked, "Are you ready, Jimmy?"

"Yeah, sure am."

"All right." Bill pressed the red record button. I sang one warm-up pass so Bill could check his levels, then one take per song, and we were finished.

Bill called Mike and said, "Hey, Mike."

"Yeah?"

"You may want to come down here and hear this," Bill said.

Surprised, Mike responded, "Y'all are finished already?"

"Yeah, man."

Apparently it was uncommon in Nashville for a vocalist to record a song that fast, accurately nailing the notes the first time, in one take. I didn't know that most artists "build" a song in the studio, laying down the vocals one line at time, and it can often take all day to sing one song. Sometimes it takes even longer, until the vocalist gets each part correct, and if the artist never gets it exactly right, through the miracles of electronics, the engineer can fine-tune the vocal until it sounds perfect.

Mike came down to the studio and listened to each song. As far as he was concerned, we were done. "Let's go to lunch," Mike said.

We went to a restaurant, where Mike talked much more than he ate. After the meal Mike promised he'd call me to let me know what the other guys at the company thought of my voice and if they wanted to sign me.

THE FOLLOWING MONTH WAS THE LONGEST MONTH OF MY life. I was constantly checking my answering machine at home and looking in the mailbox for any signs that OMG wanted me.

Finally, Mike called and asked, "Jimmy, how much money do you make working at the prison?"

"I make about twelve hundred dollars a month," I said.

"We can pay you two hundred and fifty dollars a week, if you'd like to join us."

I could not believe Mike Whelan was offering to pay me for doing something I was happy to do for free. Better yet, he was willing to pay me almost as much as I was making by risking my life every day at the prison. I didn't have to debate my next step.

"Yeah, I'll do it," I answered quickly, not even trying to sound cool, "but I'll need to give the prison a one-month notice."

"Great," Mike responded. "I'll get a formal agreement to you soon."

One more month, and my life would never be the same—but not for the reasons I hoped.

Thirty-two

GOOD-BYE, JIMMY; GOOD-BYE, BEA

For the next month I focused on packing my things, selling anything I didn't need, and tying up loose ends. But there was one loose end that I wasn't expecting—my relationship with my friend, Bea Costner.

She was eighty-one years old now, and much to her chagrin, Bea was forced to close the woodshop. For almost a year, a For Rent sign had hung in the window, but Bea still went out to the woodshop and puttered around for hours every day. Eventually the building rented, and Bea was resigned to spending her time sitting in the green-and-white metal chair in the front yard facing the woodshop. She sat there for hours on end, reading her Bible, working crossword puzzles, and watching the new people who had moved into her building.

Although I couldn't help Bea with her personal business, I picked her up and took her with me to every show I performed. Bea loved going along. It didn't matter what the event was—a cookout, a pageant, a karaoke contest, or whatever—Bea always sat on the front row, directly in front of the microphone stand.

But she rarely paid much attention to me. Instead, Bea sat on the front row and read her Bible. I couldn't help but notice, and it drove me crazy.

You mean to tell me, I drove all the way to your house to pick you up and bring you with me to this show, and you're not even going to pay attention to my performance? I thought. Of course, I never said that to her. I wouldn't offend Bea for the world.

No matter where we went, she'd sit through the entire show and read her Bible. She didn't read out loud, but I could see her pen moving across each page as she highlighted various verses.

Having Bea on the front row was a problem for me. I couldn't flirt with the pretty, young girls, and I surely couldn't sing a song about partying while Bea was sitting directly in front of me reading Scripture. It was annoying, and it affected my performance; but I loved Bea, and I wanted the beautiful, white-haired woman to be there with me.

I RECEIVED A CALL FROM CINDY BALLARD ASKING ME IF I could sing at the 1997 year-end closing ceremony for Highland Junior High. Of course, I accepted the invitation.

I called Bea and asked her to come along. But because I anticipated a number of bubbly high school girls bouncing to the beat on the front row, I planned ahead how I could circumvent Bea's Bible reading.

When we arrived, I told Bea, "I have a special chair for you tonight, right over here by the exit door, so you won't have to battle the crowd after the show is over." I ushered Bea to her special seat and told her I was going backstage to prepare for the show. Bea sat down in the seat by the door, with her purse and Bible in her lap.

Ecstatic that I had moved her out of the fan zone without offending her, I went backstage with a smile on my face. Soon the announcer's voice boomed, "Ladies and gentlemen, please welcome Jimmy Wayne Barber!" The house lights went down, the curtains opened, and the spotlight was on me. I walked out to the microphone at the edge of the stage, and as I reached for the mike, I glanced down into the audience of young girls. There, right in the middle of the girls, sat Bea on the front row, directly in front of the mike stand, reading her Bible.

Oh, well, I thought. *I tried.*

About halfway through my performance, I saw Bea close her Bible and stand up. I continued singing but kept an eye on her. She walked to the exit door and stepped out of the auditorium. Cindy Ballard followed her to make sure she was okay.

The moment I finished singing, I ran out to see where Bea was and to find out what was wrong.

"Oh, it's nothing, Jimmy," Bea said. "My leg started hurting from sitting so long, and I just needed to walk it off." I was concerned. Bea was tough, and it was highly uncharacteristic of her to even mention an ache or a pain, much less to get up and walk out of a show. I said a quick good-bye to Cindy and the staff and helped Bea to the car.

It was a short drive back to Bea's house. As I glanced over at her, she was looking down at her Bible in her lap. Her face was radiant, and her white hair was beautiful, as usual. To me, she looked the same as she did the day I met her.

The familiar voice spoke to me: *You need to tell Bea you love her and how much you appreciate all she has done for you.*

What? I thought. I had never said those words to Bea, not once. *This is weird.*

We drove on in silence for a few more minutes. We were approximately one minute from her house. We were both unusually quiet.

"Bea," I said.

She looked up but didn't speak.

I stared at the road in front of me, and thought, *I can't believe I'm getting ready to do this. This feels so cheesy.*

She simply sat there, as though waiting on me to say something.

Finally I looked at her and said, "Bea, I love you." I quickly looked away from her. I had lived with Bea for six years and had known her now for seven years, but that was the first time I'd ever uttered those words to her.

"I love you, too, Jimmy," Bea responded warmly and easily.

The door of my heart opened, like the dikes of a dam, and a Niagara of words flowed out in a rush. I began thanking her for everything I could possibly think of—for opening her home to me, for the opportunity to have a car, an education, my job. I thanked her for encouraging me to pursue my dream of being a musician. I thanked her for all the doughnuts and the Coca-Colas she gave me when I cut the grass. "I wouldn't be here if it weren't for you," I told her. "Thank you, Bea, for my clothes; thank you for all the meals you made for me." I thanked Bea for everything.

I pulled in her driveway, parked the car, and ran around to her side and opened the door. She reached out and locked her arm with mine as I helped her out of the car. We walked slowly toward her front door, and Bea commented on how much her leg was still hurting.

When Bea got to the top of the three steps leading to her door, she turned around and looked at me. It struck me that she was standing in the exact spot where she stood the day she first invited me into their home, holding open the same glass storm door. I, too, was standing in the same spot as I stood that day I showed up with my bag full of dirty clothes.

"Well, I'll be back in three days to pick you up and take you to another show," I said.

Bea looked at me and extended her arm slightly to wave at me. It was as though she was looking right through me. "Good-bye, Jimmy!" she said with so much love as she waved at me.

I thought, *This is very weird.*

We were three feet from each another. Still, I waved at Bea, and she waved at me again. I waved back, and we stood there waving at each other for what seemed like several minutes.

Bea kept saying, "Good-bye, Jimmy! Good-bye, Jimmy!" over and over.

I said, "Good-bye, Bea; I'll see ya in three days, okay?"

Bea didn't acknowledge my comment. She smiled and said again, "Good-bye, Jimmy." She continued to wave at me.

I got in the car, and Bea was still waving. I pulled out and headed down the road, but when I looked in my rearview mirror, I saw Bea, still standing there, waving.

I waved at her one last time.

She was *beautiful*.

THE FOLLOWING MORNING I RECEIVED A PHONE CALL FROM Bea's daughter, Sandie; she was crying. Somehow I knew what Sandie was going to tell me.

"She had a stroke, Jimmy," Sandie said through her tears. "They said Mother had a blood clot in her leg that moved to her brain."

Sandie and I wept together on the phone.

Over the next month or so, I visited Bea in the hospital as often as possible. Most days, she was unconscious, deep in a coma. I'd hold her hand and talk to her, but she rarely responded. Every so often, though, she roused slightly, and I tried to feed her some applesauce. She ate little and before long slipped back into the coma. Whether she knew I was there or not didn't matter; I went to visit her anyhow.

One day I slipped into her room, and she was in the coma. Some other friends were visiting, so I simply stepped to the side of the bed and held Bea's hand. "Bea? Bea, it's Jimmy," I said softly.

She opened her eyes, and they seemed to roll slightly, but then she focused just enough on me. In a soft, weak voice, she mumbled words that will motivate me till the end of time. Speaking barely above a whisper, Bea looked at me and said, "I'll be looking for you."

She closed her eyes and slipped back into the coma. Those were her last words to me, and to all who knew her. "I'll be looking for you." And she will be.

GOD PROMOTED BEA TO GLORY ON JULY 29, 1997. WHEN Sandie called and said, "Mother passed away," I was terribly sad, but I was glad that she was not suffering anymore, and I knew that because of our mutual faith in Jesus, I would see Bea again.

Still, her funeral was difficult for me. I knew that Bea would want me to sing, so I walked up to the podium and turned around to face the congregation. I looked down and saw Bea lying in front of me, in the casket. Her white hair was done perfectly, although it didn't look quite right without some sawdust in it. Her face retained the dignity of royalty even in death.

She was still *beautiful*.

I began singing "How Great Thou Art," one of her gospel favorites, but I couldn't get through it. I just cried.

I think she understood, and I thought I heard her saying from somewhere up in heaven, *I'll be looking for you, Jimmy.*

Thirty-three

SOME DREAMS REALLY DO COME TRUE

By January 1998, Mike Whelan and I had agreed in principle on the deal points for my songwriting agreement with Opryland Music Group. I still wasn't officially a professional songwriter, but the possibility of my dream coming true was one step closer. In the meantime, I went to work at the prison each day and slipped into the music room at every opportunity to practice my guitar playing. My commanding officer discovered me practicing when I should have been guarding prisoners, but he knew my time at the prison was winding down, and he graciously didn't fire me.

On March 20, 1998, the time came for me to turn in my badge and uniforms. As I walked through the gate, carrying a plastic bag filled with my prison guard uniforms, a convict yelled, "Hey, Elvis, you gonna play us a song?"

"I can't," I replied.

"Hey, everybody, Barber Mandrell is going to play us a song," the convict called out, using the parody of my name with which he often teased me. Convicts stood up from the weight benches; a couple of guys threw down their basketballs. Others laid down their cards or stopped

265

doing what they were doing and walked toward me. A crowd gathered quickly, and I knew I had to play at least one song before I left, or there was going to be trouble.

So like the pied piper, I walked toward the music room with a large group of convicts following behind me. I could hear antsy prison officials calling out over the intercom system, "Attention on the midyard! All inmates must remain in the yard." The guards must have thought something bad was about to happen since it looked as though a riot was about to break out. The army of convicts continued following me. We went inside the music room—the same music room where I sometimes met with Jody Hager and where Sergeant Newton caught me practicing guitar. Cons and killers surrounded me the same way they did on my first day during mail call. Some sat at my feet, others stood in the doorway stretching their necks to look in. Still others looked in the windows.

I took down from the cabinet the brown guitar, the same one Jody had used, with the prison number 4515 stamped on it. I was about to begin playing when the prison superintendent burst through the door. "What's going on?" he demanded.

"They want me to play them a song," I said.

He looked at me then glanced around at all the prisoners. The convicts looked back at him expectantly.

"One song, and that's it!" the superintendent said. "One song, Barber; do you understand?"

"Yes, sir," I replied.

I began strumming the guitar and singing the song I'd written with Bea in mind, "My Only Friend," describing the unconditional love of a mother. My guitar playing still wasn't great, but I was at least able to accompany myself by now. As I played and sang, I noticed several men listening with tears trickling down their faces. That could be dangerous because in prison, tears are a sign of weakness. But the men didn't seem to care.

Adult men began to groan as I sang. Others cursed. But they all missed their mamas. I understood. So did I.

After the song, the convicts applauded, not so much to thank me but to break the tension. As other men filed out of the room, some saying good-bye, others nodding in grudging respect, Ron, one of the toughest cons in the prison, approached me. Ron had been on death row and was now serving a life sentence. As he neared me, he reached in his back pocket, and I immediately was on alert. I thought, *He's reaching for a shank*—a homemade prison weapon.

An unwritten but generally known rule among convicts requires that a convict keep a six-foot distance between himself and an officer when talking to the guard, so other convicts can hear what they are saying. Otherwise, the convict will be accused of snitching, and in prison, snitches get stitches.

Ron violated the six-foot rule and got right in my face. But instead of a weapon, he pulled his wallet out of his pocket. He opened it and removed a photo of a woman.

"Here, will you sign this?" Ron asked, as he handed me the photo.

"Your mother's picture?" I asked.

"Yes," he said quietly.

I paused momentarily and looked into Ron's eyes, and he looked into mine. In some incomprehensible yet very real way, we were brothers. I took the photo and carefully signed the back of it, then handed it back to him.

Ron spoke very softly, "That way I know I won't lose your autograph."

Over the years since that day, I've signed thousands of autographs but never one more meaningful than that first one.

Now that Bea was gone, leaving North Carolina and moving to Nashville was not as difficult. Making matters even easier, my girlfriend, Tonia, hoped to relocate in Music City as well. I moved to Nashville and signed my first songwriting agreement, which required that I write eighteen songs per year, with cowrites, songs written in collaboration with other writers, counting as half a song. I thought, *This is a piece of cake. And these guys want to pay me for doing this? What a way to make a living!*

ON MARCH 23, 1998, I BEGAN MY FIRST DAY AS A SONG-writer for one of the largest music publishing companies in the world, the Opryland Music Group Publishing Company, formerly known as Acuff-Rose Music, founded by country music legends Roy Acuff and Fred Rose. The catalog included such classics as "Tennessee Waltz," "Oh, Lonesome Me," "I Can't Stop Loving You," as well as hits by Hank Williams Sr., such as "Your Cheatin' Heart," not to mention some of contemporary country music's greatest writers.

One of those writers walked down the hallway toward me on my first day of work. I recognized him immediately as the guy I had seen four years earlier on *Crook & Chase* playing some of my favorite songs: Skip Ewing, who had written "Love, Me," the song I had hoped to sing for the Opryland Theme Park audition. He had also written the three songs that Mike Whelan had sent me to learn and record. In a way, it was because of Skip Ewing that I was even at OMG. I wanted to tell him so.

I watched Skip as he stopped to say a few words and hand a work tape to Sandra Morgan, the woman who logged the company's songs in a computer, on his way out to the parking lot. I followed him all the way out to his vehicle. Skip was already in the car with the motor running and was ready to back up when I approached his window.

"Sir, can I have your autograph?" I asked.

"Sure," he said.

I told Skip how I had landed in Nashville by singing his songs, as I handed him a pen to sign my journal. But the pen was out of ink, so I ran over to my car to dig out another pen. Skip started to sign the first page of my journal, and that pen was almost empty too. Skip patiently waited as I retrieved yet another pen; he signed my journal and handed it back to me. I was thrilled!

But when I got back upstairs, Mike Whelan pulled me aside. "Jimmy," he said, quietly but firmly. "Stay out of Skip's way." He explained to me that Skip Ewing was a superstar among songwriters; he was the company's bread and butter, and he was not to be bothered.

"I'm sorry," I told Mike. "I just wanted to say thanks and to get his autograph."

Mike nodded and smiled. "Okay, fine, but don't bother him again. Come on. I'll show you around." Mike gave me a grand tour of the music complex. As we were walking across the alley to the writers' rooms next door, Mike introduced me to a guy wearing a baseball cap and standing on the curb, ready to cross.

"Jimmy, meet Kenny Chesney," Mike said. "Kenny, Jimmy is a new OMG writer."

Kenny reached out his hand and shook mine, and said, "Welcome. Good to meet you, Jimmy."

I was in awe. I thought, *I've been singing this country singer's songs at weddings and karaoke contests, and now I'm meeting him?* I was totally starstruck. "You're Kenny Chesney?" I asked.

"Yeah . . ."

"Man, I saw you at the Monroe County fairgrounds. I was on the front row, me and my girlfriend. I was that guy, yelling, '*Kenny!*' Do you remember me?"

"Er . . . ah . . ."

Mike jumped in quickly, "Jimmy, let's go inside and take a look at the writing rooms."

Kenny smiled and kept going.

I spent that Monday and the rest of the week adjusting to the new job. It was the first time in four years I didn't have to be on guard at work. The company treated me like the new kid at school, giving me all sorts of gifts bearing the company logo: shirts, jackets, hats, music from their catalog, postcards, and other items. I was so impressed by the swag, I wore one of those shirts to work every day, ironed and creased. I was honored and proud to be part of the Opryland Music Group. My dreams were coming true.

Once I settled in at work and home, I sat down and wrote a post-card to every person in my contact book. "Dear Aunt Elaine, I'm in Nashville, trying to make it big. If you'd like to keep in touch, here's my address and telephone number." Of all the postcards I mailed to friends and relatives, other than notes from Patricia and Mama, I received back only two responses—one from DD White and the other from Randy Deal, two men I had guarded in prison.

FOR THE NEXT THREE YEARS I WORKED DILIGENTLY, SEVEN days a week, on my writing, guitar playing, and singing. It was normal for me to spend thirteen hours every day honing my craft. I felt I needed to step up because everyone around me could play guitar and sing well at the same time. They all could write well too.

One of the best career moves I made was taking guitar lessons from Ellen Britton. The first day I arrived at Ellen's house, I sat in the drive-way and debated whether I really wanted to take lessons. I had heard that Ellen was a tough teacher, but she was the best. Did I really want to subject myself to certain humiliation when she heard the way I noodled at guitar playing?

I spent fifteen minutes of my first lesson sitting in her driveway. Ellen must have noticed me from inside because she came to the front door and waved at me. I got out of the car and walked into her music room and into a whole new dimension in my career.

After some small talk, Ellen asked, "Is there any specific song you would like to learn?"

"Yeah, I really love 'Sara Smile,' by Hall and Oates," I replied. I told Ellen how I had found the Daryl Hall and John Oates CD, when I was rummaging through the bargain box at a store in the mall, and how I had fallen in love instantly with it. "Have you heard that song?"

Ellen smiled. "Have I heard it? I've known John Oates since we were kids." She was originally from Philadelphia, and this was her kind of music. She and I hit it off immediately.

She wrote out the chord chart for "Sara Smile" and taught me how to read the chart. She taught me how to read the Nashville number system, the quick notation system used by studio professionals. "We're going to learn the bass line, too, because it all starts from there," Ellen said. I went home and started practicing everything Ellen taught me. Ellen encouraged me to attach a shoulder strap to my guitar and practice while standing up. True to her reputation, Ellen was tough, but she was a great teacher, extremely patient but demanding, satisfied with nothing less than excellence.

Ellen was, and still is, one of the most influential people in my music career. Any success I have achieved musically is directly attributable to Ellen Britton.

After working night and day, writing songs for more than eighteen months without a hit, I ran into a classic case of writer's block. Despite faithfully going to my writer's room at OMG every day and working all day and half the night, I still wasn't writing anything that artists wanted to record. I asked a fellow writer, Mike "Machine Gun" Kelley, what I could do to break the logjam. Mike wrote for another company, but he understood my dilemma. "You need to get out of this office," he said. "Let's go downtown."

"Okay. I'm really not writing any great songs, and I'm miserable. So I might as well go have some fun." For the first time in eighteen months, I took a break and decided to go to downtown Nashville for no real reason. Mike and I roamed around Broadway, checking out the various music venues, but my brain was still in songwriting mode. Standing on the busy corner of 4th Avenue and Broadway, I noticed tourists placing their hands inside the handprints of famous movie and music stars, indented in cement on the wall outside the Planet Hollywood restaurant, now Margaritaville.

When I went back to the office later that evening, images of those handprints stuck in my mind. That's when an idea came to me: I thought of a dad in prison and his little boy tracing his own hand on a piece of paper and giving it to his dad. The son says to his dad, "When you think of me and want to be close, anytime you want to be near me, just put your hand in mine."

I worked on the song idea late into the night and even shared it with a few writers the next day. Nobody got it; they all declined to help write it. "That's stupid, man," one writer said.

"It's not stupid. I know some people who can relate to this kind of experience."

I knew in my heart that it was a great idea, and all I needed was a hit songwriter—and the most successful writer in Nashville was right down the hall from me. Despite Mike Whelan's cautions against bothering Skip Ewing, I felt strongly that I needed to share the idea with him. I held onto the idea for a few weeks and watched for my opportunity to approach Skip.

I knew he was busy writing, but I figured he had to come out of his writing room to go to the bathroom or get a cup of coffee or something, so I positioned myself in the "Picking Parlor," the office coffee area where writers could take a break. I paced back and forth and calculated my approach to Skip. I figured I'd have only a few seconds to catch him and hit him with my idea as he made the trek from the restroom back to his office.

Sure enough, when Skip walked out of his writing room, he went straight for the restroom. I waited outside like a stalker, and the moment he came out, I was in front of him. "Stop!" I said much too loudly.

"What?"

"Skip, I know I'm not supposed to do this, but I have a song idea you need to hear."

Skip turned and looked at me. He seemed irritated, but he looked me right in the eyes and apparently saw my sincerity.

"Okay, come on in." Skip nodded toward his private writing room.

I stepped into Skip's writing room, and I was so nervous I could barely explain the idea. I didn't have any written lyrics, so I simply had to pitch the concept. "There's a kid who traces his hand," I stammered.

"What?" Skip cocked his head and looked at me as though I had dropped in from outer space.

"He traces his hand on a piece of paper and his dad is in prison . . ."

Skip was looking at me with a look that said, *How am I going to get this guy out of my room?*

I quickly blurted the rest of the idea. "The kid gives his dad the tracing of his hand, and says, 'Dad, put your hand in mine, and I'll be there anytime.'"

Skip closed the door and turned back to look at me. "That's as strong as a new piece of rope," he said emphatically. "Let's plan a writing appointment and write this idea."

I was in shock. Not because I didn't think he would like my idea but because I remembered sitting on the floor at Bea's in 1994, wishing, wondering, *What would it be like to write a song with this guy?*

For the next several weeks all I could think about was the opportunity to write a song with Skip Ewing. Although Skip liked my idea, it was several months before we finally got together to work on the song. But once we got started, it didn't take long before we came up with something good. Skip stood at the piano, and I sat on the couch, holding a notepad, my guitar nearby. We wrote the song in about two and a half hours that same day.

The company pitched the song to a bunch of producers, and on May 12, 1999, "Put Your Hand in Mine" was placed on hold for country star Tracy Byrd. Tracy was a "hat guy," and he was cranking out some hits. I was thrilled, but lots of songs get put on hold as an artist, producer, and music company consider them. That doesn't necessarily mean they will ever be recorded. But on June 2, 1999, Tracy Byrd recorded "Put Your Hand in Mine." The song soon climbed the country radio charts.

I was backing into the parking lot of Armos gym when I heard a familiar piano intro on my car radio. *I know that song!* I thought. I was so excited. It was the first time I ever heard "Put Your Hand in Mine" on the radio. That night I called Patricia and told her about hearing my song.

"Really?"

"Yeah, it really was on the radio," I said, barely able to contain my excitement.

"Are you sure it wasn't in your tape player?" Patricia asked.

"No! It was on the radio."

Sure enough, the song stayed on the radio. Every week for the next thirty weeks, I listened and recorded the Top 40 Country Countdown, waiting to see where "Put Your Hand in Mine" charted. It peaked at number nine on the charts; it was surreal to hear my name in there with all the country greats. Some dreams really do come true!

Thirty-four

YOU NEVER KNOW

THE SUCCESS OF "PUT YOUR HAND IN MINE" RESULTED IN new opportunities for me to work with other writers. By now I had written more than two hundred songs but had only one hit. I was still feeling cocky when OMG teamed me up with a visiting writer from New York. Sitting in a writing room behind the piano, he said, "Play me something you've written."

"Okay, sure," I said, and I played him "Put Your Hand in Mine." With my chest pumped up a bit, I turned the tables on him. "Now you play me something you've written," I said.

"Oh, okay," he replied. He played a simple piano intro and went into "Where everybody knows your name . . . ," the theme song from the hit television show *Cheers*. At the height of show's popularity, the song was played every day of the year in forty countries. In addition to that Emmy-nominated song, Gary Portnoy, the New York writer, had written hits for Dolly Parton and Air Supply, as well as the theme for the NBC sitcom *Punky Brewster*. I swallowed my pride; after discovering how successful Gary was, I was totally intimidated. We never did write a song that day.

ABOUT A YEAR LATER A PROBLEM CAME UP WHEN I WAS asked to concede a larger portion of my publishing royalties to a co-writer. I was a young writer in my midtwenties, and I had recently worked in prison. I wasn't very diplomatic, and I didn't realize that the music business is a small, close-knit group. I had not yet learned to play the music business game. So I refused.

I became persona non grata at that company from that day forward. A few months later, despite having a hit song and having earned enough royalties already to recoup the company's investment in me, OMG did not exercise my next option—which is publishing lingo for saying, "You're fired." Although I was disappointed, the news didn't come as a surprise.

I HIT THE STREETS LOOKING FOR A NEW SONGWRITING deal. Even with a hit song, those deals often take time, so for the next two weeks or so, I floundered, unemployed. I began to worry about how I was going to pay my rent.

Meanwhile, Jason Payne, an acquaintance of mine, called and asked me to participate in a "songwriters in the round" event at his hair salon. (Hey, it's Nashville; you never know where the next great talent might be found!) With writers in the round, one writer tells the story of how he or she wrote a song and then performs it. Then the next writer does the same. Since many writers aren't performing artists, the writers will often pitch in and help sing and play one another's hit songs. Nashville songwriters share a strong sense of camaraderie unlike anything I have experienced in any other part of the world.

As much as I was always glad to help out, I had just lost my publishing deal, so I was in no mood to entertain an audience. "Man, I am so depressed, I don't even feel like coming out of the apartment," I tried to beg off.

But Jason talked me into participating in the round, and my plans were to leave as soon as I was done playing. It was an awkward writers' night, with people crammed in the salon, and the sound system was horrible.

One of the writers in the round that evening was Steven Dale Jones. Steven had written hits for Reba McEntire, Diamond Rio, Josh Turner, and numerous other artists. His wife, Allison Jones, was the director of Artists & Repertoire at DreamWorks Records. Allison was in the audience that night, as was one of her coworkers, Jim Catino.

I performed a handful of songs and was just going through the motions, being a seat filler since I had only one hit at the time. Toward the end of the round, as I always did at such events, I said, "I didn't write this song, but I like it," and I performed "Sara Smile."

Allison had already passed on me when I was at OMG, so she didn't show any interest in me at all. Jim Catino, however, came up to me afterward, handed me his contact information, and said, "You sang 'Sara Smile' very well. Call me tomorrow."

I called Jim the next day, and he invited me to stop by the publishing company to perform a few songs I'd written. I dropped in and performed some songs, but nothing impressed him. As I was getting ready to leave, songwriter Chris Lindsey walked in.

Chris had written big hits for artists such as Faith Hill and Tim McGraw; he also cowrote the song "Amazed" for the group Lonestar. Jim introduced us and asked me to perform "Sara Smile" for Chris.

When I finished, Chris and I talked briefly, and he was quite complimentary but gave no indication what he had in mind.

Late the following night, Chris called me and said, "Hey, Jimmy, this is Chris, the guy you met at Jim's office yesterday. Will you sing a demo for me tomorrow morning at ten o'clock?"

"Ah, sure!" I said, but thinking at the same time, *Oh, no; this is going to be a disaster since I've had no time to learn the song Chris wants me to record.*

But the next morning, after several stout cups of coffee, I stood in the vocal booth at County Q recording studio, holding a lyric sheet, and I recorded a demo called "Are You Ever Going to Love Me?" I thought Chris needed a vocal demo to pitch the song to some artist.

For the next week I spent a lot of time in meetings at DreamWorks and listening to songs that Jim Catino thought were hits. I had no clue what he was doing, and I was wondering why he was playing me these songs when I needed a publishing deal. I enjoyed the music and Jim's friendship, but I really didn't care that he liked other writers' songs. I wanted him to like *my* songs and offer me a publishing deal. But he didn't.

Jim asked me several times that week if I'd consider working with Chris Lindsey, maybe have Chris produce a few of these songs on me, which meant that Chris would record me performing the songs.

I declined because I had made an informal agreement to record with another producer in town. But I hadn't heard from him since I parted ways with OMG, so I wasn't sure if he still wanted to do it. I had called him repeatedly, but my calls always went to voice mail.

That same week I was stopped at the traffic light on 17th Avenue and Wedgewood, and I saw that producer sitting in his GMC Yukon at the light, facing me in oncoming traffic. I called him and watched him pick up his cell phone to see who was calling. He looked at the phone as it was ringing and laid his phone back down beside him. From the opposite side of the intersection, I watched him purposely not take my call.

That's when I knew he was avoiding me. I called Jim and told him I was interested in working with Chris.

A FEW DAYS LATER I WAS IN JIM'S OFFICE WHEN CHRIS Lindsey walked in. We talked briefly, and Chris asked if I would walk upstairs and meet someone. I followed him up the steps to Scott Borchetta's office.

I didn't know who this guy was. I'd never even heard of him. He looked like a mad scientist, with his frizzy hair. He was standing behind his desk, wearing a headset and talking on the phone; it sounded as though he was talking with someone who worked in radio. Scott flipped the mouthpiece back away from his face and introduced himself.

"I really liked the demo you sang for Chris," he said, between breaks in his phone conversation.

"Thank you," I replied, trying not to speak too loudly, so as not to be heard on his headset mic.

I didn't know why I was in his office. I assumed I was there to discuss a publishing deal since that's what I told Jim Catino I needed. I figured the "Chris thing" was a long-term project and might never happen. My paramount thought was, *I need a publishing deal so I can pay my rent.*

When Scott got off the phone, he said, "Play me something."

Instinctively, I played "Sara Smile," despite the fact that I didn't write it, which probably seemed odd. After all, why would a writer showcase someone else's song if he were trying to get a songwriter's publishing deal?

But when I finished, Scott said, "You can't leave here until you sign with us."

Hey, great! I thought, although I didn't really understand what he meant because it didn't sound as though he was offering me a standard publishing deal. I was too naive to realize that I had just been offered a recording deal with a major Nashville music company. It never even crossed my mind since that wasn't why I was there. Nevertheless, Scott and I shook hands, and I left.

Later that afternoon Chris Lindsey called me and congratulated me. "Aren't you excited, Jimmy?" he asked.

"About what? Why, what happened?

"You got a record deal! Aren't you excited?"

"What?"

In that very moment, sitting in my four-door, beat-up, blue Honda Civic, I felt as though I had just won the lottery.

"What?" I asked again. "Are you kidding me?"

"No, I'm not joking. You just got a recording deal on DreamWorks," Chris said.

I was all by myself; Tonia was working, and I had planned to eat at

LongHorn Steakhouse, so that's where I celebrated my first recording deal, with a large glass of sweet tea and a sweet potato.

I glanced up at a television screen in the restaurant and noticed the Atlanta Braves were playing baseball. The man on the pitcher's mound looked vaguely familiar. When he turned to hurl his next pitch, I saw the name on the back of his uniform: Millwood. I could hardly believe my eyes. It was Kevin Millwood, pitching for the Atlanta Braves.

I thought back to when I was about twenty-one years old, and Kevin and I had once sat on the tailgate of an old pickup truck, talking about some of our dreams. "What do you want to do?" Kevin asked me.

"Man, I'd love to be a country music singer." We both laughed. "What about you? What are your dreams? What do you want to do when you graduate from college?"

"Well, I'd like to be a Major League Baseball player," Kevin said.

Now I was watching a ballgame on television, and Kevin Millwood was pitching for the Braves—and the other guy on the back of that pickup truck, a kid named Jimmy Wayne Barber, had just stepped into the world of country music, alongside some of the biggest names in the business.

CHRIS LINDSEY CALLED ME THE FOLLOWING DAY AND SAID that James Stroud, the president of DreamWorks Records, wanted to meet me. So on April 17, 2001, I met with James Stroud at DreamWorks. I sat on the couch in his office. James pulled a chair right up in front of me. He sat facing me, with his knees almost touching mine. And then it was as though he forgot I was there, ignoring me completely while talking shop to Chris. When I reached for my guitar, James laughed and said, "Oh, are you gonna play me something?"

"Yes, sir," I said. I immediately started picking "Sara Smile."

As soon as I finished performing, James clapped his hands together once, stood up, and said, "Let's get to work." That was the end of our meeting. I packed up my guitar as fast as I could and exited the building.

A few days after the worst day in American history, September 11, 2001, I received both a recording contract and a publishing deal from DreamWorks. Thus began one of the most tumultuous rides of my life.

Thirty-five

WHO ME?
A COUNTRY STAR?

JUST AFTER THANKSGIVING WEEKEND 2001, I BEGAN RECORD-
ing my first album for DreamWorks at Ocean Way Studios in Nashville.
The album was produced by Chris Lindsey along with James Stroud.
The first song I recorded, while still looking for other songs for the
album, was "Sara Smile." That song, however, didn't make it onto the
first album, but another very special song did.

I HAD SUSPECTED TROUBLE IN PATRICIA'S MARRIAGE AS FAR
back as when I was living with Bea. One time, Patricia and her husband
were sitting in Bea's driveway when I noticed a bruise on Patricia's face.

"Hey, what happened to your face?" I asked.

"Oh, I just bumped it," Patricia said.

I looked at her suspiciously. "Are you sure?"

"Yeah," she replied, but I knew she was unwilling to say more in
front of Steven. I later learned that throughout their marriage, he had
been violently hitting her. A few years after I moved to Nashville, I
received a desperate call from Patricia. "I need some help," she said.

She asked me to come and get her out. "Pack a bag," I said. "I'll be there as soon as I can."

When I learned that Patricia was being abused by her husband, I took the first flight to Charlotte. I had never before flown in an airplane, but I wanted to get there as fast as possible. After landing in Charlotte, I rented a car at the airport and drove like a madman to Patricia's house.

When I walked in her house, my presence must have surprised her husband. He ran to the bedroom and came back out wielding a gun. "She's not going anywhere!" he yelled.

"Oh, yes, she is," I said, and walked Patricia out of the house. He had an easy shot if he wanted it, but fortunately, he didn't shoot.

Patricia was petrified with fear as she and her son, Brian, got in the car, and I drove them away and set them up in an apartment. Following their divorce, Patricia moved farther away in an effort to keep some distance between her and her abuser, not an easy feat since her former husband was also the father of her son.

A number of months later I was driving through Nashville's Green Hills area when I received a phone call from Patricia. "He's found out where I live."

"Is there anything I can do?" I asked.

"No," she said, "I wish he would just stay gone, and I'd be fine." Her words ripped my heart out, yet they also resonated with me. I wanted to write a song that would encourage her. A songwriter, Billy Kirsch, had contacted me about writing together, so I pitched the idea for the song to him. I had little more than the idea and a melody line, and even on that, I was mimicking Michael McDonald. But Billy caught what I was trying to do, and he sat at the piano and came up with the hook, "Baby, baby, stay . . ." Billy and I wrote the song, and I sent it to Patricia. "I hope this helps," I wrote in a note to her.

We turned in the song for my producers to consider, and the song tested high. "We'd like you to record it," Scott Borchetta said. Even before we recorded the other songs on the album, Scott said, "This is going to be your first single."

The record company released "Stay Gone" to radio in January 2003, and by February 10, it hit the charts, debuting at number thirty-four, with more radio stations adding it to their playlists every day.

Patricia called me, and she was whispering. "I was in the textile mill," she said, "and the guy on the radio said they are going to play a new song by a hometown boy that he wrote for his sister. So I came out here to the car, and I'm lying down in the seat, hiding from the boss, to listen to it." About that time, I heard the WSOC deejay's voice on Patricia's radio in the background. "Coming up next, we have 'Stay Gone,' by Jimmy Wayne." What an experience! Listening to the song that I had written for Patricia along with her the first time she heard it on the radio—both of us were overcome with emotion, and our tears flowed freely.

"Stay Gone" went up the charts, all the way to number three and remained there for three weeks. My music career took off like a bullet, following the song up the *Billboard* charts.

On March 21, 2003, I performed at the world-famous Grand Ole Opry for the first time. Adding to the excitement and my nervousness, the show was broadcast live on WSM radio. Before I began my first song, I stopped at center stage and said, "Excuse me for a moment, folks. I want to write this down in my journal." And I did, writing the date and time I first played the world's longest-running music-based radio show.

In May, I opened a show for Dwight Yoakam in Chicago one night and for Don Williams in Salt Lake City the next. A few weeks later, on June 3, 2003, I performed for the first time on the stage of Nashville's famous Ryman Auditorium, the original home of the Grand Ole Opry. Playing the Ryman is a dream of every country musician, as well as bands such as Lynyrd Skynyrd, ZZ Top, and the Doobie Brothers. That night I opened for a rising country superstar, Keith Urban.

On Sunday, June 15, 2003, I met Scott Borchetta at DreamWorks, and he handed me a copy of my very first CD. Tears welled in my eyes as I looked at some of my own song titles, which included "Stay Gone,"

"After You," and "Paper Angels," a song based on a story about the paper angels on a mall Christmas tree, alluding to the Angel Tree program that provides gifts to needy children at Christmastime through the Salvation Army—the group that gave me my first guitar. On that same album was another special song, one that Don Sampson helped me to write: "I Love You This Much," about a boy who sought love from his dad, and although he never found it, he eventually discovered that God's constant love had been there all the time. As I thought about the unusual way this album of special songs had come together, I realized I was holding my first CD on Father's Day.

THE EXCITEMENT CONTINUED FOR ME THROUGHOUT THE summer of 2003. In late June, I performed three shows in El Paso and received standing ovations at every show. Then on July 4, I performed again at the Grand Ole Opry in Nashville, this time backed by the Opry's amazing musicians.

Midmonth, I opened for Patty Loveless in Atlanta. This was a special concert for me since Patty and I had grown up in the same area. Patty was doing her sound check but stopped right in the middle of it to give me a hug. I was blown away when she said, "Jimmy, I bought your record. It's great!" We talked briefly about the old days, when she had lived in a brown trailer on Second Street. We had both come a long way.

The very next day, after the concert with Patty in Atlanta, I received word that "Stay Gone" had achieved number one status on the Country Music Television (CMT) network. Considering all the great songs and videos out there, to think that the song I had written for Patricia was the most requested song on CMT was truly humbling and fabulously exciting.

Of course, the music business has its own way of keeping a person humble. While "Stay Gone" was receiving a lot of airplay, I was driving in Nashville one day when a pretty young woman in a BMW convertible sitting at the traffic light glanced over at me in my banged up Honda Civic. Tonia and I had broken up months earlier, so I smiled real big at the woman in the convertible. She rolled her eyes and drove off while singing along to "Stay Gone" on her radio. So much for having a hit song!

With the excitement over the album and the success of "Stay Gone," the record company scheduled a video shoot for "I Love You This Much" on July 18, 2003. About a week before the shoot, I walked outside my apartment on Music Row and saw a homeless guy in the alley, scavenging for food in one of the large trash bins. His arms were dirty, and I noticed his hands were cut from digging through the garbage. When I saw him, I tried not to make eye contact with him. Too late.

"Hey," he called out. "Are you Jimmy Wayne?"

Oh, man, I thought. *He's going to ask me for money.*

"Yeah, I am," I answered reluctantly.

He was a large man but had a high-pitched, squeaky voice. "I saw some of your promo posters in the garbage can over there, so I recognized you," he said. "Can I have your autograph? I heard your song 'Stay Gone,' and it really helped me."

I was intrigued. "Really? How?"

"I lost my wife and kid in a car accident, and the song helped me get through it. You know, when you hurt like that, you want the pain to go away, to stay gone."

His story touched my heart. "I have to tell you, I wasn't expecting that from you," I told him. "I thought you were going to ask me for money. I was trying to ignore you. I'm sorry. Please forgive me."

"No problem," the big guy said.

"Stay right here a minute," I said. "I want to get something." I went into my apartment and grabbed my journal. I took it back outside and handed it to the homeless man. "Would you do me a favor? Would you sign my journal? I want *your* autograph."

He signed my journal and filled an entire page with his musings. At the close, he signed his name, "John."

I saw John every so often, and he never asked me for anything. One day I saw him outside again. "Hey, Jimmy," he called. "I got you something," John said. He pulled out a brand-new journal. "I noticed that the spine of your journal was broken, so I got you a new one."

I couldn't believe it. This guy was digging through garbage to survive, and he had gotten me a journal. I thanked him profusely then asked, "What are you doing tomorrow?"

"Digging in the dumpster," he responded.

"Do you think you can get a suit somewhere, and maybe clean up just a bit?"

"Maybe."

"Well, if you can, I'm shooting a new music video tomorrow, and I want you to be in it." I gave him the shoot details.

The following day I was standing around a spread of food with a bunch of crew and publicists at the video location, when in walked John—wearing a suit. "Hey, John, great to see you," I greeted him. "Hey, everybody, this is my friend John."

"Hey, John," they all went to great lengths to make him feel welcome, hugging him, blowing air kisses, and offering him food. Nobody knew that John was homeless, so they treated him like a star. John stood around eating finger foods from the same plates as everyone else. I chuckled to myself as I watched some of the "plastic people" hugging a homeless guy who had been digging in the dumpster the day before. We had a great time, and I made sure John was seen in the video of "I Love You This Much." He did a good job.

Following his appearance in my video, John was asked by various producers to do other videos. Because of his large physical size, he made an appearance in the audience of the television show *The Biggest Loser*. He actually started making some money.

A few months later I saw John again. "I got ya something," he told me. "I was at the Johnny Cash estate sale, and I bought this for you." He handed me an old suitcase. Unbelievable. The guy who had been digging in the dumpster handed me a suitcase that had once belonged to Johnny Cash. "I can't believe you took a chance on me," he said.

"John, I really didn't do anything," I said.

"Yes, you did. Being in your video gave me a new start in life," he told me. "And I just want to say thanks."

I WAS STILL ON A ROLL THROUGHOUT JULY AND AUGUST 2003. I opened for Vince Gill a couple of nights in Boston and received standing ovations both nights. Attending one of the shows was rock-and-roll icon Steven Tyler. He was obviously there to hear Vince, but I was thrilled to meet him.

A few weeks later the video for "I Love You This Much" debuted at number one on CMT, as the most requested song of the week. That was incredible, but even more meaningful to me was a letter I received from a fellow in Indianapolis. He wrote:

Jimmy,

I just want to let you know your music has made a difference in my life. I was down on life, my wife had left me for another man after 21 years together, and we have a 4-year-old son that means so much to me. I started thinking about suicide. I bought the gun, rope, pills, and so on to do this when I was alone, since nothing was stopping me. Not the thought of family, friends, my son—nothing.

On Sunday evening, November 9th, I had the plan to go ahead. I sat on my couch in the living room with my gun in my hand from 1:00 a.m. till Monday morning at 7:45, but I never did it. I turned my TV on, and your video came on: "I Love You This Much," and I saw the little boy with his arms wide open, saying does my Daddy love me, and I just stopped and stared at my TV. I watched the whole thing and cried so hard, asking myself why I was even trying to do this. Really silly on my part, because he is a great kid, and smart. . . .

I bought your CD, and it is great. All the music on it hits my heart and soul. You really did save my life that day. And when I get that thought, I play that song over and over, and it keeps me here with him . . . so Jimmy, keep up the good songwriting and singing. You really did save my life.

That letter reminded me why I wanted to become a musician, and it really helped put the business in perspective for me.

NEVERTHELESS, NO MATTER HOW HARD YOU TRY TO MAIN-
tain perspective, the music business will change you, and *success* in the music business will change you even more. Before I knew it, I got caught up in it, as do so many others. After a while I started believing my own press and thinking I really was something special. The label didn't mind; I was selling about ten thousand units a week, and it was making money, which seemed to be all that mattered. But God had some interesting ways of keeping me humble.

For instance, when I appeared at an event sponsored by WQYK, featuring Charlie Daniels, in Tampa Bay, people in the crowd were screaming their heads off, and I was eating it up. Then I looked over and saw a Jumbotron showing a replay of the Tampa Bay Buccaneers scoring a touchdown. I thought the fans had been cheering for me!

To add to my swelling ego, in September 2003, I was selected to team up with world-class photographer Russ Harrington to do a photo shoot for *People* magazine's "Sexiest Man Alive" issue. Russ is known as a photographer to the stars and has photographed everyone, from Faith Hill to Loretta Lynn to Reba McEntire to Alan Jackson to Alison Krauss to Brooks and Dunn. I never had considered myself *sexy*, so I felt awkward and wasn't quite sure how I was supposed to look. But Russ's professionalism helped ease my concerns, and instead of looking silly, by trying to pose in some provocative way, Russ posed me fully clothed, in a tasteful manner, and the photos turned out fairly well. When the issue came out in December that year, I was surprised to see myself in the same magazine as George Clooney, Johnny Depp, and others.

The week the magazine hit the stands, I was on a flight and seated right next to an attractive woman who was looking at a copy of the issue. She was flipping through the magazine, and when she came to George Clooney's photo, it appeared that she was almost salivating. She stared at George for what seemed like five minutes. I wondered how she might respond when she realized that she was sitting right next to one of the so-called sexiest men in America. I thought, *Any minute now, the oxygen mask is going to fall from the ceiling, and I'm going to have to resuscitate this lady. She's almost kissing the pages.* She caressed the photos of George Clooney and Johnny Depp, and I continued watching her, thinking, *Any second now, she's going to turn the page and get to me.* She finally flipped to my picture, barely gave it a quick glance, and quickly turned the page. No need for any mouth-to-mouth. That was a much-needed reality check for me.

2003 WAS A GREAT YEAR FOR ME. "STAY GONE" WON AN award for being the most played song in the music business that year, in all genres. "I Love You This Much" was also a top ten hit, while two other songs on my first album, "Paper Angels" and "You Are," made the top twenty.

The following year, "Paper Angels" was one of the most played songs during the Christmas season. The song was the highest charting seasonal track in country music history, surpassing the record set by Dolly Parton's "Hard Candy Christmas" in 1982. The video we made depicting the storyline of the song was so helpful in promoting the Salvation Army's Angel Tree program that I was honored by the Salvation Army as the youngest person ever to receive the William Booth Award for my efforts to help needy children.

Life was looking good for me. Like a kite darting ever higher in the sky, my career continued to rise; but what I didn't know, and was about to find out, was that the people holding the strings were coming down.

Thirty-six

HOUSE OF CARDS

As early as November 2003, I began hearing rumors that my record label, DreamWorks Nashville, might disappear, merging into Mercury and MCA record companies, two labels owned by Universal Music Group. DreamWorks was originally the brainchild of Hollywood movie magnates Steven Spielberg and Jeffrey Katzenberg and music mogul David Geffen. While Geffen also enjoyed success in the film business, producing hits such as *Little Shop of Horrors*, *Risky Business*, and other envelope-pushing movies, he is best known for founding Asylum Records, where he recorded artists such as Jackson Browne, the Eagles, and Linda Ronstadt. He went on to form Geffen Records, which released John Lennon's album *Double Fantasy* the same month he was shot and killed. Geffen later released albums by Elton John, Nirvana, Cher, Aerosmith, Peter Gabriel, and a host of other highly successful artists. If anyone could make DreamWorks work, the three communications wizards should have been able to do it. Yet for some reason, the label was floundering.

At the time of the merger, the label's biggest artist was Toby Keith, whose career had been revived with the help of Scott Borchetta's promotional abilities, resulting in albums such as *How Do You Like Me Now?* and three other hugely successful projects. Other artists on the label were

Darryl Worley, Emerson Drive, and Jessica Andrews. I was busy writing songs and getting my career on a solid foundation, so I wasn't paying much attention to the reshuffling going on all around me, and it hadn't really affected me—yet.

I was excited because I was about to go out on the road as part of a major tour, opening for the popular band Lonestar. With the success of my first album, Scott Borchetta had suggested, "Jimmy, you really need to get a manager." I interviewed a number of potential management companies and decided to sign on with Borman Entertainment in Nashville and, in particular, with Joni Foraker, who also managed Faith Hill, Trace Adkins, Keith Urban, James Taylor, and Lonestar. So when Lonestar was going out on their Front Porch Looking In Tour, Joni put me on it.

Touring as a musical artist was a whole new experience for me. Joni arranged a deal in which I could rent Faith Hill's tour bus. I didn't have a band, so it was just the bus driver and one other person on the bus—a former member of the pop-rock group Dakota, Rick Manwiller, who served as my road manager and sound engineer. The bus was gorgeous, replete with a shower, televisions, refrigerator, and living and sleeping areas. It had everything I could possibly need. Rick had most of the front of the bus, and I lived in the back for several months.

I had grown up in trailer parks and had spent several weeks in Uncle Austin's freezing cold trailer with no electricity, heat, or water. Now, here I was in the ultimate rolling trailer home, a million-dollar motor coach with all the comforts of a luxury hotel. Except for going onstage, I could live in the bus and not come out!

I was nervous performing my first few concerts. I had sung at writers' nights and small-town events, but now I was stepping onstage in auditoriums, where people were paying money to see and hear a good show. My song selection wasn't the best at first. I performed songs that I liked rather than appealing to the crowd. It didn't take me long, however, to discover that the audiences were interested in hearing about Bea and how she and Russell had saved my life. They liked my stories that set up my songs, and the songs that illustrated the stories. Naturally, some people in the business said, "Jimmy, don't talk so much. You need to play more and talk less." I tried it. I went out and simply played some songs. But for me, that didn't work. Sharing my heart with the audience was a major part of what I wanted to do.

The guys in Lonestar treated me like a younger brother, and we got along great. They were young guys with good-old-boy attitudes and strong work ethics. They were kind to me and made me feel welcome. They also knew when to keep things lighthearted, and they were good pranksters. One night I took the stage to open the show only to discover that one of the Lonestar guys had coated my microphone in hot sauce. I started coughing and sputtering so badly I couldn't even sing. For the first ten minutes of my thirty-minute set, I was choking and wiping tears out of my eyes. The audience could tell something was up. Meanwhile the guys were laughing hysterically offstage.

I got even, though, later that night, when Lonestar gathered at the front of the stage to sing one of their biggest hits, "Amazed." Since it was the Front Porch Looking In Tour, they had a mock cabin and front porch as part of the stage set. So at one of the most serious parts of "Amazed," the audience saw some crazy guy in the doorway of the set, dressed in nothing but his underwear and cowboy boots. The audience started laughing and pointing at the figure in the doorway. I heard that the guy in his underwear looked a lot like me. I can tell you this much: it sure is hard to run in cowboy boots!

I was so green as an artist that I didn't even know I was able to sell merchandise. Midway through the tour, Lonestar's merchandise manager said to me, "Jimmy, if you want to put some CDs or other product out here on the tables, I can sell them for you, and you can just pay me a commission on whatever I sell."

"Really? Hey, that's a great idea." I bought some CDs, and from then on the merch guy made money for me every night.

Nobody from DreamWorks seemed interested in participating in the tour support. What I didn't know was the merger details had sent everyone scrambling. Although nobody verbalized it, the attitude was,

*The company is closing, so why worry about trying to sell product? We're
concerned about our jobs.*

Meanwhile, I was becoming more and more caught up in the new
world of big-time music. I truly believed that I could do anything I
wanted, that I was Superman, and that I couldn't fail. Everyone was telling me how great I was, so it quickly went to my head. I was street-smart,
so maybe that's why I didn't drink or do drugs, but I wasn't prepared for
all the female attention I received. Every teenage male fantasy became
available to me. I had grown up in small towns in North Carolina; I'd
had only two serious relationships with girls, so I was relatively naive
regarding the temptations of women throwing themselves at me, and I'm
sorry to say that I made some serious mistakes in that regard.

Before I knew it, I had fallen headfirst into the pig trough. I learned
the hard way that if a person is going to be involved in the entertainment
business, he or she better be spiritually strong and take every precaution
to avoid the evil and choose the good. It's possible to do that, but it takes
more than mere human willpower. It takes God's power. And it requires
some common sense to surround yourself with good people, to avoid
compromising situations, to call your friends or family after the show,
and to position yourself for success rather than failure. I'm ashamed to
say that at the time, I didn't do any of that.

At my weakest points, people always came up to me, pouring their
hearts out, telling me how God was using my music and stories to touch
their lives.

One night a muscular, tough-looking guy came up to the merchandise table after a show and slammed his fist on the table. "I just want to
tell you something," he said loudly.

"Yes, sir?" I said, as I noticed my road manager easing closer, just in
case.

"That song you sing, 'I Love You This Much' . . . I have a daughter,
and she's never going to have to live without a dad." Suddenly the enormous man started crying and spilling his guts to me. I understood that
his daughter meant everything to him, and I realized that some of the

girls I had been messing around with could easily be his daughter. I felt convicted and knew I needed to get right.

By the time I finished the Lonestar tour, the DreamWorks merger was complete, and my career was jammed into neutral. I thought that since I had already signed with the label and had several hit songs, I would be welcomed into a thriving relationship with the new label heads. That proved unrealistic on my part, and reality soon punctured the balloons of my idealism.

ON MAY 7, 2004, DREAMWORKS MERGED WITH UNIVERSAL, Mercury, and MCA Records. Universal's chairman and CEO, Luke Lewis, and DreamWorks Nashville's president, James Stroud, were to serve as cochairmen of the company, with artists such as Toby Keith, George Strait, Reba McEntire, Vince Gill, Lee Ann Womack, Trisha Yearwood, Gary Allan, Josh Turner, Shania Twain, and others now all under one roof.

I called James Stroud and asked him about my future. "What's going on?" I asked. "Where am I going to be? What label do you think will be a good match for me?"

James was uncharacteristically vague. "We don't know yet, Jimmy. We'll just have to wait and see." Worse yet, shortly after the new year, in the middle of working on the follow-up album to my initial effort with four hit songs on it, James Stroud fired Chris Lindsey as producer of my second album. That should have told me something, but I was still optimistic about my future with the new music consortium. I appealed to Stroud to have Chris reinstated as my producer, and James acquiesced, but I sensed trouble.

Scott Borchetta became head of promotions for both labels, so that made me feel a little better. I trusted Scott. He and I were more than business colleagues; we were friends. I knew that Scott believed in me. But Scott's future with the label was soon in jeopardy as well.

In March 2005, I met with Scott and played him a new song,

"Whatever Makes You Happy." He loved it. "I'm going to get Luke Lewis," he said excitedly. "I want him to hear this." Scott came back without Luke. The look on his face was telling. Something wasn't right.

Two days later I called Scott at home, and he sounded as though his world had collapsed. "I got fired this morning," he told me. Scott didn't say so, but I couldn't imagine the new label keeping me around either, now that Scott was gone.

Despite all the turmoil in the music company, I continued writing songs for my new album and performing at every opportunity throughout the spring and summer.

Spurred on, and with Chris Lindsey back on the project, I rerecorded "Sara Smile" at Ocean Way Studios in June. In August, I was still waiting on answers from Stroud as to whether we were moving forward or not. I was set to record tracks on several new songs within two weeks. But with DreamWorks now officially dissolved, I was an artist without a home.

In early September I finally called Stroud again. "Am I in or out?" I asked.

"You're in," he answered brusquely.

"Where? What label?"

"Maybe MCA. We're not sure yet."

In early October I was sitting in a restaurant when Mike Robertson, from my new management company, walked in and sat down across from me. "I have some bad news, Jimmy," he said. "I just received a call from the label saying they've dropped you."

"What?" I could hardly believe my ears. Just a few days earlier, Universal had indicated we were moving forward. Now they were dumping me? I called Scott Borchetta and told him the news. His response was simple. "Come home, Jimmy. Come home."

Following his dismissal from DreamWorks, Scott had been working throughout the summer to obtain funding for a new record company, a little label he called Big Machine Records. Toby Keith partnered with Scott for a while and then moved on to another label. Unfortunately for Scott, when Toby pulled out, so did potential investors.

While I was still wondering where I was going to land, Scott occasionally called me with an odd request. "Jimmy, I need you to come over and do a few songs for some friends. I just want you to come in and sing, and then leave. Don't talk, just sing." I was glad to help Scott any way that I could. After all, he was one of the first guys to help me. So I dutifully responded any time he called. I'd go in, meet his friends from Albany or New York or Pittsburgh, sing a few songs, and leave. I didn't realize it at the time, but Scott was scrambling for investors, and his time was running out. It takes a lot of money to build a new record label from scratch, and even a guy as talented as Scott couldn't do it without somebody putting up some major money.

In May 2006, I signed a recording contract with Big Machine Records, Scott's new label. Although I had reunited with the best promotions guy in Nashville, reviving my career was not a sure thing. I met with Scott and Mark Bright, my new producer, and we decided that once we had the songs we wanted, we'd go into the studio and record them.

During this time, Scott was extremely stressed. I could tell something was really bothering him. He'd come to my apartment on Music Row, and we'd sit in his Porsche, listening to songs he was pitching me to record. We finally settled on four songs, so in June 2006, I began tracking sessions at Starstruck Studios, the recording complex on Music Row originally built for Reba McEntire.

In mid-July I wrote a new song called "That's All I'll Ever Need," did a rough demo of the song, and took it in to Scott's office so he could hear it. The demo was recorded one step too high for my voice, so it was hard to sing in that key, but I figured if Scott liked the demo, Mark and I could recut it in the correct key, and it would sound even better. Scott liked the song. "That should be your next single, Jimmy," he said.

I tried to convince Scott to let me recut the song since the demo was too high for me to sing onstage every night, but Scott seemed convinced the song was a hit, just as we had recorded it. "That song is like lightning in a bottle," Scott said, "and we may not be able to capture it twice."

I trusted Scott. We were inseparable buddies, working together all over Nashville; we talked by phone or communicated by text messages nearly every day. But for the first time in our friendship and business relationship, I sensed trouble, something about Scott I hadn't seen before. It was as if he was operating in survival mode.

I'd been there, and I knew that feeling very well. I recognized that look.

Over the next few days Scott informed the label about my first single and arranged for me to meet fashion designer Sandi Spika Borchetta and the label's website guy for a photo shoot. Things were moving rapidly. Within a week the CD was out the door. The label moved forward with its efforts to promote the song, but it flopped as soon as it shipped.

Despite our disappointment, we went back into Starstruck and recorded three more songs—"Belongs to You," Counting the Days," and "All the Time in the World"—in an attempt to reestablish my reputation with radio and help Scott save his label.

In the midst of our promotion efforts, I received a call from Scott.

"Hey, Jimm . . . aay," Scott greeted me. I knew something was up since Scott only pronounced my name like that when he was in a good mood. I could tell he was excited about something.

"I've just signed this new artist," he said. "She's only fourteen years old, but listen to these lyrics she wrote." Scott proceeded to read some lyrics over the phone. I was standing at the kitchen sink in my apartment, listening to the excitement in his voice more than the lyrics. I was thrilled for Scott because he was my friend. He deserved success after all his hard work—especially after the manner in which James and Luke had dumped him.

Plus, I knew that if Scott won, I won. Even on our worst days, we still dreamed about making albums together for years to come. "Jimmy, we'll make many records together," Scott always reassured me. I believed him because we were friends. Scott knew that I would always support him, and I knew that Scott had my back, no matter what.

He was still prattling on about the lyrics, something about "When

I think Tim McGraw." Scott read the entire song to me over the phone. "She's going to be a star," he said.

I believed Scott, not because of the teenager's lyrics but simply because Scott said so. I was genuinely happy for him. It was great to hear him gushing about a new artist after he'd been down for months. I congratulated him, hung up the phone, and went back to work.

Several days went by, and I didn't hear from Scott. That was unusual. Several weeks went by, and I still hadn't heard from him, and he wasn't returning my calls even though I knew he was in town. I decided to drop by the label offices and see what was going on.

As soon as I walked into the office foyer, I saw large, framed pictures of a young girl lining the hallway. She was stunning and looked like a superstar already. Those photos had not been there a few weeks earlier. I proceeded to Scott's office and there sat a skinny young girl with golden curly hair. She looked something like the girl in the photos, and she was holding a guitar. "Hi, my name is Taylor," she said in a sweet-sounding voice. "Taylor Swift."

Scott properly introduced us then ventured, "Taylor, play a song for Jimmy." She strummed a song and sang.

It was obvious that this girl was now Scott's top priority. Fortunately for Scott, Taylor Swift was a quick study, a great songwriter, and a natural performer.

Thirty-seven

EXPOSURE

New York City is an invigorating place to visit any time, but especially during the Thanksgiving and Christmas season, which was when I first visited the Big Apple in 2006. I was doing an interview for a Sirius Radio show at 7:30 a.m. at the Sirius Tower, and, as I often did, along with my own hit singles, I sang "Sara Smile" live on the air. It is difficult to sing that early in the morning, so I really didn't do my best performance of the song. More accurately, I was horrible.

Imagine my surprise when I walked out of the studio, and there, striding straight up the hallway in my direction, were the two guys who had made that song famous, Daryl Hall and John Oates. What are the odds of that happening? When I first saw them, I thought for sure that I was being punked, that someone had set me up for a practical joke. But this was no prank.

Daryl and John were talking among themselves with some other people, walking toward me. Instinctively I moved in their direction, like the starstruck fan that I was, with my record label representatives following behind me. I was staring at Hall and Oates so intensely I barely blinked. I almost had to pinch myself to make sure this was real. After all, a few minutes earlier, I was singing their song; they were the reason

I was even there in New York. John saw me and said hello. "Hey, man, how're you doing?" he asked.

"Hey, I have something to tell you," I said. We talked briefly, and they told me they were in town to record a Christmas album. I told John and Daryl that I had gotten my recording deal by singing their song "Sara Smile."

"Really?" John said. He reached in his pocket, pulled out a card, and said, "Here's my phone number; call me. I'd like to write some songs with you."

I called John Oates that same day—several times. "Hi, John, it's me, Jimmy. We just met at the Sirius Radio building, and you said to give you a call. I want to write with you. Here's my number. For the third time. Call me, man! I'll text you to make sure you got the number."

Two weeks went by, and I hadn't heard from John Oates. I thought, *Yeah, right, I knew it. He's never going to call.*

Then one day during a writing session in Nashville, I received a phone call. I looked at my phone and saw it was a Colorado number, but I didn't recognize it. I thought, *I don't know anyone in Colorado.* But for some reason I asked my writing partner, "I'm not sure who this is. Do you mind if I take this call?"

"Sure, go ahead."

I answered the phone, and a voice said, "Hey, man, this is Oates."

I said, "Who?"

"Oates. John Oates."

I thought I was being pranked again. I walked out in the hallway and asked again, "Who *is* this?"

"John Oates. We met in New York City. Do you want to come out to Aspen, where I live, so we can write some songs?"

"Sure!"

I FLEW TO ASPEN TO WRITE WITH JOHN, BUT I WAS SO NER-vous and starstruck, my creativity level was less than zero. John was kind to me, though, welcoming me into his home, where he had his own recording studio. I gawked around the studio like a little kid, thinking, *I'm sitting in the home of John Oates, one of my heroes.*

John had a million-dollar check sealed in glass, sitting on his desk. "What's the story on that check?" I asked.

"That's a reminder," John said, "that I will never sign a bad publishing deal ever again. I had to return that amount to our record company because we had signed over our publishing rights to some of our early songs, some big hits."

I spent several days with John, and we had a good time, though we didn't write any songs worth recording. But we became fast friends as a result of that visit. One night, after another lackluster day of trying to write love songs with John, I went back to my hotel room, and I began to write some lyrics about my experience as a nine-year-old child, when I had lashed myself to the cross.

The next day I showed John the first verse to a song I called, "How Jesus Felt." "What do think about this, John?" I asked. John looked at the lyrics and listened to my ideas. He looked me right in the eyes and said, "I'm not interested in it." He continued and said straightforwardly, "But that's the kind of stuff you need to be writing. It's obviously real to you. That's what you need to be doing, Jimmy."

As Taylor Swift's success multiplied exponentially, the entire company rose with her. Everything around the label changed, from the paint on the walls, to the clothes people wore, to the cars people drove. The label was doing wonderfully well, but I was still struggling to get along, writing songs and waiting for Scott to come back and pick up where we had left off. I knew he would; Scott was a stand-up guy.

For almost a year, my career languished in limbo. Finally, in September 2007, Scott told me that he was creating a sister label to Big Machine, called Valory Records. He hoped to lure major artists such as Reba McEntire to Valory. "We're almost up and running," he said. A month later I met with Scott at Big Machine, and afterward we walked to a Mexican restaurant, where he told me he was signing Jewel and a few other artists to Valory. "But you," he said, "will be the first artist I release on this label."

I didn't know it at the time, but his words were prophetic.

Valory Music officially opened for business with three artists—Jewel, Justin Moore, and me—on November 2, 2007. It was time to get busy recording again, so one of the first songs I tracked was "Where You're Going," the song based on the story of my college visit to the detention center. Two weeks later I visited Dustin Center and HomeBase, a receiving home for foster kids in Phoenix. I sat in the middle of a room with the kids all around me as I played songs and shared my story. They loved "Where You're Going," and I helped raise $160,000 for foster kids at that event. The kids at HomeBase presented me with a special piece of art painted by one of the homeless kids. A few years later I used the painting in a music video. It remains one of my most cherished possessions.

In December 2007, a music publisher called me and asked, "Jimmy, will you write with one of my writers?" I quickly agreed.

Several weeks later I went to the old RCA building and entered the studio where songwriters Dave Pahanish and Joe West were waiting. Dave and Joe had recently moved to Nashville from Pittsburgh, and this was the first time we had met. We didn't write a song that day, but as I was heading out of the studio, Joe said, "Hey, Jimmy, would you be interested in hearing a song we wrote?"

I was still in work mode and didn't want to stall, but I remembered Skip Ewing's response when I had first asked him to hear my song idea. "Sure," I said. "Let me hear it." I set my bag and guitar down on the floor and walked over to the mixing board. Joe pressed play, and I heard Dave's voice on the demo, singing, "Do you remember . . ."

I stood behind the mixing console, listened to the entire song, and liked what I heard. I complimented the guys regarding the song and asked Joe if I could have a recording of it. By this point in my career, I had learned a little more about the psychology of songwriting, and I knew enough not to hype a song too much—especially a great song—because that ensured it would get pitched, possibly to someone else.

I called Joe several days later and asked if I could record my vocal on their song. The key was too high for me, so Joe, Dave, and I rerecorded all the instruments in my key. I played the acoustic guitar. "Hey, why don't we add a little acoustic intro," I suggested. The guys loved it, so I played the opening before the vocals. Then I recorded my vocals on the track. When we were done, I asked Joe not to play the demo for anyone, and he agreed—a major concession for a songwriter who depends on pitching songs to pay his or her light bill. But Joe and Dave trusted me with their song.

I kept the song in my vehicle for six weeks and listened to it every day. On a cold day in January, I pulled into the record label parking lot and sat in my vehicle, listening to the song several times. Finally, I ejected the CD and went inside.

"Scott, do you have a few minutes to listen to a new song?" I asked. Scott was busier than ever, and he was especially busy on this day. Someone was just leaving his office, and someone else was in the waiting room, anticipating a meeting.

"I'm busy, Jimmy." Scott was seated in his chair, facing away from me.

"Scott, please, listen to this song," I said again.

"Hand it here," he said impatiently, as he held his hand over his shoulder, not even looking at me. Scott inserted the disc into his computer and pressed play. I watched the back of his head begin to bob back and forth in sync with the groove of the music.

He twirled around in his chair and asked, "Where did you find this song?"

I told him that I had recorded it with Dave and Joe.

"I'm getting ready to go into a meeting," he said, nodding toward the waiting room. "I'll call you back in thirty minutes." I knew Scott well enough to tell whether a song excited him or not. He was definitely excited about what he'd heard on that CD.

That afternoon, my phone rang as I was walking inside my townhouse. "Hello?"

I heard the label staff cheering on the other end of the phone. Then I heard Scott's voice. "Congratulations, Jimmy! This song, 'Do You Believe Me Now?' will be your next single," Scott said. The entire label staff cheered and applauded again over the conference call.

Suddenly, I felt wanted again.

ON MARCH 10, 2008, VALORY RELEASED "DO YOU BELIEVE Me Now?" to radio. By the end of the month, it was the third most added song in the country, slightly behind hits by Kenny Chesney and Carrie Underwood.

Scott called me while I was in a hotel room in Medford, Oregon, getting ready to perform at a charity event. He sounded excited by our overnight success and wanted to strike while the iron was hot. Scott said, "We need to take all the songs you've recorded but have not released and use them to complete this CD."

"What? No way!"

I called Joe West and told him we needed to get back in the studio and record four more songs that would at least balance half of the album. "Otherwise, this CD will die after 'Do you Believe Me Now?'"

I didn't say anything to Scott about recording new songs. I simply withdrew some money from my savings account, paid for the recordings myself, and then showed up at the label and handed them to Scott. Two of those songs were "Kerosene Kid" and "Elephant Ears," two of my most meaningful songs.

I filmed a video for "Do You Believe Me Now?" in April, and in June began working with Mike Kraski, my new manager, on booking concert dates. The full album containing "Do You Believe Me Now?" released on August 26, 2008. A few days later, while I was in Las Vegas getting ready to perform on the Jerry Lewis Telethon, I received a phone call informing me that "Do You Believe Me Now?" had gone to number one on the *Billboard* charts! The song stayed at the top of the charts for three consecutive weeks. It went on to earn BMI's prestigious Million-Air Award for having aired more than a million times on radio. What a kick it was for a kerosene kid from North Carolina to see my name listed along with the music industry's finest recording artists.

"DO YOU BELIEVE ME NOW?" WAS NOT ONLY A GREAT single for me; it was a door-opening song for Joe West and Dave Pahanish and their cowriter, Tim Johnson. Joe and Dave parlayed their success with me into number one hits, such as "Without You" for Keith Urban and "American Ride" for Toby Keith.

With a number one song, I immediately set out on a grueling, three-city-per-day radio tour, waking up in one part of the country and going to bed hundreds and sometimes thousands of miles away that same night. It was a crazy schedule, but I loved meeting the radio personnel, some of whom I knew from past tours but many of whom I was meeting for the first time. Not surprisingly, the press picked up on the "revival of Jimmy Wayne's career." I had been out of circulation and prior to "Do You Believe Me Now?" off the charts for several years. That made every radio station visit or television interview all that much more special to me.

I had been going constantly for eighteen days when I woke up in Oakland, California, and had to catch a flight. I was really tired from being up late the previous night, but I was still on the radio tour, which meant a record label rep was dragging me to every radio station possible in the shortest amount of time, squeezing in every public relations opportunity down to the very last second.

Semiconscious, with not nearly enough coffee in my system, I was going through airport security at approximately 7:30 a.m. As I stepped through the metal detector, the alarms went off. A TSA agent spoke to me in broken English. "What's in your pocket?" he wanted to know.

"Nothing," I responded.

"Go through again," he nodded toward the magnetometer. I dutifully walked through the machine again. I followed his directions but to no avail. The red lights continued to flash, and the buzzers kept sounding. I took off one item of clothing after another, but nothing solved the problem. I noticed a number of people in line watching me with amused expressions; others looked on impatiently, wanting to get through the line but unable to do so because I was blocking their forward progress.

"Something is in your pocket setting off the alarm," the TSA guy said. "Go through again." This was getting embarrassing, not to mention irritating since I knew I was not carrying anything dangerous. After the third time going back through the security check, the TSA officer said something to me, but I pretended I couldn't understand him. I figured I would solve the problem once and for all. I removed my shorts and laid them on the conveyor belt. The people in line behind me quickly scattered.

When it was my turn to go through the magnetometer again, the TSA agent realized I was standing there in my boxers and T-shirt. He yelled at the top of his lungs, "Security!" From out of nowhere, a team of approximately ten men the size of Oakland Raiders football players, including some civilian undercover agents, surrounded me.

"Put your hands behind your back, now!" one of the agents gruffly barked at me. I felt my arms pulled back and handcuffs slapped onto my wrists. The agents interrogated me in rapid-fire fashion while I stood there in my underwear. They searched my wallet and threw all my cards and photos on the floor.

Seeing my family's photos lying in disarray on the airport floor made me angry. Not at the security agents but at myself. I realized that my insolent actions were a throwback to my rebellious youth. Instead of doing what was right, I bucked authority, and it got me in trouble. I blamed it on the TSA officer's dialect, but even if I hadn't understood every word he said, I knew exactly what he meant. One thing for sure: he hadn't told me to take off my shorts. I was just being a jerk.

After about twenty-five minutes of humiliation, the interrogators released me and told me not to speak about this incident to anyone for the rest of the day. Those instructions made no sense to me, but I wasn't going to argue. I was already dangerously close to missing my flight. I guess the agents simply didn't want me flaunting my actions, so they said to keep my mouth shut. Sure enough, though, as soon as I made it through security, a redneck ambled over to me and said, "That was *awesome*, man!"

Not about to miss an opportunity for publicity, the record label publicist welcomed questions from the media. I could only answer, "From my experience, the last place you want to take off your shorts in an airport is in Oakland, California. They do not play around, especially with some southern boy who's being a smarty pants!" *People* magazine picked up the story that week and cited my comments as one of their 10 Best Celeb Quotes, explaining why I thought it was okay to take off my shorts: "I mean, they show guys in boxers in Sunday paper ads, right?"

So much for the idea that if you have a number one hit song, you can get away with just about anything. I sure didn't.

IN OCTOBER THE RECORD LABEL HOSTED A "#1 PARTY" FOR "Do You Believe Me Now?" at the Nashville BMI building. It was a great celebration, and the best part for me was that John Oates was there and sang with me.

A few months later Cindy Watts, a journalist from Nashville's local newspaper, the *Tennessean*, called me. She was writing an article about artists' New Year's resolutions and wanted to know mine.

I told her I wanted to go on a full-blown major tour since I'd never been on one, other than my acoustic tour with Lonestar. Cindy included my comments in her article, and by the end of the week, I received six missed calls in rapid succession from Jenny Bohler, who, along with Mike Kraski, was now managing me.

When I finally called Jenny back, she called Mike Kraski, and we were on a three-way conference call. Jenny said, "Brad—" and before she could say another word, Mike jumped in excitedly and said, "—Paisley," and then they both nearly shouted the rest of the sentence in unison, "wants you to go on tour with him starting in June!"

I could hardly believe my ears! I was so excited. Brad was selling out concert halls and arenas around the country, and his American Saturday Night Tour was an opportunity of a lifetime for any artist. I'd have to put together a band and cancel a lot of the county fair dates that the William Morris Agency and I had been booking, but we all felt the incredible exposure with Brad would be worth it.

My career had been stuck in neutral for far too long; I was excited to get things back in gear and rolling again.

Thirty-eight

SECOND CHANCE

When I came off the road with Lonestar in 2004, I felt almost as if God was saying to me, *I gave you this marvelous opportunity, and you squandered it away, so I'm going to put you on the shelf for a while to think about how you have handled what I've given you.* Nearly five years later, when the call came for the Brad Paisley tour, I felt as though God was saying, *Okay, I'm going to give you another shot.* I knew I wasn't perfect, and I still had a lot to learn, but by that time I was a different person with different attitudes. I had learned some hard lessons, and I was thankful for the new opportunity.

As I put together my band for the tour, one of my first calls was to Rob. We had played together in Fantasyche when we were seventeen, and while Rob had never given up hope of making it in the music business, it hadn't happened for him, so he had taken a job with a roofing company. "Come play guitar for me," I asked him. For either of us to get out of our small town and perform on a Brad Paisley tour was a miracle, and it was gratifying for me to share the opportunity with Rob.

I found Jake Clayton, a great young utility player, in a club in Illinois. Jake played keyboards, fiddle, mandolin, banjo, dobro, and just about anything else he put his mind to playing. Jake was incredibly talented. Studio drummer Johnny Richardson played drums, and Luis Espaillat played bass, and of course, I played guitar. We weren't the greatest band ever assembled, but we worked hard, and the guys learned the songs exactly like the records, and that's what the fans wanted to hear.

It didn't take me long on tour to realize that my acoustic rendition of "Sara Smile" still had a special touch to it. I smiled to myself when I thought of how many industry insiders warned me away from performing the song. One pro told me point-blank, "If you ever want a career in Nashville, stop singing that song!" But I loved the song and did it anyhow, and it was constantly requested everywhere I went. I got to be known around town as the "the guy who sings 'Sara Smile,'" which was okay with me. Besides helping me land my recording deal, the song was also instrumental in my meeting one of the most respected songwriters in Nashville.

I was participating in a writer's night at the Bluebird Café, one of Nashville's best known listening rooms, where songwriters gather to perform in the round in a "heroes behind the hits" sort of format, with each writer performing his or her own songs as well as accompanying the other writers on theirs. The Bluebird boasts that it was the venue where country stars, such as Kathy Mattea and Garth Brooks, were discovered, and it is still a place where great songwriters go to play and to listen.

After playing a few of my own songs, as I usually did, I said, "I didn't write this song, but I like it," and I played and sang "Sara Smile." People loved it! Listening at the Bluebird that night was Pat Alger. Pat approached me afterward and said, "We need to write! I've only asked one other person to write together, but I'd like to write with you."

The only other person of whom Pat had made that request was Garth Brooks.

Pat and I worked together on "Summer of '85," a poignant song describing one of the most chaotic periods in my life. One line in the song is especially meaningful to me: "The reason for the pain was to lead me to the cure."

I performed "Summer of '85" at an event in Nashville; also in the show that night was the renowned singer-songwriter Jimmy Webb, who had won Grammy Awards for songs such as "By the Time I Get to Phoenix,"

"Wichita Lineman," and "MacArthur Park." His songs have been recorded by music superstars, including Glen Campbell, The Supremes, The Fifth Dimension, Art Garfunkel, Elvis Presley, Frank Sinatra, Barbra Streisand, Carly Simon, and a virtual who's who of contemporary artists.

After I had performed "Summer of '85," Jimmy Webb gave me one of the most meaningful compliments of my career to date. In front of the entire audience, Jimmy looked at me and said, "You're in."

Now that I was on tour with Brad Paisley, people still wanted to hear me perform "Sara Smile" all the more, so much so that Scott Borchetta was willing to recruit Dann Huff, one of Nashville's top musicians and producers, to help me rerecord the song. Scott knew that we were leaving money behind every night because we didn't have "Sara Smile" on CD, so he was willing to risk it.

As soon as I knew we were going into the studio—in mid-August— I called John Oates and told him. John seemed delighted; he'd heard me sing the song a number of times now, and he knew I always handled it with special care. Nevertheless, I was still a little nervous when I broached an outlandish idea to him. "Hey, John, what would you think about you and Daryl being on the song with me?"

"Oh, that's going to be hard. I don't know, Jimmy," John replied. "I'd enjoy it, but you know Daryl doesn't do much of that sort of thing."

"Yeah, that's what I was afraid of . . ."

"But you never know," John said. "I'll try. Let me mention it to him and see how he responds."

A few days later John Oates called me back. "Who loves ya, baby? Who loves ya? We got Daryl to sing on the song."

Although I had made several attempts now to record "Sara Smile," Dann Huff caught it in a fresh way, and the song came out better than we could have imagined. Adding the background vocals of Hall and Oates, with a few vocal twists of my own, made for an incredibly special piece of music.

We titled the album *Sara Smile* and surrounded the title cut with some great songs, including "Just Knowing You Love Me" and "I'll Never Leave You." In my album notes, I addressed words of thanks first to God and then to Bea and Russell Costner.

ONE OF THE HIGHLIGHTS OF WORKING WITH BRAD PAISLEY was getting to know his dad, Doug Paisley, who was out on tour with us for every date. He was always there for everyone. It wasn't just me; Doug Paisley was good to everyone on the tour. Before I joined the tour, during a show in Wichita, an arena worker collapsed one night with a heart attack. Doug performed CPR and saved the man's life, keeping him alive until the paramedics arrived. When people started calling him a hero, Doug characteristically replied, "A lot of things came together. There's nothing heroic about this. Heroic is when you're standing on the front lines in Afghanistan or Iraq." That was typical Doug.

Brad's dad took a liking to me, and I enjoyed talking and interacting with him. He called me his "second son," and I really appreciated that, especially since I never knew my real dad. Doug noticed that I carted a beat-up bicycle in the bay of the tour bus. When we rolled into town, I enjoyed riding around and seeing the sights, rather than merely hanging out in the bus all day. Doug bought me a brand-new bike as an early birthday present; it was a nice bike too. How cool was that? My own dad never bought me a birthday present of any kind in my entire life, but Brad Paisley's dad bought me a bicycle.

Brad himself was straightlaced, quiet, and businesslike on tour. He allowed no groupies backstage or on our buses. Backstage was extremely controlled; no one was permitted to linger without a reason for being there. He'd joke around a bit, but it was usually one-sided.

Brad treated his team to the very best food backstage, all day long. We had steak, chicken, lasagna, lobster, salads, special desserts—an entire feast every day on the road. Everyone, from the musicians to the sound and light guys to the roadies, was welcome to the backstage banquet. Someone said that Brad spent nearly eleven thousand dollars a day on food for his team. Brad usually ate with us, and mealtime was always a good time. It's a wonder we all didn't put on twenty or thirty pounds during the tour.

Brad, of course, was in tip-top shape, partly because as soon as we rolled into town, his crew guys set up a small portable gym on a rolling cart. Brad was disciplined about working out, and that's probably one of the reasons he is so successful as a performer.

Brad was a prankster, too, but it was hard to get him back. The closest I came was during the encore of his song, "Alcohol," when Dierks Bentley and I joined him onstage. On more than a few nights, rather than singing "Alcohol," I sang "Al Capone." Of course, with the crowd going wild and Dierks and me traipsing all over the stage, Brad never noticed. Till now. Gotcha, Brad!

Working with Brad Paisley was an education in how to do things well in the music business. I learned so much from him and will always be indebted to Brad for helping me see what really matters. I enjoyed every single tour date with the Paisley team, but after five fabulous months on tour, culminating in the amazing night at Madison Square Garden, I was ready to get off the bus and get my feet back on the ground. I just had no idea, at the time, how many new steps I would take and how far I would go in seeing America from the ground up.

Part Four

THE WALK

Thirty-nine

WALKING AWAY OR
WALKING TOWARD?

When my stint on the Paisley tour concluded in Connecticut at the end of October, I woke up on November 2, 2009, in the Litchfield Hills, with breathtaking views of the Berkshires' fall foliage. That afternoon a chauffeur picked me up in a limousine at Interlaken Inn and Resort and drove me to the home of Daryl Hall, where I was to appear on his television show, *Live from Daryl's House.*

Along with some great musicians, I met Daryl in his home studio. He greeted me, wearing his sunglasses. "Hey, man," Daryl welcomed me in his aloof sort of way. "Glad you're here." The idea of the show was for Daryl and his studio pros to jump in and sing along on some of my songs, so we recorded all afternoon. By evening we had knocked out a great show of music, the highlight again, for me, was Daryl and me singing "Sara Smile."

I received a phone call a few weeks later from John Oates. "How'd it go, man?"

"It was a dream come true," I said, "to sing with one of the greatest vocalists of all time."

"That's awesome," John said. "I've been fortunate to sing with Daryl a long time. I'm glad you got the opportunity."

JOHN AND I HAD ESTABLISHED A GENUINE FRIENDSHIP, SO it made sense for me to contact him early in December when I decided to walk halfway across America to raise awareness about foster kids aging out of the system at eighteen with nowhere to go. "Foster kids don't want a free ride," I explained to him. "They are just looking for someone to meet them halfway." I told John that I was thinking of calling my walk "Meet Me Halfway" because I hoped to walk seventeen hundred miles from Monroe Harding foster center in Nashville to HomeBase foster center in Phoenix—a distance equivalent to walking halfway across America. John caught the vision immediately. "I want to get started by the first of the year," I told him. "That way I'll be done by the time the spring and summer tour season starts. I think I can write some new songs along the way."

I asked John if he had any connections with a company that may be willing to endorse the walk. Sure enough, John had an idea. "I know someone at Marmot," John said. "Let me reach out to my friend there."

I was familiar with the outdoor sports equipment and apparel company, but had no contacts with them at the time, so John's reaching out to them was a tremendous help. On December 6, 2009, John wrote a personal e-mail to Alison Smith at Marmot:

A. My good buddy Jimmy Wayne (country singer) has a very cool project he is doing to promote awareness of homeless kids (read his story) around the country. . . . He had a huge #1 single this past summer, and his version of "Sara Smile" is in the top 30 on the country charts right now. He wants to walk around the country and sleep on the streets with kids and talk / sing to them and share their stories. . . . I thought you / Marmot might want to get involved with outfitting him and cross-promoting this. Pls. check out his sites. His bio is below.

By 10:30 a.m. the next day, Alison responded to John's request:

Subject: Re: Oates idea

Good morning,
   That is a great idea and a perfect cause for us to support. I will
review with my marketing team this week and get back to you.

P.S. I love Jimmy Wayne's music and am very familiar with him. And
his version of your song definitely honors your work and brings a new
audience to that great music.
   Did you check out the new Marmot store on Galena? Soft opening last Friday.
   Talk soon. Alison

Although Alison's note implied that it might take a week or longer to
broach the subject with her marketing team, she must have been incredibly persuasive because before that day ended, she sent another note to
John Oates.

Subject: RE: Oates idea

Hi there,
   We are happy to participate in this cause. Do you want to send
me the contact info, and I will pick it up from here?
   Looking forward to helping out.

                                                   Alison

Amazing! But not so unusual for people such as John—someone who
is willing to work behind the scenes, to lend his celebrity to help people
whether he receives any acknowledgment for it or not—and Alison—
someone who knows how to make things happen and is willing to throw
her energy into doing it with excellence. Within days Marmot sent me

more than ten thousand dollars' worth of materials—pants, shirts, jackets, windbreakers, a backpack and tent, flashlights, everything I could possibly need for surviving out in the cold Tennessee terrain, and lightweight clothing for the superheat of the Arizona desert. Their generosity was astounding!

When I told friends about my idea, some people tried to talk me out of it. "Jimmy, that's just too far!" they cautioned. But I'd traced it out on the map on the Southwest Airlines napkin, and it didn't look too far to me. More important, I could no longer avoid the conviction I felt about not keeping my promise to help those foster kids, and I was convinced that I wanted to do it.

In mid-December it occurred to me that I probably should do some conditioning before I attempted to walk across the country. I wasn't in bad physical shape, but after several months on the road, eating at the Paisley backstage banquet every day, I was in need of some vigorous workouts. I certainly wasn't in the condition of a marathon runner or even a baseball or football player. I was a musician! And starting in the midst of the Christmas season didn't exactly help matters.

A few days before Christmas I made an announcement to the media regarding the proposed walk, inviting the public to "Meet Me Halfway." Scott Borchetta called me the next day, praising the concept. "I love this idea," Scott gushed. "We'll have the entire label staff out there to walk the first mile with you on January 1."

I spent New Year's Eve in my upstairs bedroom, rolling every item of my clothing—my Marmot shirts, pants, jackets, and Smartwool socks, even my underwear—and then placing each piece of clothing into its own Ziploc freezer bag. This was a trick I had learned while living outside in the cold as a fourteen-year-old. Rolling the clothes made it possible to get more into a tight space, and the plastic bags kept my clothes dry, even in the rain or snow. Packing everything I owned in plastic is how many of my childhood poems, drawings, photos, official documents, and prison letters survived all the years of my disjointed living.

I couldn't help reliving some of those experiences, even as an adult in my nice warm townhouse, as I carefully packed each plastic bag into my backpack. When I finished packing, I turned off all the lights in my master bedroom and gazed out the large window. From my location I could see downtown Nashville's New Year's Eve celebration, which included a huge fireworks display, the dark night sky bursting with umbrellas of color every few seconds. A part of me wished I could be out there, celebrating the beginning of the new year with everyone else, but I knew I needed to get a good night's sleep. Tomorrow was going to be a big day.

ON JANUARY 1, 2010, WHILE THE REST OF THE WORLD WAS waking up to the Rose Bowl Parade, football games, and family events, I washed out my coffeepot, checked the clothes dryer and water faucets, and unplugged everything I could. I planned to be gone for at least three months. Bitterly cold winter air smacked me in the face as I left my townhouse at 9:44 a.m. and headed to Monroe Harding. When I arrived, I was met by a crowd of supporters, including my friend and record label boss Scott Borchetta and the staff of Valory Music Company. Jenny Bohler and Mike Kraski, from my management company, were there too.

Grand Ole Opry star and country music legend John Conlee braved the cold to see me off that morning as well. John gave me a special coin to carry along with me on my journey. "My son is in the Marine Corps," John said, as he gave me the coin, "and I want you to know that just as I am proud of what he is doing, I am proud of what you are doing. I'll be praying for you." John's kind gesture deeply touched me.

I went inside and spoke to the kids participating in the foster program, living at Monroe Harding. They were incredibly encouraging and appreciative. After talking briefly with the kids, I was having an interview with the media when Scott Borchetta stepped up in front of the live television news cameras and said, "I am donating fifty thousand dollars to project Meet Me Halfway." Although I was grateful for such a generous gift, I was shocked at Scott's promised contribution, especially since

I hadn't solicited funds from anyone and was merely seeking to raise awareness of the plight of foster kids through my efforts.

It was finally time to start walking, and I was ready. I stepped over to my vehicle and hoisted the heavy Marmot backpack onto my shoulders for the first time. *Whoa! Who packed this thing?* I hadn't road-tested the fifty-pound backpack until the moment I began my seventeen-hundred-mile trek. It suddenly struck me just how poorly prepared for this journey I really was, but it was too late. To the cheers and encouragement of numerous onlookers, I took the first steps out of the parking lot, toward Highway 70, eventually heading west toward Memphis. I paused momentarily and looked back. "Here we go," I called to the cheering crowd. "This is the beginning of the walk. Seventeen hundred miles!"

Despite the below-freezing temperatures, a large group of enthusiastic, exuberant people, including Scott and the Valory team, walked the first mile along with me. That initial mile seemed relatively easy; friends and associates were talking to me and laughing, and of course, I was still running on adrenaline, but I noticed the backpack was not getting any lighter. The end of the first mile was bittersweet as Scott and the Valory staff and I parted company. I didn't realize that their departure was a living metaphor, soon to be played out in my future.

By midafternoon I had barely cleared the West Nashville suburbs, and already my crowd of fellow walkers had vanished. I was on my own, alone, walking out Highway 70. Cars whizzed by at fifty-five miles per hour or faster, whipping the already chilling winds across my face as they passed. Semitrucks roared past me, as well, a few blowing their horns as they sprayed me with a mixture of road dust and diesel smoke. I didn't know if they were greeting me or telling me to get off their turf. I stopped at a Hardee's restaurant, glad to take off the backpack for a while. I gobbled down a chicken filet sandwich, stopped at the restroom, and went right back out on the road again.

Day One of the walk was a mixture of excitement, adjustment to the cold temperatures, and a sudden awareness of the horrendous loneliness I felt. Despite my best efforts to stave off the devil's attacks, depression was only a step away. The devil kept taunting me, telling me that I was stupid, that this walk was all in vain, and that I was a fool for walking away from a successful music career, leaving behind everything for which I had worked so hard the past twelve years. And for what? For a bunch of kids whom I would never know and who would never know my name.

I remembered Jesus' words, "Get behind me, Satan!" (Matt. 16:23).

And I sensed God telling me, *Keep walking, Jimmy.*

So I took the next step.

Forty

WALK ON!

WALKING SEEMS LIKE SUCH AN EASY THING TO DO, AND IT is until you know you have more than three million steps to go! As I strode out of Nashville, I felt like a soldier going off to war, not knowing what to expect. I sensed there was a possibility I may never return—and if I did, I probably would not be the same person.

I tried to keep up a good pace, hoping to cover approximately twenty-five miles per day. I was so naive; I thought I could do it! And I could—the first day—but the second day, my entire body was protesting. I was stiff and sore when I crawled out of my sleeping bag and got up off the ground. The walk took an early emotional toll too. Walking by myself allowed plenty of time for thinking, so I guess it was natural that I relived many of the significant steps of my life with every mile traveled by foot.

Day Two brought more of the same until a man named Terry Johnson stopped alongside the road and gave me a cup of hot chocolate. He'd read about Meet Me Halfway in the newspapers. Despite my warm Marmot ski clothes, the hot chocolate hit the spot, especially since the temperatures in Tennessee had plummeted into the teens. Terry decided to walk with me for a while, and I appreciated his company.

Three days into the walk I said to myself, *What was I thinking?* I

329

turned around, looked back toward Nashville, and felt sure I could still see my house. This was a *slow* process, much slower than I had anticipated. My spirits tumbled, and I wondered why I was even doing this crazy walk.

About that time, as I was walking along the side of the highway, I noticed a brick on the ground, and it had my name on it! Along with the brick was a bottle of root beer, an apple, and a handwritten letter addressed to me.

Jimmy,

You're doing this! Thank you for allowing us to join you at the kickoff. It was awesome to feel the excitement of the day. You keep walking, and we'll keep praying! From a family that loves you very much!

The letter contained no signature, but it certainly lifted my spirits and reignited my passion. I smiled as I recalled the many times when Bea Costner had revived my spirits with the help of a soft drink.

As my thoughts drifted back to my years with Bea, I thought of her best friend, Fan. I didn't realize when I agreed to cut Bea's grass, it also meant helping Fan keep her two-acre lot cut as well. I didn't mind, though, since Bea and Fan had been friends since they were nine years old, and Fan was a widow. I would have gladly cut her grass for free, but she paid me twenty dollars, just like Bea. I think Bea's arranging the deal was her way of encouraging me to become more of a businessman.

Bea always reminded me when it was time to cut Fan's grass. I'd load the riding mower in the trunk of Bea's brown four-door Buick—she preferred her car rather than Russell's pickup truck—and we'd head to Fan's place. Bea and Fan would sit on a porch swing while I cut the grass in the hot summer sun. I developed a pattern, and when I'd get to the big tree with the bottom of its trunk painted white in Fan's front yard, about an hour into mowing her lawn, that's when Fan would yell out, "You thirsty?"

I'd nod my head yes, and Fan would go inside and pour me a glass of ice-cold Coca-Cola. Meanwhile, Bea read her Bible while Fan was gone. Before long, the Coke and Bible break became a weekly ritual.

One day when I reached break time, I stood in the front yard and watched through the screen door as Fan went into her kitchen to get me a glass of Coke. She had two bottles, a new one and one that was half empty. I watched in anticipation as Fan grabbed the opened bottle of Coke, took a long swig from the bottle, and smacked her lips as if she were taste-testing it to see if it was flat. She then poured the remainder of the contents of the opened bottle into my glass, walked outside and handed it to me. I looked at the slightly used drink, then at Fan and Bea. *Oh, well.* I took a big gulp. It gave the slogan "Have a Coke and a smile" a whole new meaning for me. All these years later, Bea's memory is still with me, inspiring me, reminding me that I can do more than I ever dreamed.

That night, near Dickson, Tennessee, I found a spot in the brush, not too far off the highway, where I set up my tent. It was extremely cold, and it had been a long, lonely day. Before trying to sleep, I kept in touch with fans by posting quick highlights on Twitter, reading messages from supporters, and sending updates to Jenny Bohler at my management company. It was so quiet out in the wild that I could hear my heart beating. I huddled in my sleeping bag, attempting to keep my face under the cover. The temperature dropped to nine degrees above zero, with the windchill below zero; it was so cold in my tent that my sleeping bag froze! But inside my Marmot clothes and sleeping bag, I was toasty warm.

BY THE FOURTH DAY I WAS DEPRESSED OUT OF MY MIND. AN arctic blast moved through Tennessee, and the temperature remained at thirteen degrees, with the windchill hovering around zero. Walking into the bitter wind took even more effort than usual, impeding my progress and slowing me down. Later that same day a fireman stopped and gave me a bottle of water; I appreciated his kindness so much. Two women stopped and gave me a few hot dogs and a soda; two guys stopped and gave me some hot chocolate.

Despite the cold—or maybe because of it—I met some really good people along the way. I stopped at Collins Food Mart, where the proprietors allowed me to charge my phone and warm up inside. On Day Five, a man named Don Davis stopped roadside and gave me a bottle of milk and a bottle of water. Bill Hatley met me on the other side of the Tennessee River at the edge of the bridge. He gave me a thermos half filled with coffee and a bag of doughnuts. "My wife sent me out here two hours ago," he said, "and I've been trying to find you." I couldn't help staring at him. Although he was much younger, he reminded me so much of Bea's husband, Russell Costner.

At 8:12 p.m. that same evening, Dierks Bentley texted me: "hope u r in a hotel room."

I wasn't. I was huddled in my tent.

The following day the temperature continued to drop, but people continued to warm my heart with their kindness. A man came out of his shop and handed me twenty dollars. An elderly couple paid for my breakfast at the Down Home Restaurant. Another family paid for my dinner that evening. Anthony and Keliea McCartney brought me some water and food, and Anthony prayed for me before they left. David Hochreiter dropped by and gave me his government-issued cold weather suit that he used when he served in Iraq. It was rated for minus-fifty degrees. Keith Reilly saw me walking by his lane as he was pulling out in his pickup. When he saw me squinting into the snow, he went and got me a set of ski goggles to protect my eyes from the ice particles blowing sideways in the intense wind. People were incredibly good to me.

Again and again I heard someone say, "I just want to help." Some people brought food and water to me as I walked. Others left little care packages at various points alongside the road, by a tree or someplace they could be sure I'd find their gift. I always did.

On Day Eleven Samantha and Danny Marx and their four children traveled five hours from Indiana to Jackson, Tennessee, to show support for Meet Me Halfway. They spent the day walking and stopped with me at McKenzie's BBQ along Highway 70 to have a sandwich. The manager asked me to go out back to a house where an old man was lying in a hospital bed in his living room, apparently dying. The entire family held hands, and I prayed for the man; then I continued walking.

The media coverage of my walk went well during the slow news days of early January, and I tweeted regularly on Twitter as well. Then on January 12, 2010, a massive earthquake struck the nation of Haiti, causing catastrophic damage in and around the capital city of Port-au-Prince. Thousands of people died, and thousands more were made homeless. I was deeply saddened by the deaths and destruction. The media's attention shifted away from the crazy guy out walking along the highway to the tragedy in the Caribbean. Rightfully so, of course.

But I was still walking.

THE MORNING OF JANUARY 13, RANDY TRAVIS CALLED ME, and we talked for approximately twenty minutes. The previous day, Ben and Matt, two deejays from KNIX, a radio station in Phoenix, had pranked me terribly on live radio by pretending that one of them was Randy. I was so excited to receive a call from one of my musical heroes that I threw down my gloves so I could handle the phone easier. "I can't believe it!" I repeated about a dozen times. I was gushing all over myself, telling "Randy" what a big fan of his I was.

"Randy" was equally complimentary. "I heard what you are doing, and I think you are one of the best new singers out there," the voice said. "I love 'Sara Smile' too. I tried singing it once, but it's not in my range."

"I am so honored that you would call me . . . I'm a huge fan of your music, Randy," I said, "and have been since I was a little boy."

The pranksters at KNIX couldn't stand it and finally confessed, playing a song specially put together for the prank. We all had a big laugh. The deejays at KNIX actually supported my efforts wholeheartedly, and they called me at least three times a week so I could update their listeners about the walk. To some of their listeners, the "Jimmy Wayne Update" became a regular part of their day, like their morning cup of coffee.

I later heard from some locals in Phoenix that they laughed so hard when they heard this prank that they had to pull their vehicles over. On the other hand, some people protested the radio station because they were "picking on the guy walking for homeless kids." I had to call in from the road to clarify that the KNIX deejays and I were good friends.

Apparently the real Randy Travis heard about all the commotion, so he called me while I was walking out on the road. We had a great conversation, and he was incredibly encouraging to me.

"Whether you know it or not this side of heaven," Randy Travis told me, "you are making a huge difference in the lives of some people who need a lot of help, Jimmy."

Lieutenant Colonel Jason Garkey, a nineteen-year active duty serviceman in the US Army, drove from Richmond, Virginia, overnight and walked with me all day. Trim and fit, LTC Garkey ate with me that night at the world-famous Gus's Chicken. We then found an area along the side of the highway where we could set up our tents.

The next morning, I woke up shortly after 6:30 a.m. When I popped my head out of my tent, I saw that LTC Garkey had already shaved, brushed his teeth, and packed his sixty-pound backpack, including the tent. *This guy is good!* I thought.

Bobby Goodman, a gentleman we had met while walking the previous day, had invited us to his home for breakfast. Bobby fried up some bacon and baked some biscuits, but the biscuits caught fire, and the smoke was so intense, we had to evacuate the house. Bobby ran back in and smothered the fire, and LTC Garkey and I ate the burned biscuits and bacon anyway. We tried not to laugh at the charcoal in the corners of our mouths. LTC Garkey stayed and walked with me all week long, giving up his vacation to show support for Meet Me Halfway.

On January 18, Gary Luffman, owner of Hiscall.com, a communications company in Tennessee, donated a used car and a used recreational vehicle for me to use for several months as support vehicles, so I'd have a place to rest and have a meal during the walk. He had the vehicle wrapped, advertising his business and the Meet Me Halfway walk. The RV was quite old and didn't have any heat or air conditioning, but it was a shelter out of the cold, a place where I could make some coffee and store my clothes. It reminded me of the abandoned trailer without heat or electricity that Uncle Austin allowed me to sleep in, but this RV was much nicer. The name of Gary's company, Hiscall, reflects obedience to God's call in our lives and doing what He asks us to do. So giving the RV was part of his response to God's call on Gary's life.

Later, Geoff Penske of Penske GMC donated another support vehicle that I could use for the remainder of the walk. I really appreciated the car and the RV. I now had a support vehicle in which I could leave part of my heavy load while walking. The vehicle also made it possible for me to have my guitar sent out on the road along with me, which was a great help since I was missing my music badly. Each day I instructed the driver to position the RV five or ten miles ahead of me, making it a goal to push toward with the reward of a place to stop and rest when I achieved each incremental goal. I hired three separate drivers over the course of the walk and had several volunteer drivers.

In Memphis, I stopped by Youth Villages, a foster care facility, where I hung out for a while with the kids and performed some songs for them. In turn, they shared their stories and poems with me, and it was an emotionally moving time for all of us. Being there reminded me so much of my time at Faith Farm. My purpose for the walk was to raise awareness of foster kids' dilemmas, but increasingly I noticed that so much about the walk was reminiscent of my own experiences.

I got up at six o'clock to have breakfast with the kids at Youth Villages before continuing my journey. I walked through Highland Heights in East Memphis, an impoverished, high-crime section of the city, also known as Hurt Village. Alcoholics, drug addicts, and other homeless people lay on the sidewalks, and dirty syringes were openly evident. This was National Football League player Michael Oher's hometown and the same community on which the movie *The Blind Side* was based.

Everyone I met warned me not to walk through that part of Memphis because I'm white, but I grew up in a racially charged section of the country and had long since lost any prejudices I formerly carried regarding skin color. I encountered no serious trouble, but I never realized how huge Memphis is or, perhaps, how lost I got. I walked all day long and into the night, not stopping until 11:41 p.m. on the west side of town.

The following day, just for kicks, I dressed up like Elvis Presley and walked the few miles out of Memphis into West Memphis. I soon discovered that people in Memphis take their Elvis impersonators quite seriously, and I was warned to take the costume off before I got into real trouble. But I had fun with it anyhow.

Later that day an old homeless man pulling a grocery cart stopped me on the sidewalk in West Memphis. "Are you that famous guy I heard about?" he asked.

"I don't know," I responded. I told him why I was walking for foster kids.

He looked at me and said, "If I had any money, I'd give it to you."

Forty-one

NEW FRIENDS, SNAKES, AND A DOG

IF YOU'VE NEVER TRAVELED THROUGH THE SOUTH IN THE
dead of winter, you may not realize that Arkansas can become freezing
cold. I soon discovered that winter in the Deep South can be every bit
as chilling as a winter night in New England or Minnesota. A severe ice
storm struck about the time I was passing through Little Rock; the bliz-
zard was so bad that all the main roads were shut down. I was stranded
by the ice, so I stayed in the cold for two days, trying to sleep in my tent,
but I was repeatedly awakened by the ice pelting the canvas. When the
manager of Capital Hotel learned of my circumstances, she offered my
support driver and me two free hotel rooms along with meals. For several
days I went out and walked each day, then returned to the hotel at night.
We certainly appreciated the warmth and the food. While in town I visited Job Corps, speaking to the youth there and performing a few songs.

Whether I was fatigued or confused, I'm not sure, but somehow I
missed a turn in Little Rock and walked forty miles in the wrong direction! Fortunately, a guy named Greg Oswald from the William Morris
Agency came out and walked eighteen miles with me on Highway 8.
Greg was as clueless as I was about directions, but between the two of us,

we finally figured out how to get back on the correct route to Phoenix. But my mistake actually led to a tremendously meaningful meeting.

I met Topher and Gigi Warren at Melba's Country Restaurant in Norman, Arkansas. Topher later told me that when they saw me walking with my hoodie, trekking poles, and ski goggles, he nudged Gigi and said, "Look at this cat right here!" I stopped to talk with them, and they offered me a room for the night on the Pea Patch Ranch in Caddo Gap, Arkansas. Talk about the gift of hospitality; these folks have it. When I walked through the door, I could smell the stew simmering on the stovetop and the aroma of sweet cornbread in the oven wafting through the air. We ate supper and then swapped jokes and stories half the night. Anyone looking in through the windows might have thought we were getting high, but truth is, we were simply high on life.

Two days after Valentine's Day I reached the Oklahoma border at 7:12 p.m. I stepped into Oklahoma with a look of amazement on my face, astounded that I had made it so far. My joy was short-lived, though. A few days later I returned to the RV and was doing a telephone interview with Lauren Tingle for *Country Air Check* when I looked up and noticed that my belongings were gone. "Lauren, hold on a minute," I said. "I think somebody stole my clothes!" Sure enough, all of my clothes, a leather jacket, and other belongings had been stolen out of the RV while it was parked in Hot Springs. The only things I had left were the clothes on my back. Yet, thankfully, the thieves hadn't found my guitar.

KNIX, as well as *The Bob and Sheri Show*, from Charlotte, North Carolina, and other radio stations called in for a report, so I told them about the theft. "Can you believe that?" the deejays voiced over and over. "Jimmy's out there walking to help some kids, and somebody steals all his stuff! If you see someone out there in Arkansas wearing ski gear, give us a call!"

When Topher heard about what happened, he and Gigi drove out to pick me up. It was snowing the day they took me back home with them. I called Marmot and told them what had happened. I said, "You guys have been so good to me, I hate to even tell you this, but everything you gave me is gone. Someone stole it while I was walking."

Alison Smith didn't even hesitate. "We'll get a shipment right out to you," she said. "Let us know where you are, and we will get you everything you need." I could hardly believe my ears. Marmot replaced every item that was stolen from me.

Topher and Gigi allowed me to stay on the Pea Patch Ranch until the shipment of Marmot clothes arrived. Meanwhile, Topher's dad, Kenner Warren, bought me a pair of farmer-style bib overalls down at the feed store in Glenwood. I've never farmed a day in my life, but I thought I looked pretty good in them. I stayed with this family for four full days and loved every minute of it. Gigi made pancakes and bacon for breakfast, reminding me so much of Bea Costner's kindness to me. Those folks at the Pea Patch Ranch are something else. They won't steal your pants, but they will sure steal your heart.

BY EARLY MARCH I KNEW I WAS IN TROUBLE. I HAD ALLOWED three months for the walk, and I was not yet halfway. *This is going to take a lot longer than I thought.* LTC Jason Garkey came out to walk with me for the second time, and he helped me pick up my pace. We walked 25.4 miles, the longest distance I'd ever walked in one day.

Another dose of reality hit me in mid-March, when I walked into Del City, Oklahoma, and realized that the route I was traveling was almost identical to the road Mama, Tim, and I had driven when I was only thirteen and Tim was running from the law. But this time I was replacing the bad memories with good ones.

Touching my heart, some special friends, Mearl and Tina Trevethen, flew all the way from Sacramento to join me on the walk. Their daughter, Lauren Trevethen, met me along the roadside—in her wheelchair—to celebrate her twentieth birthday with me. Lauren lives victoriously, despite cerebral palsy, and when she heard about Meet Me Halfway, she wanted to help. LTC Garkey pushed Lauren for a while, and then

Lauren allowed me to push her along the road in her wheelchair for more than five miles. I felt as though she had given a special birthday gift to me.

Also in March the Red Roof Inn hotel chain offered to be a sponsor of Meet Me Halfway, allowing my support driver and me to stay at any of their hotels along the way. Although I tried to avoid walking on interstate highways, where many of their hotels were located, the Red Roof offer was a great blessing when I could take advantage of it. Regardless of where I spent the night, whether in a hotel, with a family willing to take me in, or out on the ground in my tent, wherever I stopped walking in the evening, I resumed the walk at the exact spot and mile marker when I returned.

Just before the first day of spring, I received a box of clothes from Marmot. They came in handy, too, since the winds had picked up and the temperature dropped rapidly each evening, plunging from the 70s to the 20s in a matter of hours after the sun went down. I finally reached the Texas state line on March 27, after walking nineteen miles that day. The sign said, "Welcome to Texas: Drive Friendly." No problem with that!

In Wheeler, Texas, I met Clint Devoll. "Hey, there, pardner," Clint said, tipping his big cowboy hat in my direction. "We got a place you can stay tonight." I went to Clint's RV that night, and he cooked me an enormous cowboy steak. After dinner I noticed an old guitar.

"Do you mind if I play your guitar?" I asked.

He hesitated. "Well, I don't know; my dad gave that guitar to me before he died."

"Never mind," I backed off.

"Oh, okay, go ahead."

I thanked him and picked up the guitar and started to pick. But the guitar's action was too high. "We should take out the bridge and sand it down so it will lower those strings," I told him. "I know how to do it, if you have a small file."

"Okay, but be careful; my dad gave me that guitar a long time ago."

Clint went to get a file. I looked over at his friend and noticed he had a big black eye. He looked like a firehouse dog. "What happened to your eye?" I asked.

He pointed in Clint's direction. "Me and him are best friends, but we got in a fight."

"You're best friends, and you fight?"

"Yeah, man," he said in a nasal sounding voice. He didn't crack a smile.

I could imagine these guys doing some heavy drinking and then getting mad at me, so I was especially careful while working on the guitar. Too careful. I filed too much off the bridge and ruined the guitar's action. I felt horribly about it, but I couldn't glue the sawdust back together.

"I think I broke your guitar, Clint," I finally admitted. "I'll buy you a new one, but I'm sorry; I've sanded it too low." I ordered a new Takamine guitar and had it sent to him, and Clint's dad's guitar became part of the musical photo I was taking in my mind and would eventually record in song. But it was time to move on.

I WAS WALKING INTO WHITE DEER, TEXAS, WHEN A rancher named Drew Hodges pulled off the road and offered me some water. "Hey, I have an extra room in my farmhouse if you and your support driver want a place to stay tonight." As was my policy, I accepted almost all invitations since my twofold goal was not only to simulate homeless life but also to raise awareness about foster kids with anyone who might listen.

"Sure, I'll be glad to come," I responded.

When we got to the house, I saw a cute, black-and-brown female dog that Drew and his girlfriend had recently rescued from a kill shelter. The tiny Chihuahua and Miniature Pinscher mix was lying in a dog bed with two other pups and looked like a lot of the kids for whom I was walking—she was the runt of the litter, scared, just out of the facility, and ignored by the other dogs. She looked up at me with her big eyes and stole my heart instantly. "This little girl needs a home," I said, thinking of my childhood dog, Sparkles.

"Do you want her?" Drew asked. "You can have her."

"She can't possibly walk with me, and I'm a long way from home," I replied. "But maybe I can have her sent back to Nashville."

When I arrived in Amarillo a few days later, the halfway point in my walk, Drew brought the dog to me, so I named her "Ruby Amarillo" and sent her back to Nashville. I couldn't wait to get back home to be with her.

ON APRIL FOOL'S DAY, ROB DANIELS, MY FORMER GUITAR player, joined me on the walk as my new support driver. It was great to be reunited with my friend. His first day out, I walked twenty miles on the famous Route 66. Rob was amazed. This was a far step from bounding across the stage at Madison Square Garden!

As I walked, I usually listened to music or audiobooks on an iPod or MP3 player, so I often had earbuds in my ears, with the audio drowning out much of the road noise. But, fortunately, I was listening to the sounds of nature as I walked alongside the road into Adrian, Texas. I was weary, having walked nearly twenty miles that day. I was about to take another step when I heard a sound that struck fear into me. I saw something raise up under my foot as I stepped down near what I thought was a piece of bowed metal. The "metal" flopped backward, and I heard the unmistakable sound of a rattlesnake. I flipped the snake back farther with my trekking pole and veered away, as the rattler coiled then slithered away. Had the reptile been a copperhead, I would have been dead. But the ominous sound was just enough of a warning to get my attention.

From then on I saw a lot of rattlers in the desert, especially in the evening. At night they'd come out and lie on the warm road, and if I wasn't careful, I could easily walk right on top of one. After my first encounter with a rattlesnake, I took precautions and no longer wore earbuds while walking; nor did I walk in the grass or gravel alongside the road but stayed on the asphalt, which was harder on my feet and knees but safer.

Another seventeen miles on a dirt road dead-ended at someone's ranch; the road abruptly ended, and there were no directional signs or people anywhere in sight. I discovered that Route 66 simply stopped near New Mexico, so as I looked at a map, trying to figure out which way to go, I drew a straight line down to Clovis, New Mexico, and connected it to Phoenix. I decided to head that way since there was nothing but freeway to walk Route 66 in that section of the country.

ON MAY 1, 2010, A MASSIVE FLOOD HIT NASHVILLE AS more than thirteen inches of rain fell on the area within a few hours. Whole sections of the city were inundated with water. Thousands of people were displaced, and even the Grand Ole Opry was flooded. Nashville music artists naturally rallied around, raising money to help in the relief of flood victims. My heart was torn between continuing the walk and wanting to return home to help, but it was soon apparent that every artist in town was participating in benefit concerts, and the Nashville music community raised millions of dollars to help in flood relief. I was proud of my colleagues, and I knew they could do what they were doing without me, so I felt compelled to keep walking.

Forty-two

PIE TOWN

IN EARLY MAY I RECEIVED GREAT NEWS. CALIFORNIA General Assembly Member Jim Beall Jr. invited me to Sacramento to speak to the California Congress. State Senator Dennis Hollingsworth introduced me on the Senate floor in Sacramento to share my story on behalf of Assembly Bill 12, a bill to extend foster care programs for kids until they turn twenty-one years of age.

It was a successful effort, and the congressmen and senators assured me that the bill would pass in September and Governor Arnold Schwarzenegger would undoubtedly sign it. I was ecstatic! Whether project Meet Me Halfway had any influence on the decision, I may never know, but I was thrilled that the goal was in sight. I was bubbling over on May 4, 2010, as I left Sacramento for Albuquerque, on my way back to Fort Sumner to resume my walk. The anticipated positive results in California motivated me to return to the walk with even greater purpose.

I had landed and was in the transport vehicle, when at 2:23 p.m. my phone rang. I noticed the call was from my management company. "Hey, Jenny," I answered, and I immediately began babbling about the victory we had experienced in Sacramento. Jenny remained surprisingly subdued as I recounted the events of the morning.

"Jimmy," she finally interrupted in a serious tone of voice. "We need to talk with you."

Another familiar voice came on the call. I recognized Mike Kraski's voice. "Jimmy, this is Mike here," he said, "and we have some bad news for you."

I listened somberly as Jenny Bohler and Mike Kraski informed me that my friend Scott Borchetta had dropped me from the Valory Music Company. The message had been delivered in an e-mail from Scott's general manager. Although I had a number-one song for three weeks, and I had "Sara Smile" on the charts at the beginning of the walk, it was "just business."

Somebody has said, "Money doesn't change people; it exposes them." I was seeing the truth of that statement revealed more and more every day in the music business.

I was devastated, not so much that my label was letting me go but that my friend—the guy who discovered me, signed me, and helped develop me as an artist—did not call me himself. Had Scott said, "Hey, Jimmy, you aren't selling enough product, and we're going to have to make some adjustments. Let me help you find another opportunity," I'm sure I could have handled it. But he didn't. It hurt me deeply because Scott was the one person besides Bea Costner I thought genuinely believed in me.

I fulfilled every obligation that had been previously scheduled. Even during the walk, I continued to perform concerts, including an appearance on the Grand Ole Opry, which by tradition gives all performers the same small fee. The payment wasn't enough to cover a one-way ticket to Nashville, let alone the flight back to my New Mexico location, where I resumed walking.

I didn't miss a single concert date due to Meet Me Halfway. I actually booked some dates along the routes I traveled. When I arrived in a town, I simply went to the hotel, where I showered and rested a bit before the evening performance. The audiences loved it when I said, "I just walked here from Nashville!"

If I wasn't selling enough product to keep the label happy, it could have easily waited until the Meet Me Halfway walk concluded. I wasn't recording any new albums while on the walk, and while I wasn't selling in large numbers, I was probably doing as well as my label-mates, Justin Moore and Jewel. Most disappointing to me, the music was increasingly my main means of getting the word out about the kids who need help.

When I received the news, I was heading into Fort Sumner, the place where Billy the Kid was killed. The parallels between Billy the Kid and me hit too close to home: He was an orphan kid who migrated west on the orphan train. His foster mother's name was Sara. He was a singer, he was rejected by the people who supposedly loved him, and he was betrayed, shot in the back by his best friend, Pat Garrett. I visited his grave that evening before the sun went down, wiping away my tears. Was I disappointed? Of course. But as I thought about it, another incident from Bea's life helped me put my own loss in perspective.

I recalled a time shortly before Bea closed the woodshop. She sent out notes to her long-term clients who had purchased churns and baskets from her over the years to resell them in their shops all around America. She informed her customers that she was closing her doors and this would be the last time they could order from her. One customer from Ohio ordered more than five hundred churns from Bea! That was the good news; she had a huge order. The bad news, of course, was that it took a lot of work to make one churn, and she now had hundreds to make—all by herself.

Bea spent the next four months working and sweating over the saws and hammers and building those handmade churns, one by one. When she finished, she shipped the entire order to the client, along with an invoice. Months went by, and she received no payment. Bea sent more invoices, but the customer never paid her.

When I found out that someone had ripped off Bea, I was ready to drive to Ohio and get Bea's money. But Bea wouldn't hear of that. "No, Jimmy," she said. "Don't worry about it." And she just walked across the yard with a smile.

The way Bea handled that situation was an example I would never forget. Had she been done wrong? Definitely. Had someone she trusted taken advantage of her good nature? Absolutely.

But Bea refused to harbor a grudge. Rather than allowing herself to get bitter, she chose to forgive, cut her losses, and move on.

As I tossed and turned that night, thinking about my lost recording deal, I knew what Bea would do. She had a lot more experience at forgiving than I did, so following her example in that area wouldn't come easily for me, but I determined that, with God's help, I would try.

Amazingly, at daybreak, I was not nearly as despondent as I expected to be. There was work to be done and kids to be helped, and I was still a long way from Phoenix. Some people have asked me why I didn't give up and go home when I received the news that my music career was taking a downturn. That's easy. The walk was never about my music career; it was about raising awareness about foster kids who were at risk. And I could do that whether I had any support from a record label or not. If you really want to do something, you can *find the way.*

IN THE MIDST OF ENCOUNTERING DANGERS FROM RATTLE-snakes, being dropped by my record label, and a growing fatigue, an opportunity arose for a whirlwind trip to Washington, DC, to speak on behalf of FosterClub, a national network for four hundred thousand kids in foster care. I met with several US senators and congressmen and sat as part of a congressional information panel. I quickly realized that if I was going to influence legislators, I had to learn their language. For instance, when the senator said, "Jimmy, I'm going to take you down to the floor," he was not picking a fight!

The next day my nephew, Brian, joined me on the walk as my support driver, replacing Rob. I was glad to have Patricia's son share this experience with me, especially since his mom and I had benefited so much from the help of foster parents during our childhoods. Brian added a comedic element, too, with his deadpan sense of humor, and I enjoyed teasing him as well. I hired him and fired him at least a dozen times each day.

Part of Brian's responsibilities was to keep the support vehicle far enough away that it provided an incentive but not so far that he couldn't be of help if I needed anything. Unfortunately, when a spooky sort of guy pulled up beside me in a compact car as I was walking near Mountainair, New Mexico, Brian was nowhere in sight. I was walking up a long stretch of desert, the heat rising in waves from the road. When the man got out of his car, he looked to be six foot four and around two hundred forty pounds. He curtly said, "I want to walk with you."

"Okay," I said, "What's your name?"

"You don't need to know my name. I just want to walk with you."

"Oh, all right. Well, let me take your picture," I said. I always took a picture or a video of everyone who walked with me because I wanted to remember each person.

"No, no pictures," he said.

"Can I take a picture *with* you?"

"No."

"Well, if you won't give me your name and you won't let me take a picture of you, then you can't walk with me," I said.

I continued walking, and the man walked along beside me in total silence. I pretended that I was looking at my phone as I sent out a tweet on Twitter, asking the question, "What would you think if someone showed up in the middle of the desert, and he won't tell you his name or let you take a picture?"

The initial Twitter responses were mostly whimsical. Many people thought I was joking. So I sent out another tweet, noting the most recent mile marker I had passed. By my third tweet, I said, "I need help." The man still had said nothing to me, walking close beside me for more than a mile. He simply would not go away.

Approximately two thousand people who were following me on Twitter called 911 and reported that I was asking for help. A park ranger showed up and drove on past me. He stopped at the support car where Brian was immersed in playing games on a cell phone.

"Hey, is everything okay?" the ranger asked.

Brian hadn't been paying attention to my tweets, so he said, "Yeah, everything's fine." The park ranger drove off. Shortly after that I sent out another tweet asking for help. This time a state trooper showed up and stopped in front of me. "Is everything okay?" he asked.

"Oh, yeah, we're fine," I replied, winking at the officer several times while the silent man stood near me.

The trooper got out of the car and called out to the walker, "Hey, you. Stand in front of the car and put your hands on the hood." The officer patted him down, handcuffed him, took him back to his car, searched his vehicle, and escorted him out of the desert.

I later received a tweet from the man who had silently walked with me: "Sorry, the suspect did not mean to harm you." Meanwhile, Brian played on.

IF YOU'VE EVER WONDERED WHERE ALL THE OLD HIPPIES have gone, I can tell you: Pie Town, New Mexico. A real town with about sixty inhabitants, Pie Town is located atop the Western Continental Divide at an elevation of 7,796 feet. The Divide intersects the US from north to south, and it is the point where rivers and streams break either east toward the Mississippi River and the Atlantic Ocean or west toward the Gulf of Mexico and the Pacific.

Brian and I arrived in Pie Town on June 10, 2010. There was no one around, just twelve rusty windmills in one yard, dust, and the hot desert sun beating down. As I looked around at the mixture of log cabin–style structures, old buildings, and an assortment of patched-together homes and stores, the quaint village reminded me of an episode of *The Twilight Zone.* Either that or we had found the Eagles' "Hotel California," where you can check in but you can never leave! But if you get to Pie Town, you may not want to leave.

I wasn't really planning to go to Pie Town, but Highway 60 runs right through it, so I didn't have much choice. I had stopped to remove a rock out of my shoe when, out of nowhere, a white truck pulled up beside me. A man with a long white beard—somewhere between the guys in ZZ Top and Duck Dynasty—got out of the truck. "Hi, I'm Tony Shannon," he said. "This is my wife, Joan." He nodded toward a woman with straight gray hair in the passenger's seat. She looked like a throwback from Haight-Ashbury, and she had a warm, sweet smile. "We heard about your walk on the radio and got word that you were coming through Pie Town. Come on over to the house, and Joan will rustle us up some spaghetti."

Who could refuse an offer like that?

Brian and I followed them approximately three miles out into the desert to an odd-looking rectangular home with solar-powered windmills, old cars in the yard, colored glass jars decorating the shelves, and wind chimes—lots of wind chimes, everywhere!

There were also two wolves in a fenced lot, a dog on a chain, an old bus, and a ram's skull sitting on the hood of a tractor.

Tony and Joan had an outdoor shower and a chicken coop covered with a trampoline, a greenhouse filled with tomatoes, and a pile of jasmine on the ground. The exterior of the house looked like a junkyard, but the interior of their home was clean. They had a woodstove in the center of the room and a bear's head, with elk antlers attached to it, sitting on a shelf above the kitchen table. Not the standard kitchen décor, to say the least.

Joan served spaghetti while Tony shared his life story. Tony was extremely bright, and Joan was perceptive, as well, with great insights on life. We had a special time, and meeting these two wild, wacky, wonderful people was a truly gratifying experience. Much too soon, I had to leave for Albuquerque and catch a plane to perform some concerts.

When I returned to Pie Town to resume walking where I had left off, I was shocked. It was as if someone had yelled, "Action!" and a cast of characters had come to life. Unlike the day Brian and I had visited Tony and Joan, there were now people everywhere, smiling and laughing.

I walked into the Pie-O-Neer café, sat at the counter, and ordered a piece of cherry pie and a cup of coffee. Megan, the waitress, asked me what brought me to Pie Town.

I explained to her that I was walking halfway across America, and Pie Town was on the way to Phoenix.

She looked surprised. "Did you hear that Jimmy Buffett is also walking through here today?"

"Really?" I said, gulping hard and stirring my coffee. "He is?" Suddenly, it all made sense. That's why the town was so alive and bustling with activity; everyone was excited and waiting on Jimmy Buffett.

I learned that Tony and Joan, the old hippie couple I'd met a few days earlier, had told everyone that "Jimmy" was going to pick up his walk in Pie Town after he returned from a few concerts. Jimmy Buffett was in the Gulf, performing a charity concert for the oil spill victims, and thus the confusion. Or maybe Tony and Joan only half heard what I had said.

Regardless, I knew we were in trouble. Kathy, the owner of the Pie-O-Neer, was busy peeling peaches in the corner. She was so excited, anticipating Jimmy Buffett's arrival. "I'm going to give him a piece of homemade pie, and maybe he'll tell the world about my delicious Margaritaville pie!" Kathy said.

I didn't say a word.

Not only did I not want to break Kathy's heart, but there were no police in this town. I didn't know what would happen when they learned it was only me, instead of Jimmy Buffett, passing through.

I finished my coffee and pie, left an extra-generous tip, and then headed out the door.

A woman named Nita stopped me on the porch and invited Brian and me to the Jimmy Buffett party that evening at the Toaster House, a popular hotspot with hikers and bikers passing through town.

I politely declined her offer and told her I needed to go. I began walking down Highway 60, out of Pie Town, when a sudden hailstorm blew up, as they often do in the desert. I didn't mind the hail that stung as it struck me then quickly melted as it hit the ground, but the vicious thunder and lightning strikes made walking unwise. I knew I had to find shelter—fast. Brian? He was already miles down the road.

Shelter? I reluctantly headed back toward the Toaster House and the Margaritaville party.

As I approached the Toaster House, it was easy to figure out where it got the name. Old toasters hung all around and above the creaky wrought-iron gate leading to the house, on the lintels, in the trees—there were toasters everywhere. I discovered that Nita, the woman I had met earlier, owned the house and had raised her five children in the home, but since she moved in the early 1980s, no one had lived there. Instead, Nita allowed bikers, hikers, and other passersby to stay in the cabin for free, as sort of a haven and hostel for hippies. A hand printed sign on the front door read: No one lives here anymore—please make yourselves at home.

Inside, the cabin was furnished with an old wood range for heat and cooking, two bedrooms, a washing machine, and shower. There was even a wall of shoes, where guests are invited to trade footwear if they see something more to their liking. A donation jar and guest book were the only hints regarding payment, but most guests leave some money in the freezer so Nita can restock it with food for the next travelers who might stop by.

When I arrived, there were already people gathered in the large living room. Some folks carried in pies, and others hauled in musical instruments. People brought along everything from a banjo, fiddle, and string bass, to a tuba and tambourine. They were all excited and waiting on Jimmy Buffett to show up. Looking around at all the excited faces, I mentally rehearsed the words to "Margaritaville."

By the time the sun went down, the Toaster House was packed with people, picking and grinning, sharing songs and laughter. The chicken soup flowed freely, as did some other things. Everyone was having such a good time; it was almost as if they had forgotten why they were there. For all they knew, Jimmy Buffett walked through Pie Town after they had passed out.

I found a spot on the floor where I could catch some sleep, get up before everyone else did, and split. "May your moccasins leave many happy tracks," a bleary-eyed musician said as I slipped out the door.

Pie Town: come for the pie, and stay for the show.

Forty-three

NOT COMPLAININ', JUST EXPLAININ'

Between walking long stretches of hot desert high-way, I performed several concerts in venues along the way and did numerous phone interviews, as well as segments for Great American Country and Country Music Television. Alanna Conaway, a writer for *Country Weekly*, came out on the road and wrote several outstanding articles, including one titled "Still Going Strong," with a photo of me trudging up the highway, wearing Marmot clothes, with large steers eyeing me suspiciously in the background. *People* magazine sent out a reporter and a photographer and spent three days with me in Socorro, New Mexico. *People* later designated me as one of their hottest men in country music. How could I miss on that one? I was walking in the desert!

It was always interesting to note the differences between the ways people treated me. At concerts or media events, when I was onstage, girls were screaming at me or clamoring for autographs or pictures. The next day, when I was back out on the road, many people passed right by, reluctant to even look at me, perhaps assuming I was a homeless vaga-bond or worse.

For instance, earlier in the walk a church leader stopped along the road and told me in glowing terms about his church. "Jimmy Wayne, so great to meet you!" he exuded. "If you need a place to stay tonight, come on over to the church. We have lots of room. I'll stop back and check on you this evening."

I thanked the man, and he went on his way. Later that day I accepted another invitation after having visited a city mission. When the church leader returned, I told him that I was covered for the evening. "But I met two homeless guys at the city mission, and they could really use a place to stay tonight," I said.

"Oh, we couldn't do that," he said. "No, thanks."

On June 30, 2010, at 8:40 p.m., I finally crossed over the Arizona state line. I still had a long way to go, but just seeing that Welcome to Arizona sign lifted my spirits. That's where I resumed the walk on July 1, and on the first day in the state, a group of young supporters came out to walk along with me. Someone in the media asked me if I was trying to get homeless teens involved. I said, "No, they're already involved. I'm trying to get everyone else involved."

Picking me up even more, the following week Eric "Barrel Boy" Gruneisen, from KNIX Radio in Phoenix, came out to walk with me. Wearing only a large barrel and bowling shoes, he looked hilarious! He quickly discovered that walking in the barrel was impossible, so he put his clothes back on and kept pace with me. We walked eighteen miles the first day he was with me.

Barrel Boy's sense of humor was as quirky as mine, or worse, so when we walked past a sign advertising Barry Wong, a local politician, we both cracked up laughing. Two nights later, when we arrived in Show Low, Arizona, at Barrel Boy's insistence I entered a karaoke contest as "Barry Wong," dressed in a pink tank top, tight black jeans, cowboy boots, and a cowboy hat. I looked ridiculous!

I sang a Brooks & Dunn song, "Neon Moon," to a room filled with cowboys, truckers, and rednecks, and I intentionally tried to annoy them. I succeeded in getting booed right out of the bar.

Some special friends from the state of Indiana, Samantha Marx and her entire family, had come out to join me on the walk, and they had come along to karaoke night with me. When they saw the reaction of the crowd to my Barry Wong character, they feared for my health and well-being. Samantha's daughter, Kayla, overheard one cowboy talking about me to another cowboy, saying, "You hold him, and I'll hit him!"

Even when I went back and tried to sing a song as myself, the tough crowd was unforgiving. The media picked up the story, so our craziness indirectly raised a lot of awareness about Meet Me Halfway. Samantha and her family hung out with me for nearly a week, walking more than sixty miles through the hot desert.

I WAS HEADING DOWN THE HOME STRETCH TOWARD Phoenix; that was the good news. The bad news? During daylight hours, I was walking distances of 22.2 miles in temperatures that reached 117 degrees! Despite some great new shoes from Merrell, I had eight blisters on my feet, including one under my toenail—ouch!

Barrel Boy had returned to walk with me, as well as drive the gorgeous, new KNIX support vehicle donated by Beaudry RV. Brian had gone back home to college. I was sorry to see Brian go; I joked hard with him, but I love him dearly, and I appreciated his service. And he made me laugh—a lot!

As we drew closer to Phoenix, more people came out to support us. Some walked along with me; others simply cheered or offered kind words of encouragement. At one point John Erlandson from Famous Dave's restaurant brought out food for us. Sonic drive-in restaurant provided bunches of gift cards. Kohl's Ranch delivered steaks to us. "Doughnut Dan," from a local Krispy Kreme doughnut shop, brought out eight hundred boxes of fresh doughnuts so we could give them away to passing motorists, drawing more attention to Meet Me Halfway. We were doing great until a policeman came along in Show Low and ordered us to stay off the main highway with the doughnuts because we were creating a traffic problem.

About sixty miles out of Phoenix, I noticed a dull pain in my right foot. That wasn't unusual since I had been dealing with blisters and muscle spasms for more than six months. But this was different; the farther I walked, the more my foot hurt.

I had been trudging up the White Mountain range, crossing over at an elevation about eleven thousand feet above sea level. The scenery of the surrounding natural environment was absolutely breathtaking! Now I had to walk *down* the White Mountains, which was actually more difficult than walking up. If you've ever trudged down a big hill, you know the toll it takes on your knees, shins, and feet as you negotiate the downhill grade. I wore a knee brace to help compensate for the intense 6 percent slope as I walked nineteen miles downhill coming out of the White Mountains. That night my right foot was really hurting. When I awakened the next morning, my foot felt slightly better, so we took off again, walking 20.5 miles, from Star Valley through Payson, Arizona, and down the steepest mountain I'd seen yet.

THE THIRTEENTH ANNIVERSARY OF BEA'S DEATH, JULY 29, 2010, somehow motivated me. I knew I was running behind schedule and didn't want to miss our target date of August 1. Even though I was hurting, and it was growing dark, with rattlesnakes shining on the road in the moonlight, I wanted to keep walking in Bea's honor. My left hip was now hurting from favoring my right foot. It was raining and cold in the mountains, so I took a quick break at the RV. "Okay," I said to Barrel Boy, "I'm going to do it." I strapped on the Marmot reflective gear and headed back out to walk four more miles.

Going down the mountain with a headlamp on my hat, I was "pulled over" by Arizona state trooper Eric Lamb. He was concerned for my safety. "This is the deadliest state route in Arizona," Officer Lamb told us. I believed him. Besides the many sharp curves, twists, and turns coming down the mountain, there were numerous snakes lying on the warm asphalt. Officer Lamb kindly followed me in his patrol car with his emergency lights on as I made my way down the mountain.

On July 30, just two days away from the finish line, I walked thirteen miles, much less than usual, but that was as far as I could go with the excruciating pain in my foot. Every step hurt. I had caught a cold and had a fever as well. I was miserable at a time when the adrenaline should have been pushing me past my abilities. But the pain was unbearable. *I don't think I can take another step*, I worried.

At one point that day I lay down on the concrete because I was in so much pain. Barrel Boy picked me up and carried me to the support vehicle. Barrel Boy said he knew a bit about icing and wrapping ankles from back in his sports days, so he did an excellent job using plastic trash bags to form an ice-sock, icing and taping me up at the end of the day. My foot was so numb from the pain that I barely noticed the ice. The finish of the walk was definitely in doubt.

About the time I was ready to quit, two foster parents brought their son out to meet me on the road. We took some photographs together, and when that boy shook my hand and looked into my eyes, my heart leaped, and I knew I could take another step, regardless of the pain.

THE NEXT MORNING THE SWELLING ON MY FOOT WAS worse. I was sad, angry, and determined all in the same mishmash of emotions. *I can't believe this!* I thought. *After all these miles, here I am five miles from the finish line, and I can hardly walk. This is unreal!*

But God was still connecting the dots. Officer Lamb, who had escorted me down the mountain a few days earlier, had a squadmate whose brother was a podiatrist. Dr. Brian Allen came into his Mesa office on his day off and X-rayed my foot. He looked at me and said, "Jimmy, I'm sorry to tell you this, but the bone on the back of your right foot has broken. It is as though one part of your heel has broken off. More than likely, it was a progressive injury, getting worse the farther you walked, but the worst probably happened as a result of walking down the White Mountains." He estimated that I had walked more than fifty-seven miles on a broken bone.

The doctor suggested I keep my foot in a boot cast and stay off my leg for six to eight weeks. I knew that wasn't going to happen, even if I had to drag my foot across that finish line. So Dr. Allen gave me a protective boot to wear on my right foot and some strong pain medications to see me through the next few days.

"Thanks, Doc; how much do I owe you?" I asked, reaching for my wallet.

"No charge," Dr. Allen responded without blinking. "I read about you in the *People* article, and this is my contribution to Meet Me Halfway."

I thanked him and left his office, literally on my last leg. I still had five miles to go to get to the Phoenix city limit sign and then on to HomeBase, where we planned a celebration and concert. With three miles to go, it started pouring rain, but I didn't care. I was determined to get there.

A number of people who had followed our walk, from various locations around the country, joined us for the finale. Lauren returned from Sacramento so she could cross the finish line in her wheelchair shortly after I did. She was incredibly courageous, and I felt awful when she turned bright red from the hot desert sun. But I was honored that she felt compelled to be there. Barrel Boy stayed with me, and Alanna Conaway, who had written so many articles about my journey, was there at the end as well. Dreama Gentry came to celebrate with us too. Dreama had facilitated the Meet Me Halfway website from the very beginning, and it was deeply meaningful for her to join us for the culmination of the walk.

On Sunday, August 1, 2010, the Bear regiment of the Basha High School Marching Band led the parade of several hundred supporters as we walked through Phoenix to HomeBase Youth Services. Wearing my usual combination of khaki shorts and a green Marmot T-shirt, I burst through the welcome banner and raised my arms and walking sticks high in the air. I smiled broadly but was nearly overcome by emotion as an enthusiastic group of foster care kids greeted me. It had taken seven months—213 days—to walk from Monroe Harding to HomeBase.

That night, hobbling around on my designer boot, I performed for a packed house at Toby Keith's I Love This Bar and Grill. The following evening I did a special performance, especially for the foster kids and our supporters, at Hard Rock Café in Phoenix. Despite the pain and my lack of mobility, it was one of my most enjoyable performances ever! I felt as though Bea was sitting in the front row—and it was *Bea*utiful!

Forty-four

FIRST STEPS TO A
NEW JOURNEY

Returning to Nashville after the walk was almost anticlimactic—until I reached the airport waiting area. I couldn't walk well and had to be pushed in a wheelchair from the plane to the concourse, with my large Marmot clothes bag on my knee. I was looking for my drummer, Johnny, whom I had contacted to pick me up that Tuesday. But when I turned the corner, I heard a loud cheer and saw about sixty people—the majority of whom were foster kids from Monroe Harding, the foster center from which I had set out more than seven months earlier—carrying signs and banners welcoming me home and thanking me for doing the walk. It was emotionally overwhelming. I had to fight back tears through my smiles. I was *home* at last, full circle.

Pouring some GoodBean coffee into one of my favorite mugs, topping it off with hazelnut Coffee-Mate creamer, in my comfortably air-conditioned Nashville townhome in the heat of August, I wondered if I could ever be the same. The obvious answer was no. I still enjoyed my coffee and the comforts of life, but the walk had changed me, deeply transformed me within.

As I sipped my coffee, my mind drifted back to Bea's funeral. I remembered standing at the front of the church, looking into the faces in the crowd. Bessemer City was a small town, and most people were familiar with one another, but there were several families in the congregation that day I didn't recognize.

After the funeral I asked Sandie, "Who are those people?"

"Oh, that's Cynthia and her family," Sandie replied without hesitation. "When Cynthia was a teenager, Mom took her into their home. She lived with Mom and Dad for several years." I nodded toward another group of strangers across the room. Sandie smiled. "Yes, them too." She looked at an adult man and mentioned his name. "That's his family; Mom took him in, back in the early 1980s."

Clearly, I was not the first young straggler whose life was influenced by Bea and Russell. They had never mentioned a word about how they had helped other kids like me. Bea and Russell didn't *talk* about loving God and loving people; they just did it.

Several weeks later Sandie and I were at Bea's house; we were going through Bea's belongings and cleaning up. I pushed back the bedroom door and took Bea's housecoat off the hook. Beneath the robe, a few old calendars were still hanging on the back of the door. One of them was dated 1980. I flipped through each month and saw where Bea had written a note on every page, including the name of various children's orphanages that she and Russell had donated to each month.

Beautiful.

IN SEPTEMBER 2010, THE CALIFORNIA BILL PASSED, RAISing foster care to age twenty-one. I was juiced! If they did it there, we can do it in other states as well.

The positive response in the California legislature encouraged me to press harder. Tennessee state treasurer David H. Lillard Jr. introduced me to Heather Sczepezenski, legislative assistant to Representative Mark White from Memphis, a strong child advocate, and Doug Overbey, a state senator. They asked me to show up at the state legislature every time the issue of foster care came before committees. The major issue, of course, was money. With the help of a number of researchers who knew the facts and figures, I studied to prove that it was actually less expensive for the state to keep kids in foster care longer than to kick them to the streets at age eighteen. I went in armed with statistics about drug usage and sales, premarital pregnancies, and prison incarcerations, all of which took state money to deal with. On the other hand, it was relatively inexpensive to allow an eighteen-year-old a few more years to mature and set some feasible goals. A bill to change state funding for foster care from eighteen to twenty-one years of age finally made it to the House in the spring of 2012.

I showed up. Monroe Harding brought some children over, and they sat in the balcony during the vote. I saw an African-American boy looking over the balcony as the votes were cast. It was his eighteenth birthday. I knew that one way or the other, this boy's life was going to be affected immediately. Given an opportunity to speak on the House floor, I pointed up at the young man and said to the representatives, "Please pay attention because if this bill does not pass, that young man's life changes—today!"

As the votes came in on Tennessee House Bill 2337, all but one person voted for the bill. That was marvelous, but I could not imagine anyone voting against the bill. The legislator who voted against the bill had felt the additional money was an unnecessary handout.

The following day I reached out to Laura Bond, Representative White's legislative assistant, and asked for the name and address of the legislator who had voted against the bill. I sent the legislator a letter, including the story about Bea helping me and changing my life.

The next day that legislator went back to the House floor and changed his vote to yes, making it a unanimous vote.

The vote in the Tennessee Senate followed suit. I put on one of the three suits I owned and sang "The Star Spangled Banner" to begin the session. I figured, *Whatever it takes!* Doug Overbey led the charge, proving to his fellow senators that they could save money by changing the program, and the Tennessee State Senate passed the bill unanimously.

On May 29, 2012, Tennessee governor Bill Haslam signed the bill into law, one of the first in America.

Was walking across America to raise awareness of foster kids worth the sacrifices? Oh, yes.

I could fill several books with stories of people such as Anna, who became a foster parent after hearing Bea's and my story. She has already directly and permanently changed the lives of six children placed in her care. Plus, she sought out and was hired in a position training other foster parents. Bea's influence continues to multiply.

Foster parenting came full circle in my family when my sister, Patricia, remarried and established a safe, happy home with her new husband, Tim Looper. During a transitional season in Patricia's life, she got a job working as a fund-raiser for the Cleveland County Kidney Foundation in North Carolina. You can guess who received most of her requests for gratis benefit concerts. Yep, and I was always glad to help her. Hey, I was thrilled she was out of the textile mills and working at a desk job!

At several shows in North Carolina, I noticed a vivacious little girl dancing in the audience. *Who is that little girl?* I wondered.

She attended with her foster parents, and she fell in love with Patricia. When the foster parents said they had to send the little girl back to the system, Patricia and Tim cringed. "No!" they protested. "Please don't put her back into the system."

"We're sorry; we have to," the foster parents said.

Patricia and Tim were not about to let that happen, so they took immediate steps to adopt the little girl. Her name is Charleigh Storm, and although she has no blood relationship to our family, she looks almost identical to the way Patricia looked at that same age. She is now my niece, and she is the light of my life.

"HOW DID WALKING ACROSS AMERICA AFFECT YOU?" I AM often asked.

For one thing, I was pleasantly surprised at how many really good people I met in America—salt-of-the-earth types of people who would go out of their way to bring me a cup of coffee or allow me to stay in their homes. Sure, I met a few strange folks and a few mean, cantankerous types. But I met far more good-hearted people, people who care about others and are willing to lend a hand.

In many ways the walk was cleansing for me and brought me back to reality. The walk brought my life back into focus. It opened my eyes to what really matters, what is important, and it gave me perspective on my own purpose and significance.

It also allowed me enormous amounts of time to think about my past, especially my relationships with my family, about being hungry and homeless. Through it all, in a much more effective way, I found the grace to forgive my mom for rejecting and abandoning me and for doing so many harmful things during my childhood.

While walking through the desert all by myself one evening, with the big, orange sun setting in front of me, I was thinking about how Jesus felt, hanging on that cross. But I was still feeling sorry for myself too. I thought of Mary, the mother of Jesus. I looked skyward and asked, "Jesus, why can't my mom be more like Your mom? She was there for You to the bitter end."

Almost immediately He spoke to my heart and mind. *I'm not trying to get your mom to be more like Mine. I'm trying to get you to be more like Me.*

That placed the emphasis right where it needed to be—on me—and made it easier to forgive my mom. The *FTW* initials on my chest immediately took on new meaning. I had "Found the Way." I can honestly look at my mom now and say, "Mama, I love you. I forgive you. Let's move on together."

I returned to writing and performing music, but my motivation was different. I wasn't concerned about promoting an image or a product, nor was I concerned about being a country music star. I want to do something that will matter a million years from now. Something like what Bea and Russell did for me.

COMING THROUGH THE AIRPORT ONE DAY, I SAW MY SONG-writer friend Pat Alger. We'd been talking about writing songs together for years—and had even written "Summer of '85," one of my most meaningful songs—but now it was time to write something really special.

Pat and I got together and wrote an entire concept album based on stories surrounding the walk. We worked together for eight months and wrote about Pea Patch Ranch, Billy the Kid, my dog Ruby, and so much more. Pat, the master songwriter, finessed the physical journey into a musical story par excellence. We wrote the song "How Jesus Felt," a song that encapsulates what I've learned, especially in relationship to forgiveness. How did Jesus feel on the cross? Even after people had hurt Him so deeply, He didn't feel like condemning; He felt like forgiving.

Each day during my walk, as I got off the ground and rolled up my sleeping bag, I remembered why I was doing it, not simply for troubled kids but for all kids. Whenever I felt like quitting—which I often did—I remembered Bea and Russell Costner and how they sacrificed for me. And how Jesus sacrificed for all of us.

The walk also reminded me not to give up, regardless of other people's opinions. People responded in various ways; some shook their heads in amazement or amusement while others lent support. Some turned their backs; others turned around their lives.

I know the walk changed me. I grew closer to God in many ways I am still only beginning to understand. But one thing I know: I'll never be the same. I'll never again let time slip by without getting involved in life—not merely in my life but in the lives of others who need a helping hand, who need someone to meet them halfway.

I THANK GOD FOR THE GIFT OF MY EXPERIENCES—BOTH the good and the bad. They have changed me forever, and I can no longer tolerate any phoniness or fakeness in myself. I live transparently: when I'm happy, you see me smile; when I'm sad, you see my tears; when I am angry, you hear it! But I'm attempting to do as the book of James suggests: get real. Don't just talk about how much you love God. Do something. Take care of the widows and orphans (1:27). Looking back on it now, I don't think it was an accident that my mom named me *James*.

Nor do I think it is coincidence that the first three letters of Bea's name are also the first three letters in *beautiful*. Bea Costner changed every cell in my body; she was a living, breathing example of Jesus in my life. If you have trouble figuring out what Jesus would do, ask yourself, "What would Bea do?" You will likely find yourself close to the heart of God.

And if you ever become "weary in doing good" (Galatians 6:9), think of Bea. When you are tempted to think your life is insignificant, remember the little woman who took in a homeless teenager and saved his life; ask God what He wants you to do. When circumstances drag on you, weighing you down to the point you think you can't take another step, muster your courage, stay strong; keep walking.

Don't walk only when it is convenient; don't merely walk till you get tired; keep walking through it all. Walk to Beautiful.

Epilogue

BE SOMEBODY!

NEARLY EVERYWHERE I GO NOWADAYS, I ATTEMPT TO RAISE awareness for at-risk kids, especially foster kids who are soon to age out of the system with nowhere to go but the streets. Inevitably, when I tell tenderhearted people about the circumstances of these kids, somebody will say something like, "That's awful! Somebody needs to do something."

"That's right," I say. "Be somebody."

The response often comes, "How? What can one person do?"

There are several ways you can help if you want to *be somebody* in a foster child's life. Certainly you can begin by becoming aware of the issues involved for these kids. You can become a youth advocate; you can mentor or even adopt a child. You can open your home to a kid like Bea and Russell did for me. You can donate to an organization that helps children.

One of the most important keys to helping foster kids is to elect public officials who have a heart for children and the courage to take the necessary stands that will truly make a difference, especially for the forgotten foster kids aging out of the system. Certainly, this is true on a national level, but you may not be aware that each state within the US sets its own standards regarding foster care. Presently, a handful of states have raised the age that children transition out of the foster care system to twenty-one. That's great, but we need every state to do something similar. That can happen if we elect people who genuinely care about foster children.

Almost every day now, I meet someone who understands what it means to *be somebody*. I met Elizabeth on a plane, during my walk halfway across America. I had performed a concert the night before and was on my way back to the Meet Me Halfway walk. I spoke to Elizabeth before the plane taxied down the runway. She seemed reserved and quite skeptical of me, but for some reason, I felt compelled to share with her my mission. In her own words, here is how Elizabeth responded:

As I waited in line to board the plane, I saw him . . . the man and his guitar were in the boarding group ahead of me, and he was finishing up a conversation with another passenger in the waiting area. As he headed for the plane, I heard him say, "Nice to meet you. I'm Jimmy Wayne."

I walked onto the plane and quickly scanned the seats, searching for that prized window seat. There he was again, having taken an aisle seat. Before I could even get my luggage into the overhead bin and stick my nose in my magazine (my usual method of fending off conversations from strangers on airplanes), the questions began: "What do you do?" "Where are you from?" "Where are you going?" I quickly realized this was not going to be a typical flight. After not-so-politely answering his questions, it was my turn to ask questions. Without giving his name, my fellow passenger began to tell me about his mission to walk halfway across the United States to raise awareness of foster kids aging out of the system. My skepticism kicked in, and my thought process was something like, *"Oh, sure, buddy . . . you're 'walking' across America. That's why you're sitting next to me on an airplane!"*

Over the next hour and a half, he proceeded to tell me about his mission, showed me pictures of people and kids he'd met along the way, and explained that the reason he was on the plane was he had played a concert the past weekend and was headed back to pick up his walk where he left off, somewhere near Oklahoma City. As we talked, his passion for his project became evident, and I began to soften a little. Although lingering somewhere in the back of my mind was the thought, *This can't be legit. Any minute now this guy is going to ask me for money!*

He continued talking, telling stories of foster kids and homeless kids and kids with no adults in their lives to help guide them into their own adulthood. I was struck by his intensity and his passion and his obvious conviction to this cause. Somewhere in the conversation, we finally introduced ourselves, and he handed me his card: Meet Me Halfway. Follow Jimmy Wayne on Twitter.

He never did ask me for money, but he did ask me if I would join him on his walk the following day. Admittedly, being asked to go somewhere with a stranger, especially one with a guitar, long hair, and a knit stocking cap, was something I'm sure my mother warned me not to do, so I politely declined.

I got off the plane, went home to my comfortable house and my three kids, and my two dogs and cat, content in the thought that my mother would have been proud I had the good sense to turn down a stranger's offer.

But that night I couldn't sleep. I finally went to the computer and typed in the website listed on the card Jimmy Wayne had given me, and I began to read . . . and read . . . and read. Before long, tears were running down my face as I learned more about this man's mission and the deeply moving story of his own troubled childhood and the young people he was now determined to help. I also learned he was a country music star . . . *who knew?*

The next morning I signed up for a Twitter account and "tweeted" Jimmy that I wanted to walk with him that day. Soon, he sent me directions on where to meet him, and off we went. Six miles and many stories later, I knew the direction of my future volunteer efforts—working with older foster kids. I walked with Jimmy a few more times as he made his way through Oklahoma, each time learning more about the world of foster kids and the system and his own experiences.

Through several twists of fate and shared connections that I can only attribute to divine intervention, I was connected with a local Oklahoma City organization, Citizens Caring for Children, whose mission is to serve foster kids in our county and surrounding counties. I signed up to begin the vetting process to become a mentor. After a couple months of background checks and interviews, I was given my match. I was hoping to be able to be matched with a teenage boy, since I had spent the last several years with that age group traveling and serving as team mom for my son's competitive basketball team. But because of strict rules put in place to keep there from being even the slightest appearance of impropriety, and for the good of all involved, women are only matched with girls, and men with boys.

While I certainly understand this policy, it still breaks my heart to know that there are so many young boys who are eagerly awaiting a male mentor but can't be matched because not enough men choose to step up.

I was matched with thirteen-year-old Keke. Bright, beautiful, funny, moral, athletic, sensitive—we hit it off immediately. She and her siblings were in a kinship home, living with their aunt. Her mother had been in and out of jail for drugs, and from what little she knew of her father, he had been in prison since she was three. Keke had been in the foster care system since she was eight, taken from her home during a drug raid. Her life was not easy, as she was the oldest of six kids and was many times left to care for the other five while her aunt worked a job forty-five minutes away, most nights late into the evening. When I met Keke, her aunt had begun the process of adopting all six of the kids.

One night I went to pick up Keke for our weekly visit. No one was home. The next day I was informed that Keke had been removed from the home. Her aunt told me she did not know where Keke was, only that she was moved to a house in the country and would not be returning. It took me more than two months to track her down, in the meantime, missing Thanksgiving, her birthday, and Christmas celebrations with her. I later learned Keke's aunt had changed her mind about adopting her and had asked DSS to find a new place for her.

Before we could arrange to resume our visits, Keke was moved again. Her foster mom was engaged to be married, and soon she and her husband-to-be began the process of adopting Keke. Then, unexpectedly, one day I learned Keke had been removed from this home as well.

It didn't take as long to track Keke down this time, but it was still too long for me. When we finally visited again, Keke confided in me that this foster mom had also changed her mind, didn't want to complete the process, and had asked DSS to remove her from her home.

Another new home. Four homes in fourteen months . . . four new schools . . . four new families . . . four new sets of rules . . . four new sets of foster siblings. Not to mention Keke's child welfare worker had changed during this time as well. I became the one constant, the one familiar face in those months of turmoil. In each home, when I would connect with Keke's new foster families, one of the first things they would tell me is that Keke had been asking for me and wanting to know if they would let her continue our relationship. She and I had forged a bond.

This past spring, Keke met her forever family at an adoption party hosted by DSS. She moved to another town in Oklahoma and is thriving. Keke's adoptive parents invited me to her adoption celebration three weeks ago. To say Keke is happy is an enormous understatement. The sparkle in her eyes and the smile on her face say it all. She is surrounded by people who truly love and accept her, from her new parents and extended family, to her giant church community, to her new school friends. I got a lump in my throat when I heard Keke call her new parents "Mom and Dad."

My first experience as a mentor has been incredible, and I thank

God for putting me next to Jimmy Wayne on that plane more than three years ago. Without him, I never would have stepped so far out of my comfort zone or learned to see past the lifelong stereotypes I held about foster kids, to open my eyes to a world I never wanted to acknowledge even existed.

Today I am awaiting a new mentee match. While somewhat anxious about what lies ahead, I know I am not the same person I was three years ago, and neither is Keke. As I left Keke's adoption party, she actually hugged me back for the first time, and even held on for a long time, something that had never happened before. When I asked what she has learned from her new adoptive family, she responded, "That I am loved."

What better ending could there be?

Elizabeth discovered what it means to be somebody. The fact that you have read this book speaks loudly that you, too, want to be somebody in the life of a child. Maybe you are like me: I want to be the kind of guy who is not afraid to take a stand; I want to be the kind of friend who will be there when needed.

One person really can make a difference. I know that is true because one person—Bea Costner—changed every fiber of my being. Bea made a difference in my life; now I want to "Bea" somebody for other kids who need someone to meet them halfway.

From the depths of my heart, I hope you will Walk to Beautiful with me.

For more information, contact me at jimmywayne.com.

ACKNOWLEDGMENTS

THANK YOU TO THE FOLLOWING, WITHOUT WHOM NEITHER
my personal walk nor this book would have been possible:

God	Brandon Stewart	Ralph Ballard	Alicia Null
Jesus Christ	Jonathan Stewart	Madge Ballard	Michael Frady
Bea Costner	Rhonda Barber	Rodney Ballard	Charity Frady
Russell Costner	Heather Akers	Cathy Ballard	Treston Frady
Patricia Looper	Gavin Akers	Jacob Ballard	Peyton Frady
Brian Burgess	Rebecca Reed	Mallory Ballard	Lloyd Kelso
Charleigh Looper	Nicholas Reed	Barrett	Debra Kelso
Tim Looper	Zachary Horlacher	Brian Barrett	Becky Kelso
Mom	Lawrence Barber	Casey Ballard	Reese Kelso
Ruby Amarillo	Charles Barber	Bridges	Sandie Conrad
Tate	Chad England	Samuel Bridges	James Conrad
Sparkles	Brittni England	Cooper Bridges	Josh Conrad
Dad	Diane England	Somer Ballard	Julie Conrad
Don Miller	Derek England	Fortenberry	Jason Conrad
Pat Miller	April Bost	Craig Fortenberry	Jody Hogshead
Tina Miller	Evan Bost	Noah Carter	Ms. Crystal Friday
Kathey Stewart	Evans Bost	Joshua Carter	James Tillman
Eric Stewart	Carla Moore Foy	Tonia Creviston	Ruby Friday
Christopher Stewart	Mark Foy	Rex Creviston Jr.	Lorenzo Friday Sr.
Joshua Stewart	Joseph Foy	Rex Creviston III	Robert Friday
Kenneth Wayne	Kathryn Foy	Jazora Creviston	Martha Friday
Stewart	Mark Moore	Zailah Creviston	Lowery
Kenneth Wayne	Amy Moore	Dorothy Keever	Lorenzo Friday Jr.
Stewart ll	Marvin Foy	Charlie Keever	Rufus Friday
Brittany Stewart	Sherry Foy	Marline Frady	Thomasina Friday
Bentley Carter	Bobby Moore	Larry Frady	Bessie Friday Hopper
Aubree Carter	Margaret Moore	Pam Null	Lisa Friday
Kenny Stewart	Cindy Ballad	Gregory Null	Tammy Friday

377

Lewis Carpenter
Tony Baker
Donna Baker
Rick Davis
Patsy Davis
Ginger Beam
Don Lawerence
Mr. Goldman
Jason Bazon
Jamie Montgomery
Lisa Montgomery
Lisa Abraham
Ken Abraham
Alyssa Abraham
Debbie Wickwire
Doug Wickwire
Susan Ligon
Max Lucado
Steve Green
Matt Baugher
Carol Martin
Meaghan Porter
Paula Major
Emily Sweeney
Kristi Smith
Andrea Lucado
Caroline Green
Kristen Vasgaard
Trina Hunn
Jennifer Stair
Norma Bates
Allison Grimenstein
Carol Reid
Gabe Wicks
Travis Thrasher
Sharon Thrasher
Kylie Thrasher
Mackenzie Thrasher
Brianna Thrasher
Deborah Evans Price
Cindy Watts
Jackie Pillers
Cynthia Sanz
Danielle Anderson
Kevin Ellis
Mark Price
Mark Martin
Melissa Moon
Jim Garbee
Jim Beall
Laura Bond
Lily Bond
Mark White

Kathy White
Doug Overbey
Kay Overbey
Leah Dupree
David H. Lillard Jr.
Janice Cunningham
Heather
  Sczepczenski
Josh Stites
Governor Bill
  Haslam
Sherry Jones
Tre Hargett
Dawn Hargett
Cole Hargett
Connor Hargett
Sister Mary Justin
Sister Mary Michael
Frank Harrison
Jan Harrison
James Harrison
Caroline Harrison
Morgan Everett
Carter Glenn
Terri Todd
Keith Todd
Darrelee Bare
Sue Anne Wells, PHD
Thompson Wells
Todd Wells
Clark Neilson
Anne Neilson
Blakely Neilson
Catherine Neilson
Taylor Neilson
Ford Neilson
Marcus Smith
Cassi Smith
Graham Smith
Gracie Smith
Graeme Keith
Gloria Keith
India Keith
Greg Keith
Dowd Keith
  Simpson
Barrett Keith
Tanner Keith
Cody Keith
Bubba & Cindy
  Cathy
Dan & Rhonda
  Cathy

Tom & Gayle Benson
John Craighead
Jan Craighead
Josh Craighead
Scott Craighead
Chad Adcock
Brandon Adcock
Suzanne Craighead
Patrick Bradley
Lisa Bradley
Heather Bradley
Matthew Bradley
Becky Duncan
Chris Duncan
Victoria Duncan
Tyler Duncan
Caleb Duncan
Jeff Newton
Jeremy Robinson
Tony Arata
Pat Alger
Betty Jo Alger
Susan Alger
Ryan Alger
Julia Hollis-Alger
Lindsay Hill
Jill Wood
Bob Regan
Jamie Regan
Brett Regan
Miriam Mimms
Billy Kirsch
Julie Simpson
Isabel
  Simpson-Kirsch
Julian
  Simpson-Kirsch
Don Sampson
Larry Beaird
Skip Ewing
Slam Duncan
Sonya Isac
Tony Haselden
Michael "Verbs"
  Boyer
Mark Evitts
Curt Casassa
Julie Casassa
Ryan Casassa
Austin Casassa
Chris Casassa
Joe West
Kim West

Zach West
Dave Pahanish
Cole Wright
Tim Johnson
Don Poythress
Donna Hughes
Doug Rich
Sarah Majors
Don Henry
Ken Harrell
James D Hicks
AJ Masters
Mark Nesler
Tony Martin
Abbe Nameche
Ellen Britton
Alex King
Bobby King
Caroline King
Richard Harris
Cheryl Harris
Lisa Meijer
Jenny Bohler
Mike Kraski
Coach Kraski
Mike Robertson
Joni Foraker
Greg Oswald
LeAnn Phelan
Will Trapp
Sandi Spika
Jim Ed Brown
Steve & Karen
  Warnier
Jerry Bradley
Connie Bradley
Clay Bradley
Troy Tomlinson
Mike Whelan
Karen Rochelle
Willie Boozer
John Rolf
Rusty Jones
Darrel Brown
Darwin Spain
David Vincent
Debbie Parsley
T. Kareem Powell
Pat Flynn
Jim Catino
Jim Weatherly
Jo Dee Messina
Jim Graham

Buddy Peacock
JoAnn Graf
John Conlee
Doug Paisley
Sandy Paisley
Jasper Paisley
Kim Paisley
Brad Paisley
Brent Long
Cheryl Martin
Connie Harrington
John Shomby
Jeff Pierson
John Ritter
Jon Brockman
Josh Turner
Marv Green
Rob Daniels
Chad Houser
Richard Calhoune
Eric Pruitt
Luis Espaillat
Johnny Richardson
Jake Clayton
Ron Hemby
Brian Oakes
Brian Hayes
Jack Kincade
Nioshi Jackson
Matt Billingslea
Bobby Messano
Chad Carlson
Joe Baldridge
Nathan Chapman
Kirk "Jelly Roll"
  Johnson
Wes Hightower
Tony Lucido
Tom Bukovac
Marshal Bukovac
Sarah Buxton
  Bukovac
Jacob Lowery
Johnathan Yudkin
Dan Dugmore
Bill Miller
Charlie Worsham
Bobby Terry
Russ Paul
John Jarvis
Craig Young
Shawn Fichter
Mike Rojas

The McCrary Sisters
Jennifer Kummer
Larry Paxton
Joe Morris
Gene Dries
Jeremy Wayne
  Overall
Rick Manwiller
Buddy Manwiller
Will Byrd
Karen Keely
Storme Warren
Kimberly Murphy
Anthony McCartney
Keliea McCartney
Twila Devoll
Clint Devoll
Jenee Devoll
Paisley Devoll
Gentry Devoll
Tucker Duvoll
Coy Devoll
Stefani Devoll
Josh Jackson
Darby Jackson
Tony Shannon
Joan Shannon
Kathy & the Pie-
  O-Neer family
Nita the Trail Angel
Jason Saiz
Quannah Saiz
Seth Saiz
Tyler Saiz
Knox Cortese
Elaine & Gary
Topher Warren
Gigi Price
Donna Warren
Kenner Warren
Marci Warren
Alanna Conaway
LTC Jason Garkey
Kathy Garkey
Tyler Garkey
Natalie Garkey
Scott Rogers
Kristi Barto
Dr. Brian Allen
Trooper Eric Lamb
Barrel Boy
Ben & Matt
Shawn Cain

Ana Cain
Enrique Cain
Contessa Cain
Justin Jackson
  & Paris
Chris Ladd
Butch & Debbie
  Hardie
Lupe Tovar
Lani Clark
Lisa Sanders
Mandy Hale
Marcy Mynatt
Carmen Burgos
Kevin Kisamore
Cindy Kisamore
Drew Kisamore
Jacob Kisamore
Julie Coulter
Mary Baker
Monroe Harding
Amy Rathburg
Cynthia Sparks
Trish O'Neil
Patrick O'Neil
Anna Boyce
Anthony Mazza
Beth Roden
Barbara Brown-Hill
Jeff Brown-Hill
Brian Brown-Hill
Drew Hodges
Lew Cowan
Connie Lee Cowan
Holly Cowan
Chelsea Cowan
Sierra Cowan
Maureen Ferrante
Vincent Ferrante
Victoria Ferrante
Kenny Robertson
Elizabeth Boraczek
Nicholas Boraczek
Brayden Boraczek
Tauni Newman
Hank Martin
Cheri Martin
Karen Warnick
Jeanne J. Preisler
John Baker
Kathy Ramper
Debbie Tod
Sue Brown

Scooby
Kasey Fitts
Sue Ellen Coffee
Zach Parolin
Julie Wehner
Wendy Semler
Dan Semler
Eva Nimark
Amanda Grieves
Jaye Eubanks
Kendall Combes
Stephanie Nemec
Dreama Gentry
Hasan Davis
Malcolm Davis
Christopher Davis
Sharon Lucasi
BindyShay Fachin
Gary Johnston
Amie Kelly
Sara Jouret
Susie Scott
Jonathan West
Stephen Bowlby
Windi Raper
Danielle Huffman
Alison Young
Patti Allen
Rhonda Alcorn
Danielle
  Gentry-Barth
Danny Orton
David V. Williams
Collin Bokker
David Duncan
Gary Luffman
Hally Phillips
Eric Lulow
David Lee Murphy
David Masters
David McLaughlin
Gina Keltner
Sandy Judge
David Pack
Darryl Worley
Glen Worf
Hank Williams
Jack Keller
Danielle Peck
Debbie Vought
Dawn McDonald
Jackie Lee King
Alex Moore

Amanda Young
Russell Young
Andrea Poe
Terry Atkins
Angela Atkins
Kelly A. Fry
Lauren Tingle
Marion E. Hallim
Jacob Reid
Keith Riley
Matt Weber
Tammy Meyers
Maura Dunbar
Kelly Rich
Ray Pronto
Tami Jo
Rick Daly
Ken Morton
Melvin Proctor
Marie Moffitt
Carrie Jahnke
LuAnn Tacke
Renee Espinoza
Rick West
Debbie Dunlap
Rima Barkett
Ryan Griffin
Stacey Montoya
Todd Klug
Sue Klug
Shelby Klug
Sean Klug
Carole Christianson
Paul Christianson
Amanda
  Christianson
Ashlee Christianson
Carroll Collins
Decarlos White
Lucille White
Dazzia White
DeMallon White
Rod Littlejohn
DeNya White
Jerin Truesdale

Maily Gainer
Tawanda White
Jody Lee Hager
Tonia Frady
Heather Elkin
Chad Owens
Bill & Willodean
  Wise
Julie Roberts
Tony's Ice Cream
Christina Fontana
Alison Smith
Marmot
Helga Breyfogle
Tom Fritz
Andy Meyer
John Oates
Aimee Oates
Tanner Oates
JCPenney
Roper
Merrell
Red Roof Inn
Geoff Penske
Ernest Tubb
  Record Shop
Capitol
Hotel-Arkansas
Southwest Airlines
Hiscall
Grand Ole Opry
Ryman Auditorium
Pete Fisher
Brenda Colladay
Country Music
  Hall of Fame
Songwriters Hall
  of Fame
Virginia & Don
Kevin Harrison
  and family
Amanda French
Jim French
Lisa French
Paige French

Phyllis French
Ryan Green
Julie Green
Ethan Green
Brandon Green
Vanessa Green
Stephanie Babbs
Jeremy Babbs
Susan Howard
Sandy Cox
Shelby Cox
Casey Cox
Betty Cox
Sam Cox
Scott McClain
Vickie Coleman
Robin McClain
Tommy Ring
Keri Ring
Catherine Ring
Ethan Ring
Ronnie Robbins
Cathy Robbins
Nancy Alcorn
Dana Glover
Jennifer O'Brien
  Enoch
Russ Harrington
Brenda Harrington
Matthew Harrington
Brent Harrington
Suzanne Niles
Barbara Fisher
David Winning
The Bob &
  Sheri Show
Todd Haller
Jaymie Gordon
Zeke
Mike Kennedy
T J McEntire
Tonya Campos
Jeni Taylor
Scott Gaines
Shannon McComb

KNCI
KNIX
Joe Wallace
Ben Campbell
Matt McAllister
DJ Stout
Rick McCracken
Rob Tanner
Chris Allen
Guenn Schneider
Catherine Lane
Charlie & Debbie
Big Sexy
Chele Fassig
Jeff Roper
Jesse Tack
Travis Moon
Jim Mantel
Jerry Hufford
Kerry Wolfe
Mike Coulatta
Chad Douglas
Lia Douglas
Keith Bilbrey
Emy Jo Bilbrey
Vince Benedetto
Paul Ciliberto
Rodney Baldridge
Shane LaCount
Tina Thomas
Judge Cheryl
  McCally
Senator Mary
  Landrieu
Jason Wain
Scott Splawn
Chris Bochenek
Pastor David &
  Elaine Mason
Pastor David
  Chadwick
Susan Ashton
Suzanne Durham
James Phinney
Walter Petrie